THE LETTERS OF
PLINY THE
YOUNGER

REVIVE *classics*

The Letters of Pliny the Younger
Pliny the Younger 61 AD – C. 113
Translated by William Melmoth
Melmoth, William 1665 – 1743
Revised by Frederick Charles Tindal
Tindal, Frederick Charles 1847 – 1928

Text edits © 2025 Revive
Design © 2025 Revive

Text set in Adobe Caslon Pro.
Chapter headings set in Franklin Gothic.

ISBN: 978-1-83412-023-2

THE LETTERS OF PLINY THE YOUNGER

GAIUS PLINIUS CAECILIUS SECUNDUS

Translated by William Melmoth
Revised by F. C. T. Bosanquet

REVIVE

CONTENTS

Prologue

GAIUS PLINIUS CAECILIUS SECUNDUS, usually known as Pliny the Younger, was born at Como in 62 A. D. He was only eight years old when his father Caecilius died, and he was adopted by his uncle, the elder Pliny, author of the Natural History. He was carefully educated, studying rhetoric under Quintilian and other famous teachers, and he became the most eloquent pleader of his time. In this and in much else he imitated Cicero, who had by this time come to be the recognized master of Latin style. While still young he served as military tribune in Syria, but he does not seem to have taken zealously to a soldier's life. On his return he entered politics under the Emperor Domitian; and in the year 100 A. D. was appointed consul by Trajan and admitted to confidential intercourse with that emperor. Later while he was governor of Bithynia, he was in the habit of submitting every point of policy to his master, and the correspondence between Trajan and him, which forms the last part of the present selection, is of a high degree of interest, both on account of the subjects discussed and for the light thrown on the characters of the two men. He is supposed to have died about 113 A. D. Pliny's speeches are now lost, with the exception of one, a panegyric on Trajan delivered in thanksgiving for the consulate. This, though diffuse and somewhat too complimentary for modern taste, became a model for this kind of composition. The others were mostly of two classes, forensic and political, many of the latter being, like Cicero's speech against Verres, impeachments of provincial governors for cruelty and extortion toward their subjects. In these, as in his public activities in general, he appears as a man of public spirit and integrity; and in his relations with his native town he was a thoughtful and munificent benefactor.

The letters, on which to-day his fame mainly rests, were largely written with a view to publication, and were arranged by Pliny himself. They thus lack the spontaneity of Cicero's impulsive utterances, but to most modern readers who are not special students of Roman history they are even more interesting. They deal with a great variety of subjects: the description of a Roman villa; the charms of country life; the reluctance of people to attend author's readings and to listen when they were present; a dinner party; legacy-hunting in ancient Rome; the acquisition of a piece of statuary; his love for his young wife; ghost stories; floating islands, a tame dolphin, and other marvels. But by far the best known are those describing the great eruption of Vesuvius in which his uncle perished, a martyr to scientific curiosity, and the letter to Trajan on his attempts to suppress Christianity in Bithynia, with Trajan's reply approving his policy. Taken altogether, these letters give an absorbingly vivid picture of the days of the early empire, and of the interests of a cultivated Roman gentleman of wealth. Occasionally, as in the last letters referred to, they deal with important historical events; but their chief value is in bringing before us, in somewhat the same manner as "The Spectator" pictures the England of the age of Anne, the life of a time which is not so unlike our own as its distance in years might indicate. And in this time by no means the least interesting figure is that of the letter-writer himself, with his vanity and self-importance, his sensibility and generous affection? his pedantry and his loyalty.

The Letters of Pliny the Younger

TO SEPTITTUS

YOU HAVE FREQUENTLY PRESSED me to make a select collection of my Letters (if there really be any deserving of a special preference) and give them to the public. I have selected them accordingly; not, indeed, in their proper order of time, for I was not compiling a history; but just as each came to hand. And now I have only to wish that you may have no reason to repent of your advice, nor I of my compliance: in that case, I may probably enquire after the rest, which at present be neglected, and preserve those I shall hereafter write. Farewell.

TO ARRIANUS

I FORESEE YOUR JOURNEY in my direction is likely to be delayed, and therefore send you the speech which I promised in my former; requesting you, as usual, to revise and correct it. I desire this the more earnestly as I never, I think, wrote with the same empressment in any of my former speeches; for I have endeavoured to imitate your old favourite Demosthenes and Calvus, who is lately become mine, at least in the rhetorical forms of the speech; for to catch their sublime spirit, is given, alone, to the "inspired few." My subject, indeed, seemed naturally to lend itself to this (may I venture to call it?) emulation; consisting, as it did, almost entirely in a vehement style of address, even to a degree sufficient to have awakened me (if only I am capable of being awakened) out of that indolence in which I have long reposed. I have not however altogether neglected the flowers of rhetoric of my favourite Marc-Tully, wherever I could with propriety step out of my direct road, to enjoy a more flowery path: for it was energy, not austerity, at which I aimed. I would not have you imagine by this that I am bespeaking your indulgence: on the contrary, to make your correcting pen more vigorous, I will confess that neither my friends nor myself are averse from the publication of this piece, if only you should join in the approval of what is perhaps my folly. The truth is, as I must publish something, I wish it might be this performance rather than any other, because it is already finished: (you hear the wish of laziness.) At all events, however, something I must publish, and for many reasons; chiefly because of the tracts which I have already sent in to the world, though they have long since lost all their recommendation from novelty, are still, I am told, in request; if, after all, the booksellers are not tickling my ears. And let them; since, by that innocent deceit, I am encouraged to pursue my studies. Farewell.

TO VOCONIUS ROMANUS

DID YOU EVER MEET with a more abject and mean-spirited creature than Marcus Regulus since the death of Domitian, during whose reign his conduct was no less infamous, though more concealed, than under Nero's? He began to be afraid I was angry with him, and his apprehensions were perfectly correct; I was angry. He had not only done his best to increase the peril of the position in which Rusticus Arulenus[1] stood, but had exulted in his death; insomuch that he actually recited and published a libel upon his memory, in which he styles him "The Stoics' Ape": adding, "stigmated[2] with the Vitellian scar."[3] You recognize Regulus' eloquent strain![4], [5], [6]

---

1   A pupil and intimate friend of Paetus Thrasea, the distinguished Stoic philosopher. Arulenus was put to death by Domitian for writing a panegyric upon Thrasea.

2   The impropriety of this expression, in the original, seems to he in the word stigmosum, which Regulus, probably either coined through affectation or used through ignorance. It is a word, at least, which does not occur in any author of authority: the translator has endeavoured, therefore, to preserve the same sort of impropriety, by using an expression of like unwarranted stamp in his own tongue. M.

3   An allusion to a wound he had received in the war between Vitellius and Vespasian.

4   A brother of Piso Galba's adopted son. He was put to death by Nero.

5   Sulpicius Camerinus, put to death by the same emperor, upon some frivolous charge.

6   A select body of men who formed a court of judicature, called the centurnviral court. Their jurisdiction extended chiefly, if not entirely, to questions of wills and intestate estates. Their number, it would seem, amounted to 100. M.

He fell with such fury upon the character of Herennius Senecio that Metius Carus said to him, one day, "What business have you with my dead? Did I ever interfere in the affair of Crassus' or Camerinus'?" Victims, you know, to Regulus, in Nero's time. For these reasons he imagined I was highly exasperated, and so at the recitation of his last piece, I got no invitation. Besides, he had not forgotten, it seems, with what deadly purpose he had once attacked me in the Court of the Hundred. Rusticus had desired me to act as counsel for Arionilla, Titnon's wife: Regulus was engaged against me. In one part of the case I was strongly insisting upon a particular judgment given by Metius Modestus, an excellent man, at that time in banishment by Domitian's order. Now then for Regulus. "Pray," says he, "what is your opinion of Modestus?" You see what a risk I should have run had I answered that I had a high opinion of him, how I should have disgraced myself on the other hand if I had replied that I had a bad opinion of him. But some guardian power, I am persuaded, must have stood by me to assist me in this emergency. "I will tell you my opinion," I said, "if that is a matter to be brought before the court." "I ask you," he repeated, "what is your opinion of Modestus?" I replied that it was customary to examine witnesses to the character of an accused man, not to the character of one on whom sentence had already been passed. He pressed me a third time. "I do not now enquire," said he, "your opinion of Modestus in general, I only ask your opinion of his loyalty." "Since you will have my opinion then," I rejoined, "I think it illegal even to ask a question concerning a person who stands convicted." He sat down at this, completely silenced; and I received applause and congratulation on all sides, that without injuring my reputation by an advantageous, perhaps, though ungenerous answer, I had not entangled myself in the toils of so insidious a catch-question. Thoroughly frightened upon this then, he first seizes upon Caecilius Celer, next he goes and begs of Fabius Justus, that they would use their joint interest to bring about a reconciliation between us. And lest this should not be sufficient, he sets off to Spurinna as well; to whom he came in the humblest way (for he is the most abject creature alive, where he has anything to be afraid of) and says to him, "Do, I entreat of you, call on Pliny to-morrow morning, certainly in the morning, no later (for I cannot endure this anxiety of mind longer), and endeavour by any means in your power to soften his resentment." I was already up, the next day, when a message arrived from Spurinna, "I am coming to call on you." I sent word back, "Nay, I will wait upon you;" however, both of us setting out to pay this visit, we met under Livia's portico. He acquainted me with the commission he had received from Regulus, and interceded for him as became so worthy a man in behalf of one so totally dissimilar, without greatly pressing the thing. "I will leave it to you," was my reply, "to consider what answer to return Regulus; you ought not to be deceived by me. I am waiting for Mauricus'[7] return" (for he had not yet come back out of exile), "so that I cannot give you any definite answer either way, as I mean to be guided entirely by his decision, for he ought to be my leader here, and I simply to do as he says." Well, a few days after this, Regulus met me as I was at the praetor's; he kept close to me there and begged a word in private, when he said he was afraid I deeply resented an expression he had once made use of in his reply to Satrius and myself, before the Court of the Hundred, to this effect, "Satrius Rufus, who does not endeavour to rival Cicero, and who is content with the eloquence of our own day." I answered, now I perceived indeed, upon his own confession, that he had meant it ill-naturedly; otherwise it might have passed for a compliment. "For I am free to own," I said, "that I do endeavour to rival Cicero, and am not content with the eloquence of our own day. For I consider it the very height of folly not to copy the best models of every kind. But, how happens it that you, who have so good a recollection of what passed upon this occasion, should have forgotten that other, when you asked me my opinion of the loyalty of Modestus?" Pale as he always is, he turned simply pallid at this, and stammered out, "I did not intend to hurt you when I asked this question, but Modestus." Observe the vindictive cruelty of the fellow, who made no concealment of his willingness to injure a banished man. But the reason he alleged in justification of his conduct is pleasant. Modestus, he explained, in a letter of his, which was read to Domitian, had used the following expression, "Regulus, the biggest rascal that walks upon two feet:" and what Modestus had written was the simple truth, beyond all manner of controversy. Here, about, our conversation came to an end, for I did not wish to proceed further, being desirous to keep matters open until Mauricus returns. It is no easy matter, I am well aware of that, to destroy Regulus; he is rich, and at the head of a party; courted[8] by many, feared by more: a passion that will sometimes prevail even beyond friendship itself. But, after all, ties of this sort are not

---

7   Junius Mauricus, the brother of Rusticus Arulenus. Both brothers were sentenced on the same day, Arulenue to execution and Mauricui to banishment.

8   There seems to have been a cast of uncommon blackness in the character of this Regulus; otherwise the benevolent Pliny would scarcely have singled him out, as he has in this and some following letters, for the subject of his warmest contempt and indignation. Yet, infamous as he was, he had his flatterers and admirers; and a contemporary poet frequently represents him as one of the most finished characters of the age, both in eloquence and virtue. M.

so strong but they may be loosened; for a bad man's credit is as shifty as himself. However (to repeat), I am waiting until Mauricus comes back. He is a man of sound judgment and great sagacity formed upon long experience, and who, from his observations of the past, well knows how to judge of the future. I shall talk the matter over with him, and consider myself justified either in pursuing or dropping this affair, as he shall advise. Meanwhile I thought I owed this account to our mutual friendship, which gives you an undoubted right to know about not only all my actions but all my plans as well. Farewell.

TO CORNELIUS TACITUS

YOU WILL LAUGH (and you are quite welcome) when I tell you that your old acquaintance is turned sportsman, and has taken three noble boars. "What!" you exclaim, "Pliny!"—Even he. However, I indulged at the same time my beloved inactivity; and, whilst I sat at my nets, you would have found me, not with boar spear or javelin, but pencil and tablet, by my side. I mused and wrote, being determined to return, if with all my hands empty, at least with my memorandums full. Believe me, this way of studying is not to be despised: it is wonderful how the mind is stirred and quickened into activity by brisk bodily exercise. There is something, too, in the solemnity of the venerable woods with which one is surrounded, together with that profound silence which is observed on these occasions, that forcibly disposes the mind to meditation. So for the future, let me advise you, whenever you hunt, to take your tablets along with you, as well as your basket and bottle, for be assured you will find Minerva no less fond of traversing the hills than Diana. Farewell.

TO POMPEIUS SATURNINUS

NOTHING COULD BE MORE seasonable than the letter which I received from you, in which you so earnestly beg me to send you some of my literary efforts: the very thing I was intending to do. So you have only put spurs into a willing horse and at once saved yourself the excuse of refusing the trouble, and me the awkwardness of asking the favour. Without hesitation then I avail myself of your offer; as you must now take the consequence of it without reluctance. But you are not to expect anything new from a lazy fellow, for I am going to ask you to revise again the speech I made to my fellow-townsmen when I dedicated the public library to their use. You have already, I remember, obliged me with some annotations upon this piece, but only in a general way; and so I now beg of you not only to take a general view of the whole speech, but, as you usually do, to go over it in detail. When you have corrected it, I shall still be at liberty to publish or suppress it: and the delay in the meantime will be attended with one of these alternatives; for, while we are deliberating whether it is fit for publishing, a frequent revision will either make it so, or convince me that it is not. Though indeed my principal difficulty respecting the publication of this harangue arises not so much from the composition as out of the subject itself, which has something in it, I am afraid, that will look too like ostentation and self-conceit. For, be the style ever so plain and unassuming, yet, as the occasion necessarily led me to speak not only of the munificence of my ancestors, but of my own as well, my modesty will be seriously embarrassed. A dangerous and slippery situation this, even when one is led into it by plea of necessity! For, if mankind are not very favourable to panegyric, even when bestowed upon others, how much more difficult is it to reconcile them to it when it is a tribute which we pay to ourselves or to our ancestors? Virtue, by herself, is generally the object of envy, but particularly so when glory and distinction attend her; and the world is never so little disposed to detract from the rectitude of your conduct as when it passes unobserved and unapplauded. For these reasons, I frequently ask myself whether I composed this harangue, such as it is, merely from a personal consideration, or with a view to the public as well; and I am sensible that what may be exceedingly useful and proper in the prosecution of any affair may lose all its grace and fitness the moment the business is completed: for instance, in the case before us, what could be more to my purpose than to explain at large the motives of my intended bounty? For, first, it engaged my mind in good and ennobling thoughts; next, it enabled me, by frequent dwelling upon them, to receive a perfect impression of their loveliness, while it guarded at the same time against that repentance which is sure to follow on an impulsive act of generosity. There arose also a further advantage from this method, as it fixed in me a certain habitual contempt of money. For, while mankind seem to be universally governed by an innate passion to accumulate wealth, the cultivation of a more generous affection in my own breast taught me to emancipate myself from the slavery of so predominant a principle: and I thought that my honest intentions would be the more meritorious as they should appear to proceed, not from sudden impulse, but from the dictates of cool and deliberate reflection. I considered, besides, that I was not engaging myself to exhibit public games or gladiatorial combats, but to establish an annual fund for the support and education of young men of good families but scanty means. The pleasures of the senses are so far from wanting the oratorical arts to recommend them that we stand in need of all the powers of eloquence to moderate and restrain rather than stir up their influence. But the work of getting anybody to cheerfully undertake the monotony and drudgery of education must be effected not by pay merely, but by a skilfully worked-up appeal to the emotions as well. If physicians find it expedient to use the most insinuating address in recommending to their patients a wholesome though, perhaps, unpleasant regimen, how much more occasion had he to exert all the powers of persuasion who, out of regard to the public welfare, was endeavouring to reconcile it to a most useful though not equally popular benefaction? Particularly, as my aim was to recommend an institution, calculated solely for the benefit of those who were parents to men who, at present, had no children; and to persuade the greater number to wait patiently until they should be entitled to an honour of which a few only could immediately partake. But as at that time, when I attempted to explain and enforce the general design and benefit of my institution, I considered more the general good of my countrymen, than any reputation which might result to myself; so I am apprehensive lest, if I publish that piece, it may perhaps look as if I had a view rather to my own personal credit than the benefit of others, Besides, I am very sensible how much nobler it is to place the reward of virtue in the silent approbation of one's own breast than in the applause of the world. Glory ought to be the consequence, not the motive, of our actions; and although it happen not to attend the worthy deed, yet it is by no means the less fair for having missed the applause it deserved. But the world is apt to suspect that those who celebrate their own beneficent acts performed them for no other motive than to have the pleasure of extolling them. Thus, the splendour of an action which would have been deemed illustrious if related by another is totally extinguished when it becomes the subject of one's own applause. Such is the disposition of mankind, if they cannot blast the action, they will censure its display; and whether you do what does not deserve particular notice, or set forth yourself what does, either way you incur reproach. In my own case there is a peculiar circumstance that weighs much with me: this speech was delivered not before the people, but the Decurii;[9] not in the forum, but the senate; I am afraid therefore it will look inconsistent that I, who, when I delivered

9   The Decurii were a sort of senators in the municipal or corporate cities of Italy. M.

it, seemed to avoid popular applause, should now, by publishing this performance, appear to court it: that I, who was so scrupulous as not to admit even these persons to be present when I delivered this speech, who were interested in my benefaction, lest it, might be suspected I was actuated in this affair by any ambitious views, should now seem to solicit admiration, by forwardly displaying it to such as have no other concern in my munificence than the benefit of example. These are the scruples which have occasioned my delay in giving this piece to the public; but I submit them entirely to your judgment, which I shall ever esteem as a sufficient sanction of my conduct. Farewell.

TO ATRIUS CLEMENS

IF EVER POLITE LITERATURE flourished at Rome, it certainly flourishes now; and I could give you many eminent instances: I will content myself, however, with naming only Euphrates[10] the philosopher. I first became acquainted with this excellent person in my youth, when I served in the army in Syria. I had an opportunity of conversing with him familiarly, and took some pains to gain his affection: though that, indeed, was not very difficult, for he is easy of access, unreserved, and actuated by those social principles he professes to teach. I should think myself extremely happy if I had as fully answered the expectations he, at that time, conceived of me, as he exceeds everything I had imagined of him. But, perhaps, I admire his excellencies more now than I did then, because I know better how to appreciate them; not that I sufficiently appreciate them even now. For as none but those who are skilled in painting, statuary, or the plastic art, can form a right judgment of any performance in those respective modes of representation, so a man must, himself, have made great advances in philosophy before he is capable of forming a just opinion of a philosopher. However, as far as I am qualified to determine, Euphrates is possessed of so many shining talents that he cannot fail to attract and impress the most ordinarily educated observer. He reasons with much force, acuteness, and elegance; and frequently rises into all the sublime and luxuriant eloquence of Plato. His style is varied and flowing, and at the same time so wonderfully captivating that he forces the reluctant

10   "Euphrates was a native of Tyre, or, according to others, of Byzantium. He belonged to the Stoic school of philosophy. In his old age he became tired of life, and asked and obtained from Hadrian permission to put an end to himself by poison." Smith's Dict. of Greek and Roman Biog.

attention of the most unwilling hearer. For the rest, a fine stature, a comely aspect, long hair, and a large silver beard; circumstances which, though they may probably be thought trifling and accidental, contribute, however, to gain him much reverence. There is no affected negligence in his dress and appearance; his countenance is grave but not austere; and his approach commands respect without creating awe. Distinguished as he is by the perfect blamelessness of his life, he is no less so by the courtesy and engaging sweetness of his manner. He attacks vices, not persons, and, without severity, reclaims the wanderer from the paths of virtue. You follow his exhortations with rapt attention, hanging, as it were, upon his lips; and even after the heart is convinced, the ear still wishes to listen to the harmonious reasoner. His family consists of three children (two of which are sons), whom he educates with the utmost care. His father-in-law, Pompeius Julianus, as he greatly distinguished himself in every other part of his life, so particularly in this, that though he was himself of the highest rank in his province, yet, among many considerable matches, he preferred Euphrates for his son-in-law, as first in merit, though not in dignity. But why do I dwell any longer upon the virtues of a man whose conversation I am so unfortunate as not to have time sufficiently to enjoy? Is it to increase my regret and vexation that I cannot enjoy it? My time is wholly taken up in the execution of a very honourable, indeed, but equally troublesome, employment; in hearing cases, signing petitions, making up accounts, and writing a vast amount of the most illiterate literature. I sometimes complain to Euphrates (for I have leisure at least to complain) of these unpleasing occupations. He endeavours to console me, by affirming that, to be engaged in the public service, to hear and determine cases, to explain the laws, and administer justice, is a part, and the noblest part, too, of philosophy; as it is reducing to practice what her professors teach in speculation. But even his rhetoric will never be able to convince me that it is better to be at this sort of work than to spend whole days in attending his lectures and learning his precepts. I cannot therefore but strongly recommend it to you, who have the time for it, when next you come to town (and you will come, I daresay, so much the sooner for this), to take the benefit of his elegant and refined instructions. For I do not (as many do) envy others the happiness I cannot share with them myself: on the contrary, it is a very sensible pleasure to me when I find my friends in possession of an enjoyment from which I have the misfortune to be excluded. Farewell.

TO FABIUS JUSTUS

IT IS A LONG time since I have had a letter from you, "There is nothing to write about," you say: well then write and let me know just this, that "there is nothing to write about," or tell me in the good old style, If you are well that's right, I am quite well. This will do for me, for it implies everything. You think I am joking? Let me assure you I am in sober earnest. Do let me know how you are; for I cannot remain ignorant any longer without growing exceedingly anxious about you. Farewell.

TO CALESTRIUS TIRO

I HAVE SUFFERED THE heaviest loss; if that word be sufficiently strong to express the misfortune which has deprived me of so excellent a man. Corellius Rufus is dead; and dead, too, by his own act! A circumstance of great aggravation to my affliction: as that sort of death which we cannot impute either to the course of nature, or the hand of Providence, is, of all others, the most to be lamented. It affords some consolation in the loss of those friends whom disease snatches from us that they fall by the general destiny of mankind; but those who destroy themselves leave us under the inconsolable reflection, that they had it in their power to have lived longer. It is true, Corellius had many inducements to be fond of life; a blameless conscience, high reputation, and great dignity of character, besides a daughter, a wife, a grandson, and sisters; and, amidst these numerous pledges of happiness, faithful friends. Still, it must be owned he had the highest motive (which to a wise man will always have the force of destiny), urging him to this resolution. He had long been tortured by so tedious and painful a complaint that even these inducements to living on, considerable as they are, were over-balanced by the reasons on the other side. In his thirty-third year (as I have frequently heard him say) he was seized with the gout in his feet. This was hereditary; for diseases, as well as possessions, are sometimes handed down by a sort of inheritance. A life of sobriety and continence had enabled him to conquer and keep down the disease while he was still young, latterly as it grew upon him with advancing years, he had to manfully bear it, suffering meanwhile the most incredible and undeserved agonies; for the gout was now not only in his feet, but had spread itself over his whole body. I remember, in Domitian's reign, paying him a visit at his villa, near Rome. As soon as I entered his chamber, his servants went out: for it was his rule, never to allow them to be in the room when any intimate friend was with him; nay, even his own wife, though she could have kept any secret, used to go too. Casting his eyes round the room, "Why," he exclaimed, "do you suppose I endure life so long under these cruel agonies? It is with the hope that I may outlive, at least for one day, that villain." Had his bodily strength been equal to his resolution, he would have carried his desire into practical effect. God heard and answered his prayer; and when he felt that he should now die a free, un-enslaved, Roman, he broke through those other great, but now less forcible, attachments to the world. His malady increased; and, as it now grew too violent to admit of any relief from temperance, he resolutely determined to put an end to its uninterrupted attacks, by an effort of heroism. He had refused all sustenance during four days when his wife Hispulla sent our common friend Geminius to me, with the melancholy news, that Corellius was resolved to die; and that neither her own entreaties nor her daughter's could move him from his purpose; I was the only person left who could reconcile him to life. I ran to his house with the utmost precipitation. As I approached it, I met a second messenger from Hispulla, Julius Atticus, who informed me there was nothing to be hoped for now, even from me, as he seemed more hardened than ever in his purpose. He had said, indeed to his physician, who pressed him to take some nourishment, "'Tis resolved": an expression which, as it raised my admiration of the greatness of his soul, so it does my grief for the loss of him. I keep thinking what a friend, what a man, I am deprived of. That he had reached his sixty-seventh year, an age which even the strongest seldom exceed, I well know; that he is released from a life of continual pain; that he has left his dearest friends behind him, and (what was dearer to him than all these) the state in a prosperous condition: all this I know. Still I cannot forbear to lament him, as if he had been in the prime and vigour of his days; and I lament him (shall I own my weakness?) on my account. And—to confess to you as I did to Calvisius, in the first transport of my grief—I sadly fear, now that I am no longer under his eye, I shall not keep so strict a guard over my conduct. Speak comfort to me then, not that he was old, he was infirm; all this I know: but by supplying me with some reflections that are new and resistless, which I have never heard, never read, anywhere else. For all that I have heard, and all that I have read, occur to me of themselves; but all these are by far too weak to support me under so severe an affliction. Farewell.

TO SOCIUS SENECIO

THIS YEAR HAS PRODUCED a plentiful crop of poets: during the whole month of April scarcely a day has passed on which we have not been entertained with the recital of some poem. It is a pleasure to me to find that a taste for polite literature still exists, and that men of genius do come forward and make themselves known, notwithstanding the lazy attendance they got for their pains. The greater part of the audience sit in the lounging-places, gossip away their time there, and are perpetually sending to enquire whether the author has made his entrance yet, whether he has got through the preface, or whether he has almost finished the piece. Then at length they saunter in with an air of the greatest indifference, nor do they condescend to stay through the recital, but go out before it is over, some slyly and stealthily, others again with perfect freedom and unconcern. And yet our fathers can remember how Claudius Cæsar walking one day in the palace, and hearing a great shouting, enquired the cause: and being informed that Nonianus[11] was reciting a composition of his, went immediately to the place, and agreeably surprised the author with his presence. But now, were one to bespeak the attendance of the idlest man living, and remind him of the appointment ever so often, or ever so long beforehand; either he would not come at all, or if he did would grumble about having "lost a day!" for no other reason but because he had not lost it. So much the more do those authors deserve our encouragement and applause who have resolution to persevere in their studies, and to read out their compositions in spite of this apathy or arrogance on the part of their audience. Myself indeed, I scarcely ever miss being present upon any occasion; though, to tell the truth, the authors have generally been friends of mine, as indeed there are few men of literary tastes who are not. It is this which has kept me in town longer than I had intended. I am now, however, at liberty to go back into the country, and write something myself; which I do not intend reciting, lest I should seem rather to have lent than given my attendance to these recitations of my friends, for in these, as in all other good offices, the obligation ceases the moment you seem to expect a return. Farewell.

---

11   A pleader and historian of some distinction, mentioned by Tacitus, Ann. XIV. 19, and by Quintilian, X, I, 102.

TO JUNSUS MAURICUS

YOU DESIRE ME TO look out a proper husband for your niece: it is with
justice you enjoin me that office. You know the high esteem and affection I bore that great man her father, and with what noble instructions
he nurtured my youth, and taught me to deserve those praises he was
pleased to bestow upon me. You could not give me, then, a more important, or more agreeable, commission; nor could I be employed in
an office of higher honour, than that of choosing a young man worthy
of being father of the grandchildren of Rusticus Arulenus; a choice I
should be long in determining, were I not acquainted with Minutius
Aemilianus, who seems formed for our purpose. He loves me with all
that warmth of affection which is usual between young men of equal
years (as indeed I have the advance of him but by a very few), and re-
veres me at the same time, with all the deference due to age; and, in a
word, he is no less desirous to model himself by my instructions than I
was by those of yourself and your brother.

He is a native of Brixia, one of those provinces in Italy which still
retain much of the old modesty, frugal simplicity, and even rusticity, of
manner. He is the son of Minutius Macrinus, whose humble desires were
satisfied with standing at the head of the equestrian order: for though he
was nominated by Vespasian in the number of those whom that prince
dignified with the praetorian office, yet, with an inflexible greatness of
mind, he resolutely preferred an honourable repose, to the ambitious,
shall I call them, or exalted, pursuits, in which we public men are engaged.
His grandmother, on the mother's side, is Serrana Procula, of Patavium:[12]
you are no stranger to the character of its citizens; yet Serrana is looked
upon, even among these correct people, as an exemplary instance of strict
virtue, Acilius, his uncle, is a man of almost exceptional gravity, wisdom,
and integrity. In short, you will find nothing throughout his family unworthy of yours. Minutius himself has plenty of vivacity, as well as application, together with a most amiable and becoming modesty. He has
already, with considerable credit, passed through the offices of quaestor,
tribune, and praetor; so that you will be spared the trouble of soliciting for him those honourable employments. He has a fine, well-bred,
countenance, with a ruddy, healthy complexion, while his whole person
is elegant and comely and his mien graceful and senatorian: advantages,
I think, by no means to be slighted, and which I consider as the proper
tribute to virgin innocence. I think I may add that his father is very rich.

12   Padua.

When I contemplate the character of those who require a husband of my choosing, I know it is unnecessary to mention wealth; but when I reflect upon the prevailing manners of the age, and even the laws of Rome, which rank a man according to his possessions, it certainly claims some regard; and, indeed, in establishments of this nature, where children and many other circumstances are to be duly weighed, it is an article that well deserves to be taken into the account. You will be inclined, perhaps, to suspect that affection has had too great a share in the character I have been drawing, and that I have heightened it beyond the truth: but I will stake all my credit, you will find everything far beyond what I have represented. I love the young fellow indeed (as he justly deserves) with all the warmth of a most ardent affection; but for that very reason I would not ascribe more to his merit than I know it will bear. Farewell.

TO SEPTITIUS CLARUS

AH! YOU ARE A pretty fellow! You make an engagement to come to supper and then never appear. Justice shall be exacted;—you shall reimburse me to the very last penny the expense I went to on your account; no small sum, let me tell you. I had prepared, you must know, a lettuce a-piece, three snails, two eggs, and a barley cake, with some sweet wine and snow, (the snow most certainly I shall charge to your account, as a rarity that will not keep.) Olives, beet-root, gourds, onions, and a thousand other dainties equally sumptuous. You should likewise have been entertained either with an interlude, the rehearsal of a poem, or a piece of music, whichever you preferred; or (such was my liberality) with all three. But the oysters, sows'-bellies, sea-urchins, and dancers from Cadiz of a certain—I know not who, were, it seems, more to your taste. You shall give satisfaction, how, shall at present be a secret.

Oh! you have behaved cruelly, grudging your friend,—had almost said yourself;—and upon second thoughts I do say so;—in this way: for how agreeably should we have spent the evening, in laughing, trifling, and literary amusements! You may sup, I confess, at many places more splendidly; but nowhere with more unconstrained mirth, simplicity, and freedom: only make the experiment, and if you do not ever after excuse yourself to your other friends, to come to me, always put me off to go to them. Farewell.

TO SUETONIUS TRANQUILLUS

You TELL ME IN your letter that you are extremely alarmed by a dream; apprehending that it forebodes some ill success to you in the case you have undertaken to defend; and, therefore, desire that I would get it adjourned for a few days, or, at least, to the next. This will be no easy matter, but I will try:

"For dreams descend from Jove."

Meanwhile, it is very material for you to recollect whether your dreams generally represent things as they afterwards fall out, or quite the reverse. But if I may judge of yours by one that happened to myself, this dream that alarms you seems to portend that you will acquit yourself with great success. I had promised to stand counsel for Junius Pastor; when I fancied in my sleep that my mother-in-law came to me, and, throwing herself at my feet, earnestly entreated me not to plead. I was at that time a very young man; the case was to be argued in the four centumviral courts; my adversaries were some of the most important personages in Rome, and particular favourites of Cæsar;[13] any of which circumstances were sufficient, after such an inauspicious dream, to have discouraged me. Notwithstanding this, I engaged in the cause, reflecting that,

"Without a sign, his sword the brave man draws,
And asks no omen but his country's cause."[14]

for I looked upon the promise I had given to be as sacred to me as my country, or, if that were possible, more so. The event happened as I wished; and it was that very case which first procured me the favourable attention of the public, and threw open to me the gates of Fame. Consider then whether your dream, like this one I have related, may not pre-signify success. But, after all, perhaps you will think it safer to pursue this cautious maxim: "Never do a thing concerning the rectitude of which you are in doubt;" if so, write me word. In the interval, I will consider of some excuse, and will so plead your cause that you may be able to plead it your self any day you like best. In this respect, you are in a better situation than I was: the court of the centumviri, where I was to plead, admits of no adjournment: whereas, in that where your case is to be heard, though no easy matter to procure one, still, however, it is

---

13   Domitian
14   Iliad, XII. 243. Pope.

possible. Farewell.

TO ROMANUS FIRMUS

As you are my towns-man, my school-fellow, and the earliest companion of my youth; as there was the strictest friendship between my mother and uncle and your father (a happiness which I also enjoyed as far as the great inequality of our ages would admit); can I fail (thus biassed as I am by so many and weighty considerations) to contribute all in my power to the advancement of your honours? The rank you bear in our province, as decurio, is a proof that you are possessed, at least, of an hundred thousand sesterces;[15] but that we may also have the satisfaction of seeing you a Roman Knight,[16] I present you with three hundred thousand, in order to make up the sum requisite to entitle you to that dignity. The long acquaintance we have had leaves me no room to apprehend you will ever be forgetful of this instance of my friendship. And I know your disposition too well to think it necessary to advise you to enjoy this honour with the modesty that becomes a person who receives it from me; for the advanced rank we possess through a friend's kindness is a sort of sacred trust, in which we have his judgment, as well as our own character, to maintain, and therefore to be guarded with the greater caution. Farewell.

---

15   Equal to about $4,000 of our money. After the reign of Augustus the value of the sesterces.

16   "The equestrian dignity, or that order of the Roman people which we commonly call knights, had nothing in it analogous to any order of modern knighthood, but depended entirely upon a valuation of their estates; and every citizen, whose entire fortune amounted to 400,000 sesterces, that is, to about $16000 of our money, was enrolled, of course, in the list of knights, who were considered as a middle order between the senators and common people, yet, without any other distinction than the privilege of wearing a gold ring, which was the peculiar badge of their order." Life of Cicero, Vol. I. III. in note. M.

TO CORNELIUS TACITUS

I HAVE FREQUENT DEBATES with a certain acquaintance of mine, a man of skill and learning, who admires nothing so much in the eloquence of the bar as conciseness. I agree with him, that where the case will admit of this precision, it may with propriety be adopted; but insist that, to leave out what is material to be mentioned,—or only briefly and curso-rily to touch upon those points which should be inculcated, impressed, and urged well home upon the minds of the audience, is a downright fraud upon one's client. In many cases, to deal with the subject at greater length adds strength and weight to our ideas, which frequently produce their impression upon the mind, as iron does upon solid bodies, rather by repeated strokes than a single blow. In answer to this, he usually has recourse to authorities, and produces Lysias[17] amongst the Grecians, together with Cato and the two Gracchi, among our own countrymen, many of whose speeches certainly are brief and curtailed. In return, I name Demosthenes, Aeschines, Hyperides,[18] and many others, in op-position to Lysias; while I confront Cato and the Gracchi with Cæsar, Pollio,[19] Caelius,[20] but, above all, Cicero, whose longest speech is gener-ally considered his best. Why, no doubt about it, in good compositions, as in everything else that is valuable, the more there is of them, the better. You may observe in statues, basso-relievos, pictures, and the hu-man form, and even in animals and trees, that nothing is more graceful than magnitude, if accompanied with proportion. The same holds true in pleading; and even in books a large volume carries a certain beauty and authority in its very size. My antagonist, who is extremely dexterous at evading an argument, eludes all this, and much more, which I usu-ally urge to the same purpose, by insisting that those very individuals, upon whose works I found my opinion, made considerable additions to their speeches when they published them. This I deny; and appeal to the harangues of numberless orators, particularly to those of Cicero, for Murena and Varenus, in which a short, bare notification of certain

---

17   An elegant Attic orator, remarkable for the grace and lucidity of his style, also for his vivid and accurate delineations of character.
18   A graceful and powerful orator, and friend of Densosthenes.
19   A Roman orator of the Augustan age. He was a poet and historian as well, but gained most distinction as an orator.
20   A man of considerable taste, talent, and eloquence, but profligate and extravagant. He was on terms of some intimacy with Cicero.

charges is expressed under mere heads. Whence it appears that many things which he enlarged upon at the time he delivered those speeches were retrenched when he gave them to the public. The same excellent orator informs us that, agreeably to the ancient custom, which allowed only of one counsel on a side, Cluentius had no other advocate than himself; and he tells us further that he employed four whole days in defence of Cornelius; by which it plainly appears that those speeches which, when delivered at their full length, had necessarily taken up so much time at the bar were considerably cut down and pruned when he afterwards compressed them into a single volume, though, I must confess, indeed, a large one. But good pleading, it is objected, is one thing, just composition another. This objection, I am aware, has had some favourers; nevertheless, I am persuaded (though I may, perhaps, be mistaken) that, as it is possible you may have a good pleading which is not a good speech, so a good speech cannot be a bad pleading; for the speech on paper is the model and, as it were, the archetype of the speech that was delivered. It is for this reason we find, in many of the best speeches extant, numberless extemporaneous turns of expression; and even in those which we are sure were never spoken; as, for instance, in the following passage from the speech against Verres: —"A certain mechanic—what's his name? Oh, thank you for helping me to it: yes, I mean Polyclitus." It follows, then, that the nearer approach a speaker makes to the rules of just composition, the more perfect will he be in his art; always supposing, however, that he has his due share of time allowed him; for, if he be limited of that article, no blame can justly be fixed upon the advocate, though much certainly upon the judge. The sense of the laws, I am sure, is on my side, which are by no means sparing of the orator's time; it is not conciseness, but fulness, a complete representation of every material circumstance, which they recommend. Now conciseness cannot effect this, unless in the most insignificant cases. Let me add what experience, that unerring guide, has taught me: it has frequently been my province to act both as an advocate and a judge; and I have often also attended as an assessor.[21] Upon those occasions, I have ever found the judgments of mankind are to be influenced by different modes of application, and that the slightest circumstances frequently produce the most important consequences. The dispositions and understandings of men vary to such an extent that they seldom agree in their opinions concerning any one

---

21   The praetor was assisted by ten assessors, five of whom were senators, and the rest knights. With these he was obliged to consult before he pronounced sentence. M.

point in debate before them; or, if they do, it is generally from different motives. Besides, as every man is naturally partial to his own discoveries, when he hears an argument urged which had previously occurred to himself, he will be sure to embrace it as extremely convincing. The orator, therefore, should so adapt himself to his audience as to throw out something which every one of them, in turn, may receive and approve as agreeable to his own particular views. I recollect, once when Regulus and I were engaged on the same side, his remarking to me, "You seem to think it necessary to go into every single circumstance: whereas I always take aim at once at my adversary's throat, and there I press him closely." ('Tis true, he keeps a tight hold of whatever part he has once fixed upon; but the misfortune is, he is extremely apt to fix upon the wrong place.) I replied, it might possibly happen that what he called the throat was, in reality, the knee or the ankle. As for myself, said I, who do not pretend to direct my aim with so much precision, I test every part, I probe every opening; in short, to use a vulgar proverb, I leave no stone unturned. And as in agriculture, it is not my vineyards or my woods only, but my fields as well, that I look after and cultivate, and (to carry on the metaphor) as I do not content myself with sowing those fields simply with corn or white wheat, but sprinkle in barley, pulse, and the other kinds of grain; so, in my pleadings at the bar, I scatter broadcast various arguments like so many kinds of seed, in order to reap whatever may happen to come up. For the disposition of your judges is as hard to fathom as uncertain, and as little to be relied on as that of soils and seasons. The comic writer Eupolis,[22] I remember, mentions it in praise of that excellent orator Pericles, that

> *"On his lips Persuasion hung,*
> *And powerful Reason rul'd his tongue:*
> *Thus he alone could boast the art*
> *To charm at once, and pierce the heart."*[23]

But could Pericles, without the richest variety of expression, and merely by the force of the concise or the rapid style, or both (for they are very different), have thus charmed and pierced the heart. To delight and to persuade requires time and great command of language; and to leave a sting in the minds of the audience is an effect not to be expected from an orator who merely pinks, but from him, and him only, who thrusts in.

---

22 A contemporary and rival of Aristophanes.
23 Aristophanes, Ach. 531

Another comic poet,[24] speaking of the same orator, says:

> *"His mighty words like Jove's own thunder roll;*
> *Greece hears, and trembles to her inmost soul."*

But it is not the close and reserved; it is the copious, the majestic, and the sublime orator, who thunders, who lightens, who, in short, bears all before him in a confused whirl. There is, undeniably, a just mean in everything; but he equally misses the mark who falls short of it, as he who goes beyond it; he who is too limited as he who is too unrestrained. Hence it is as common a thing to hear our orators condemned for being too jejune and feeble as too excessive and redundant. One is said to have exceeded the bounds of his subject, the other not to have reached them. Both, no doubt, are equally in fault, with this difference, however, that in the one the fault arises from an abundance, in the other, from a deficiency; an error, in the former case, which, if it be not the sign of a more correct, is certainly of a more fertile genius. When I say this, I would not be understood to approve that everlasting talker[25] mentioned in Homer, but that other' described in the following lines:

> *"Frequent and soft, as falls the winter snow,*
> *Thus from his lips the copious periods flow."*

Not but that I extremely admire him,[26] too, of whom the poet says,

> *"Few were his words, but wonderfully strong."*

Yet, if the choice were given me, I should give the preference to that style resembling winter snow, that is, to the full, uninterrupted, and diffusive; in short, to that pomp of eloquence which seems all heavenly and divine. But (it is replied) the harangue of a more moderate length is most generally admired. It is:—but only by indolent people; and to fix the standard by their laziness and false delicacy would be simply ridiculous. Were you to consult persons of this cast, they would tell you, not only that it is best to say little, but that it is best to say nothing at all. Thus, my friend, I have laid before you my opinions upon this subject, and I am willing to change them if not agreeable to yours. But should you disagree with me,

---

24   Thersites. Iliad, II. V. 212.
25   Ulysses. Iliad, III. V. 222.
26   Menelaua. Iliad, III. V. 214.

pray let me know clearly your reasons why. For, though I ought to yield in this case to your more enlightened judgment, yet, in a point of such consequence, I had rather be convinced by argument than by authority. So if I don't seem to you very wide of the mark, a line or two from you in return, intimating your concurrence, will be sufficient to confirm me in my opinion: on the other hand, if you should think me mistaken, let me have your objections at full length. Does it not look rather like bribery, my requiring only a short letter, if you agree with me; but a very long one if you should be of a different opinion. Farewell.

TO PATERNUS

As I RELY VERY much upon the soundness of your judgment, so I do upon the goodness of your eyes: not because I think your discernment very great (for I don't want to make you conceited), but because I think it as good as mine: which, it must be confessed, is saying a great deal. Joking apart, I like the look of the slaves which were purchased for me on your recommendation very well; all I further care about is, that they be honest: and for this I must depend upon their characters more than their countenances. Farewell.

TO CATILIUS SEVERUS[27]

I AM AT PRESENT (and have been a considerable time) detained in Rome, under the most stunning apprehensions. Titus Aristo,[28] whom I have a singular admiration and affection for, is fallen into a long and obstinate illness, which troubles me. Virtue, knowledge, and good sense, shine out with so superior a lustre in this excellent man that learning herself, and every valuable endowment, seem involved in the danger of his single person. How consummate his knowledge, both in the political and civil laws of his country! How thoroughly conversant is he in every branch of history or antiquity? In a word, there is nothing you might wish to know which he could not teach you. As for me, whenever I would acquaint myself with any abstruse point, I go to him as my store-house. What an engaging sincerity, what dignity in his conversation! how chastened and becoming is his caution! Though he conceives, at once, every point in debate, yet he

---

27   Great-grandfather of the Emperor M. Aurelius.
28   An eminent lawyer of Trajan's reign.

is as slow to decide as he is quick to apprehend; calmly and deliberately sifting and weighing every opposite reason that is offered, and tracing it, with a most judicious penetration, from its source through all its remotest consequences. His diet is frugal, his dress plain; and whenever I enter his chamber, and view him reclined upon his couch, I consider the scene before me as a true image of ancient simplicity, to which his illustrious mind reflects the noblest ornament. He places no part of his happiness in ostentation, but in the secret approbation of his conscience, seeking the reward of his virtue, not in the clamorous applauses of the world, but in the silent satisfaction which results from having acted well. In short, you will not easily find his equal, even among our philosophers by outward profession. No, he does not frequent the gymnasia or porticoes[29] nor does he amuse his own and others' leisure with endless controversies, but busies himself in the scenes of civil and active life. Many has he assisted with his interest, still more with his advice, and withal in the practice of temperance, piety, justice, and fortitude, he has no superior. You would be astonished, were you there to see, at the patience with which he bears his illness, how he holds out against pain, endures thirst, and quietly submits to this raging fever and to the pressure of those clothes which are laid upon him to promote perspiration. He lately called me and a few more of his particular friends to his bedside, requesting us to ask his physicians what turn they apprehended his distemper would take; that, if they pronounced it incurable, he might voluntarily put an end to his life; but if there were hopes of a recovery, how tedious and difficult soever it might prove, he would calmly wait the event; for so much, he thought, was due to the tears and entreaties of his wife and daughter, and to the affectionate intercession of his friends, as not voluntarily to abandon our hopes, if they were not entirely desperate. A true hero's resolution this, in my estimation, and worthy the highest applause. Instances are frequent in the world, of rushing into the arms of death without reflection and by a sort of blind impulse but deliberately to weigh the reasons for life or death, and to be determined in our choice as either side of the scale prevails, shows a great mind. We have had the satisfaction to receive the opinion of his physicians in his favour: may heaven favour their promises and relieve me at length from this painful anxiety. Once easy in my mind, I shall go back to my favourite Laurentum, or, in other words, to my books, my papers and studious leisure. Just now, so much of my time and thoughts are taken up in attendance upon my friend, and anxiety for him, that I have neither

---

29   The philosophers used to hold their disputations in the gymnasia and porticoes, being places of the most public resort for walking, &c. M.

leisure nor inclination for any reading or writing whatever. Thus you have my fears, my wishes, and my after-plans. Write me in return, but in a gayer strain, an account not only of what you are and have been doing, but of what you intend doing too. It will be a very sensible consolation to me in this disturbance of mind, to be assured that yours is easy. Farewell.

TO VOCONIUS ROMANUS

ROME HAS NOT FOR many years beheld a more magnificent and memorable spectacle than was lately exhibited in the public funeral of that great, illustrious, and no less fortunate man, Verginius Rufus. He lived thirty years after he had reached the zenith of his fame. He read poems composed in his honour, he read histories of his achievements, and was himself witness of his fame among posterity. He was thrice raised to the dignity of consul, that he might at least be the highest of subjects, who[30] had refused to be the first of princes. As he escaped the resentment of those emperors to whom his virtues had given umbrage and even rendered him odious, and ended his days when this best of princes, this friend of mankind[31] was in quiet possession of the empire, it seems as if Providence had purposely preserved him to these times, that he might receive the honour of a public funeral. He reached his eighty-fourth year, in full tranquillity and universally revered, having enjoyed strong health during his lifetime, with the exception of a trembling in his hands, which, however, gave him no pain. His last illness, indeed, was severe and tedious, but even that circumstance added to his reputation. As he was practising his voice with a view of returning his public acknowledgements to the emperor, who had promoted him to the consulship, a large volume he had taken into his hand, and which happened to be too heavy for so old a man to hold standing up, slid from his grasp. In hastily endeavouring to recover it, his foot slipped on the smooth pavement, and he fell down and broke his thigh-bone, which being clumsily set, his age as well being

---

30   "Verginius Rufus was governor of Upper Germany at the time of the revolt of Julius Vindex in Gaul. A.D. 68. The soldiers of Verginius wished to raise him to the empire, but he refused the honour, and marched against Vindex, who perished before Vesontio. After the death of Nero, Verginius supported the claims of Galba, and accompanied him to Rome. Upon Otho's death, the soldiers again attempted to proclaim Verginius emperor, and in consequence of his refusal of the honour, he narrowly escaped with his life." (See Smith's Dict. of Greek and Rom. Biog., &c.)

31   Nerva.

against him, did not properly unite again. The funeral obsequies paid to the memory of this great man have done honour to the emperor, to the age, and to the bar. The consul Cornelius Tacitus[32] pronounced his funeral oration and thus his good fortune was crowned by the public applause of so eloquent an orator. He has departed from our midst, full of years, indeed, and of glory; as illustrious by the honours he refused as by those he accepted. Yet still we shall miss him and lament him, as the shining model of a past age; I, especially, shall feel his loss, for I not only admired him as a patriot, but loved him as a friend. We were of the same province, and of neighbouring towns, and our estates were also contiguous. Besides these accidental connections, he was left my guardian, and always treated me with a parent's affection. Whenever I offered myself as a candidate for any office in the state, he constantly supported me with his interest; and although he had long since given up all such services to friends, he would kindly leave his retirement and come to give me his vote in person. On the day on which the priests nominate those they consider most worthy of the sacred office[33] he constantly proposed me. Even in his last illness, apprehending the possibility of the senate's appointing him one of the five commissioners for reducing the public expenses, he fixed upon me, young as I am, to bear his excuses, in preference to so many other friends, elderly men too, and of consular rank and said to me, "Had I a son of my own, I would entrust you with this matter." And so I cannot but lament his death, as though it were premature, and pour out my grief into your bosom; if indeed one has any right to grieve, or to call it death at all, which to such a man terminates his mortality, rather than ends his life. He lives, and will live on for ever; and his fame will extend and be more celebrated by posterity, now that he is gone from our sight. I had much else to write to you but my mind is full of this. I keep thinking of Verginius: I see him before me: I am for ever fondly yet vividly imagining that I hear him, am speaking to him, embrace him. There are men amongst us, his fellow-citizens, perhaps, who may rival him in virtue; but not one that will ever approach him in glory. Farewell.

---

32   The historian,

33   Namely, of augurs. "This college, as regulated by Sylla, consisted of fifteen, who were all persons of the first distinction in Rome; it was a priesthood for life, of a character indelible, which no crime or forfeiture could efface; it was necessary that every candidate should be nominated to the people by two augurs, who gave a solemn testimony upon, oath of his dignity and fitness for that office." Middleton's Life of Cicero, I. 547. M.

TO NEPOS

THE GREAT FAME OF Isaeus had already preceded him here; but we find him even more wonderful than we had heard. He possesses the utmost readiness, copiousness, and abundance of language: he always speaks extempore, and his lectures are as finished as though he had spent a long time over their written composition. His style is Greek, or rather the genuine Attic. His exordiums are terse, elegant, attractive, and occasionally impressive and majestic. He suggests several subjects for discussion, allows his audience their choice, sometimes to even name which side he shall take, rises, arranges himself, and begins. At once he has everything almost equally at command. Recondite meanings of things are suggested to you, and words—what words they are! exquisitely chosen and polished. These extempore speeches of his show the wideness of his reading, and how much practice he has had in composition. His preface is to the point, his narrative lucid, his summing up forcible, his rhetorical ornament imposing. In a word, he teaches, entertains, and affects you; and you are at a loss to decide which of the three he does best. His reflections are frequent, his syllogisms also are frequent, condensed, and carefully finished, a result not easily attainable even with the pen. As for his memory, you would hardly believe what it is capable of. He repeats from a long way back what he has previously delivered extempore, without missing a single word. This marvellous faculty he has acquired by dint of great application and practice, for night and day he does nothing, hears nothing, says nothing else. He has passed his sixtieth year and is still only a rhetorician, and I know no class of men more single-hearted, more genuine, more excellent than this class. We who have to go through the rough work of the bar and of real disputes unavoidably contract a certain unprincipled adroitness. The school, the lecture-room, the imaginary case, all this, on the other hand, is perfectly innocent and harmless, and equally enjoyable, especially to old people, for what can be happier at that time of life than to enjoy what we found pleasantest in our young days? I consider Isaeus then, not only the most eloquent, but the happiest, of men, and if you are not longing to make his acquaintance, you must be made of stone and iron. So, if not upon my account, or for any other reason, come, for the sake of hearing this man, at least. Have you never read of a certain inhabitant of Cadiz who was so impressed with the name and fame of Livy that he came from the remotest corner of the earth on purpose to see him, and, his curiosity gratified, went straight home again. It is utter want of taste, shows simple ignorance, is almost an actual disgrace to a man, not to set any high value upon a proficiency in so pleasing, noble, refining a science. "I have au-

REVIVE | *The Letters of Pliny the Younger*

thors," you will reply, "here in my own study, just as eloquent." True: but then those authors you can read at any time, while you cannot always get the opportunity of hearing eloquence. Besides, as the proverb says, "The living voice is that which sways the soul;" yes, far more. For notwithstanding what one reads is more clearly understood than what one hears, yet the utterance, countenance, garb, aye and the very gestures of the speaker, alike concur in fixing an impression upon the mind; that is, unless we disbelieve the truth of Aeschines' statement, who, after he had read to the Rhodians that celebrated speech of Demosthenes, upon their expressing their admiration of it, is said to have added, "Ah! what would you have said, could you have heard the wild beast himself?" And Aeschines, if we may take Demosthenes' word for it, was no mean elocutionist; yet, he could not but confess that the speech would have sounded far finer from the lips of its author. I am saying all this with a view to persuading you to hear Isaeus, if even for the mere sake of being able to say you have heard him. Farewell.

TO AVITUS

IT WOULD BE A long story, and of no great importance, to tell you by what accident I found myself dining the other day with an individual with whom I am by no means intimate, and who, in his own opinion, does things in good style and economically as well, but according to mine, with meanness and extravagance combined. Some very elegant dishes were served up to himself and a few more of us, whilst those placed before the rest of the company consisted simply of cheap dishes and scraps. There were, in small bottles, three different kinds of wine; not that the guest might take their choice, but that they might not have any option in their power; one kind being for himself, and for us; another sort for his lesser friends (for it seems he has degrees of friends), and the third for his own freedmen and ours. My neighbour,[34] reclining next me, observing this, asked me if I approved the arrangement. Not at all, I told him. "Pray then," he asked, "what is your method upon such occasions?" "Mine," I returned, "is to give all my visitors the same recep-

---

34   The ancient Greeks and Romans did not sit up at the table as we do, but reclined round it on couches, three and sometimes even four occupying one conch, at least this latter was the custom among the Romans. Each guest lay flat upon his chest while eating, reaching out his hand from time to time to the table, for what he might require. As soon as he had made a sufficient meal, he turned over upon his left side, leaning on the elbow.

tion; for when I give an invitation, it is to entertain, not distinguish, my company: I place every man upon my own level whom I admit to my table." "Not excepting even your freedmen?" "Not excepting even my freedmen, whom I consider on these occasions my guests, as much as any of the rest." He replied, "This must cost you a great deal." "Not in the least." "How can that be?" "Simply because, although my freedmen don't drink the same wine as myself, yet I drink the same as they do." And, no doubt about it, if a man is wise enough to moderate his appetite, he will not find it such a very expensive thing to share with all his visitors what he takes himself. Restrain it, keep it in, if you wish to be true economist. You will find temperance a far better way of saving than treating other people rudely can be. Why do I say all this? Why, for fear a young man of your high character and promise should be imposed upon by this immoderate luxury which prevails at some tables, under the specious notion of frugality. Whenever any folly of this sort falls under my eye, I shall, just because I care for you, point it out to you as an example you ought to shun. Remember, then, nothing is more to be avoided than this modern alliance of luxury with meanness; odious enough when existing separate and distinct, but still more hateful where you meet with them together. Farewell.

TO MACRINUS

THE SENATE DECREED YESTERDAY, on the emperor's motion, a triumphal statue to Vestricius Spurinna: not as they would to many others, who never were in action, or saw a camp, or heard the sound of a trumpet, unless at a show; but as it would be decreed to those who have justly bought such a distinction with their blood, their exertions, and their deeds. Spurinna forcibly restored the king of the Bructeri[35] to his throne; and this by the noblest kind of victory; for he subdued that warlike people by the terror of the mere display of his preparation for the campaign. This is his reward as a hero, while, to console him for the loss of his son Cottius, who died during his absence upon that expedition, they also voted a statue to the youth; a very unusual honour for one so young; but the services of the father deserved that the pain of so severe a wound should be soothed by no common balm. Indeed Cottius himself evinced such remarkable promise of the highest qualities that it is but fitting his short limited term of life should be extended, as it were, by this kind of

35   A people of Germany.

immortality. He was so pure and blameless, so full of dignity, and commanded such respect, that he might have challenged in moral goodness much older men, with whom he now shares equal honours. Honours, if I am not mistaken, conferred not only to perpetuate the memory of the deceased youth, and in consolation to the surviving father, but for the sake of public example also. This will rouse and stimulate our young men to cultivate every worthy principle, when they see such rewards bestowed upon one of their own years, provided he deserve them: at the same time that men of quality will be encouraged to beget children and to have the joy and satisfaction of leaving a worthy race behind, if their children survive them, or of so glorious a consolation, should they survive their children. Looking at it in this light then, I am glad, upon public grounds, that a statue is decreed Cottius: and for my own sake too, just as much; for I loved this most favoured, gifted, youth, as ardently as I now grievously miss him amongst us. So that it will be a great satisfaction to me to be able to look at this figure from time to time as I pass by, contemplate it, stand underneath, and walk to and fro before it. For if having the pictures of the departed placed in our homes lightens sorrow, how much more those public representations of them which are not only memorials of their air and countenance, but of their glory and honour besides? Farewell.

TO PAISCUS

As I KNOW YOU eagerly embrace every opportunity of obliging me, so there is no man whom I had rather be under an obligation to. I apply to you, therefore, in preference to anyone else, for a favour which I am extremely desirous of obtaining. You, who are commander-in-chief of a very considerable army, have many opportunities of exercising your generosity; and the length of time you have enjoyed that post must have enabled you to provide for all your own friends. I hope you will now turn your eyes upon some of mine: as indeed they are but a few Your generous disposition, I know, would be better pleased if the number were greater, but one or two will suffice my modest desires; at present I will only mention Voconius Romanus. His father was of great distinction among the Roman knights, and his father-in-law, or, I might more properly call him, his second father, (for his affectionate treatment of Voconius entitles him to that appellation) was still more conspicuous. His mother was one of the most considerable ladies of Upper Spain: you know what character the people of that province bear, and how remarkable they are for their strictness of their manners. As for himself, he lately held the post of flamen.[36] Now, from the time when we were first students together, I have felt very tenderly attached to him. We lived under the same roof, in town and country, we joked together, we shared each other's serious thoughts: for where indeed could I have found a truer friend or pleasanter companion than he? In his conversation, and even in his very voice and countenance, there is a rare sweetness; as at the bar he displays talents of a high order; acuteness, elegance, ease, and skill: and he writes such letters too that were you to read them you would imagine they had been dictated by the Muses themselves. I have a very great affection for him, as he has for me. Even in the earlier part of our lives, I warmly embraced every opportunity of doing him all the good services which then lay in my power, as I have lately obtained for him from our most gracious prince[37] the privilege[38] granted to those who have three children: a favour which, though Cæsar very rarely bestows, and always with great caution, yet he conferred, at my request, in such a matter as to give it the air and grace of being his own choice.

The best way of showing that I think he deserves the kindnesses he has already received from me is by increasing them, especially as he always accepts my services so gratefully as to deserve more. Thus I have shown you what manner of man Romanus is, how thoroughly I have proved his worth, and how much I love him. Let me entreat you to honour him with your patronage in a way suitable to the generosity of your heart, and the eminence of your station. But above all let him have your affection; for though you were to confer upon him the utmost you have in your power to bestow, you can give him nothing more valuable than your friendship- That you may see he is worthy of it, even to the closest degree of intimacy, I send you this brief sketch of his tastes, character, his whole life, in fact. I should continue my intercessions in his behalf, but that I know you prefer not being pressed, and I have already repeated them in every line of this letter: for, to show a good reason for what one asks is true intercession,

---

36   "Any Roman priest devoted to the service of one particular god was designated Flamen, receiving a distinguishing epithet from the deity to whom he ministered. The office was understood to last for life; but a flamen might be compelled to resign for a breach of duty, or even on account of the occurrence of an ill-omened accident while discharging his functions." Smith's Dictionary of Antiquities.

37   Trajan.

38   By a law passed A. D. 76, it was enacted that every citizen of Rome who had three children should be excused from all troublesome offices where he lived. This privilege the emperors sometimes extended to those who were not legally entitled to it.

and of the most effectual kind. Farewell.

TO MAIMUS

YOU GUESSED CORRECTLY: I am much engaged in pleading before the Hundred. The business there is more fatiguing than pleasant. Trifling, inconsiderable cases, mostly; it is very seldom that anything worth speaking of, either from the importance of the question or the rank of the persons concerned, comes before them. There are very few lawyers either whom I take any pleasure in working with. The rest, a parcel of impudent young fellows, many of whom one knows nothing whatever about, come here to get some practice in speaking, and conduct themselves so forwardly and with such utter want of deference that my friend Attilius exactly hit it, I think, when he made the observation that "boys set out at the bar with cases in the Court of the Hundred as they do at school with Homer," intimating that at both places they begin where they should end. But in former times (so my elders tell me) no youth, even of the best families, was allowed in unless introduced by some person of consular dignity. As things are now, since every fence of modesty and decorum is broken down, and all distinctions are levelled and confounded, the present young generation, so far from waiting to be introduced, break in of their own free will. The audience at their heels are fit attendants upon such orators; a low rabble of hired mercenaries, supplied by contract. They get together in the middle of the court, where the dole is dealt round to them as openly as if they were in a dining-room: and at this noble price they run from court to court. The Greeks have an appropriate name in their language for this sort of people, importing that they are applauders by profession, and we stigmatize them with the opprobrious title of table-flatterers: yet the dirty business alluded to increases every day. It was only yesterday two of my domestic officers, mere striplings, were hired to cheer somebody or other, at three denarii apiece:[39] that is what the highest eloquence goes for. Upon these terms we fill as many benches as we please, and gather a crowd; this is how those rending shouts are raised, as soon as the individual standing up in the middle of the ring gives the signal. For, you must know, these honest fellows, who understand nothing of what is said, or, if they did, could not hear it, would be at a loss without a signal, how to time their applause: for many of them don't hear a syllable, and are as noisy as any

---

39   About 54 cents.

of the rest. If, at any time, you should happen to be passing by when the court is sitting, and feel at all interested to know how any speaker is acquitting himself, you have no occasion to give yourself the trouble of getting up on the judge's platform, no need to listen; it is easy enough to find out, for you may be quite sure he that gets most applause deserves it the least. Largius Licinus was the first to introduce this fashion; but then he went no farther than to go round and solicit an audience. I know, I remember hearing this from my tutor Quinctilian. "I used," he told me, "to go and hear Domitius Afer, and as he was pleading once before the Hundred in his usual slow and impressive manner, hearing, close to him, a most immoderate and unusual noise, and being a good deal surprised at this, he left off: the noise ceased, and he began again: he was interrupted a second time, and a third. At last he enquired who it was that was speaking? He was told, Licinus. Upon which, he broke off the case, exclaiming, 'Eloquence is no more!'" The truth is it had only begun to decline then, when in Afer's opinion it no longer existed — whereas now it is almost extinct. I am ashamed to tell you of the mincing and affected pronunciation of the speakers, and of the shrill-voiced applause with which their effusions are received; nothing seems wanting to complete this sing-song performance except claps, or rather cymbals and tambourines. Howlings indeed (for I can call such applause, which would be indecent even in the theatre, by no other name) abound in plenty. Up to this time the interest of my friends and the consideration of my early time of life have kept me in this court, as I am afraid they might think I was doing it to shirk work rather than to avoid these indecencies, were I to leave it just yet: however, I go there less frequently than I did, and am thus effecting a gradual retreat. Farewell.

TO GALLUS

YOU ARE SURPRISED THAT I am so fond of my Laurentine, or (if you prefer the name) my Laurens: but you will cease to wonder when I acquaint you with the beauty of the villa, the advantages of its situation, and the extensive view of the sea-coast. It is only seventeen miles from Rome: so that when I have finished my business in town, I can pass my evenings here after a good satisfactory day's work. There are two different roads to it: if you go by that of Laurentum, you must turn off at the fourteenth mile-stone; if by Astia, at the eleventh. Both of them are sandy in places, which makes it a little heavier and longer by carriage, but short and easy on horseback. The landscape affords plenty of vari-

ety, the view in some places being closed in by woods, in others extending over broad meadows, where numerous flocks of sheep and herds of
cattle, which the severity of the winter has driven from the mountains,
fatten in the spring warmth, and on the rich pasturage. My villa is of a
convenient size without being expensive to keep up. The courtyard in
front is plain, but not mean, through which you enter porticoes shaped
into the form of the letter D, enclosing a small but cheerful area between. These make a capital retreat for bad weather, not only as they are
shut in with windows, but particularly as they are sheltered by a projection of the roof. From the middle of these porticoes you pass into a
bright pleasant inner court, and out of that into a handsome hall running out towards the sea-shore; so that when there is a south-west
breeze, it is gently washed with the waves, which spend themselves at
its base. On every side of this hall there are either folding-doors or
windows equally large, by which means you have a view from the front
and the two sides of three different seas, as it were: from the back you
see the middle court, the portico, and the area; and from another point
you look through the portico into the courtyard, and out upon the
woods and distant mountains beyond. On the left hand of this hall, a
little farther from the sea, lies a large drawing-room, and beyond that,
a second of a smaller size, which has one window to the rising and
another to the setting sun: this as well has a view of the sea, but more
distant and agreeable. The angle formed by the projection of the dining-room with this drawing-room retains and intensifies the warmth
of the sun, and this forms our winter quarters and family gymnasium,
which is sheltered from all the winds except those which bring on
clouds, but the clear sky comes out again before the warmth has gone
out of the place. Adjoining this angle is a room forming the segment of
a circle, the windows of which are so arranged as to get the sun all
through the day: in the walls are contrived a sort of cases, containing a
collection of authors who can never be read too often. Next to this is a
bed-room, connected with it by a raised passage furnished with pipes,
which supply, at a wholesome temperature, and distribute to all parts of
this room, the heat they receive. The rest of this side of the house is appropriated to the use of my slaves and freedmen; but most of the rooms
in it are respectable enough to put my guests into. In the opposite wing
is a most elegant, tastefully fitted up bed-room; next to which lies another, which you may call either a large bed-room or a modified dining-room; it is very warm and light, not only from the direct rays of the
sun, but by their reflection from the sea. Beyond this is a bed-room
with an ante-room, the height of which renders it cool in summer, its

thick walls warm in winter, for it is sheltered, every way from the winds. To this apartment another anteroom is joined by one common wall. From thence you enter into the wide and spacious cooling-room belonging to the bath, from the opposite walls of which two curved basins are thrown out, so to speak; which are more than large enough if you consider that the sea is close at hand. Adjacent to this is the anointing-room, then the sweating-room, and beyond that the bath-heating room: adjoining are two other little bath-rooms, elegantly rather than sumptuously fitted up: annexed to them is a warm bath of wonderful construction, in which one can swim and take a view of the sea at the same time. Not far from this stands the tennis-court, which lies open to the warmth of the afternoon sun. From thence you go up a sort of turret which has two rooms below, with the same number above, besides a dining-room commanding a very extensive look-out on to the sea, the coast, and the beautiful villas scattered along the shore line. At the other end is a second turret, containing a room that gets the rising and setting sun. Behind this is a large store-room and granary, and underneath, a spacious dining-room, where only the murmur and break of the sea can be heard, even in a storm: it looks out upon the garden, and the gestatio,[40] running round the garden. The gestatio is bordered round with box, and, where that is decayed, with rosemary: for the box, wherever sheltered by the buildings, grows plentifully, but where it lies open and exposed to the weather and spray from the sea, though at some distance from the latter, it quite withers up. Next the gestatio, and running along inside it, is a shady vine plantation, the path of which is so soft and easy to the tread that you may walk bare-foot upon it. The garden is chiefly planted with fig and mulberry trees, to which this soil is as favourable as it is averse from all others. Here is a dining-room, which, though it stands away from the sea enjoys the garden view which is just as pleasant: two apartments run round the back part of it, the windows of which look out upon the entrance of the villa, and into a fine kitchen-garden. From here extends an enclosed portico which, from its great length, you might take for a public one. It has a range of windows on either side, but more on the side facing the sea, and fewer on the garden side, and these, single windows and alternate with the opposite rows. In calm, clear, weather these are all thrown open; but if it blows, those on the weather side are closed, whilst those away from the wind can remain open without any inconvenience. Before this enclosed portico lies a terrace fragrant with the scent of violets, and

---

40   Avenue

warmed by the reflection of the sun from the portico, which, while it retains the rays, keeps away the north-east wind; and it is as warm on this side as it is cool on the side opposite: in the same way it is a protection against the wind from the south-west; and thus, in short, by means of its several sides, breaks the force of the winds, from whatever quarter they may blow. These are some of its winter advantages, they are still more appreciable in the summer time; for at that season it throws a shade upon the terrace during the whole of the forenoon, and upon the adjoining portion of the gestatio and garden in the afternoon, casting a greater or less shade on this side or on that as the day increases or decreases. But the portico itself is coolest just at the time when the sun is at its hottest, that is, when the rays fall directly upon the roof. Also, by opening the windows you let in the western breezes in a free current, which prevents the place getting oppressive with close and stagnant air. At the upper end of the terrace and portico stands a detached garden building, which I call my favourite; my favourite indeed, as I put it up myself. It contains a very warm winter-room, one side of which looks down upon the terrace, while the other has a view of the sea, and both lie exposed to the sun. The bed-room opens on to the covered portico by means of folding-doors, while its window looks out upon the sea. On that side next the sea, and facing the middle wall, is formed a very elegant little recess, which, by means of transparent[41] windows, and a curtain drawn to or aside, can be made part of the adjoining room, or separated from it. It contains a couch and two chairs: as you lie upon this couch, from where your feet are you get a peep of the sea; looking behind you see the neighbouring villas, and from the head you have a view of the woods: these three views may be seen either separately, from so many different windows, or blended together in one. Adjoining this is a bed-room, which neither the servants' voices, the murmuring of the sea, the glare of lightning, nor daylight itself can penetrate, unless you open the windows. This profound tranquillity and seclusion are occasioned by a passage separating the wall of this room from that of the garden, and thus, by means of this intervening space, every noise is drowned. Annexed to this is a tiny stove-room, which, by opening or shutting a little aperture, lets out or retains the heat from underneath, according as you require. Beyond this lie a bed-room and ante-room, which enjoy the sun, though obliquely indeed, from the time it rises, till

---

41   "Windows made of a transparent stone called lapis specularis (mica), which was first found in Hispania Citerior, and afterwards in Cyprus, Cappadocia, Sicily, and Africa; but the best caine from Spain and Cappadocia. It was easily split into the thinnest sheets. Windows, made of this stone were called specularia." Smith's Dictionary of Antiquities.

the afternoon. When I retire to this garden summer-house, I fancy myself a hundred miles away from my villa, and take especial pleasure in it at the feast of the Saturnalia,[42] when, by the licence of that festive season, every other part of my house resounds with my servants' mirth: thus I neither interrupt their amusement nor they my studies. Amongst the pleasures and conveniences of this situation, there is one drawback, and that is, the want of running water; but then there are wells about the place, or rather springs, for they lie close to the surface. And, altogether, the quality of this coast is remarkable; for dig where you may, you meet, upon the first turning up of the ground, with a spring of water, quite pure, not in the least salt, although so near the sea. The neighbouring woods supply us with all the fuel we require, the other necessaries Ostia furnishes. Indeed, to a moderate man, even the village (between which and my house there is only one villa) would supply all ordinary requirements. It has three public baths, which are a great convenience if it happen that friends come in unexpectedly, or make too short a stay to allow time in preparing my own. The whole coast is very pleasantly sprinkled with villas either in rows or detached, which whether looking at them from the sea or the shore, present the appearance of so many different cities. The strand is, sometimes, after a long calm, perfectly smooth, though, in general, through the storms driving the waves upon it, it is rough and uneven. I cannot boast that our sea is plentiful in choice fish; however, it supplies us with capital soles and prawns; but as to other kinds of provisions, my villa aspires to excel even inland countries, particularly in milk: for the cattle come up there from the meadows in large numbers, in pursuit of water and shade. Tell me, now, have I not good reason for living in, staying in, loving, such a retreat, which, if you feel no appetite for, you must be morbidly attached to town? And I only wish you would feel inclined to come down to it, that to so many charms with which my little villa abounds, it might have the very considerable addition of your company to recommend it. Farewell.

TO CEREALIS

---

42   A feast held in honour of the god Saturn, which began on the 19th of December, and continued as some say, for seven days. It was a time of general rejoicing, particularly among the slaves, who had at this season the privilege of taking great liberties with their masters. M.

You ADVISE ME TO read my late speech before an assemblage of my friends. I shall do so, as you advise it, though I have strong scruples. Compositions of this sort lose, I well know, all their force and fire, and even their very name almost, by a mere recital. It is the solemnity of the tribunal, the concourse of advocates, the suspense of the event, the fame of the several pleaders concerned, the different parties formed amongst the audience; add to this the gestures, the pacing, aye the actual running, to and fro, of the speaker, the body working[43] in harmony with every inward emotion, that conspire to give a spirit and a grace to what he delivers. This is the reason that those who plead sitting, though they retain most of the advantages possessed by those who stand up to plead, weaken the whole force of their oratory. The eyes and hands of the reader, those important instruments of graceful elocution, being engaged, it is no wonder that the attention of the audience droops, without anything extrinsic to keep it up, no allurements of gesture to attract, no smart, stinging impromptus to enliven. To these general considerations I must add this particular disadvantage which attends the speech in question, that it is of the argumentative kind; and it is natural for an author to infer that what he wrote with labour will not be read with pleasure. For who is there so unprejudiced as not to prefer the attractive and sonorous to the sombre and unornamented in style? It is very unreasonable that there should be any distinction; however, it is certain the judges generally expect one style of pleading, and the audience another; whereas an auditor ought to be affected only by those parts which would especially strike him, were he in the place of the judge. Nevertheless it is possible the objections which lie against this piece may be surmounted in consideration of the novelty it has to recommend it: the novelty I mean with respect to us; for the Greek orators have a method of reasoning upon a different occasion, not altogether unlike that which I have employed. They, when they would throw out a law, as contrary to some former one unrepealed, argue by comparing those together; so I, on the contrary, endeavour to prove that the crime, which I was insisting upon as falling within the intent and meaning of the law relating to public extortions, was agreeable, not only to that law, but likewise to other laws of the same nature. Those who are ignorant of the jurisprudence of their country can have no taste for reasonings of this kind, but those who are not ought to

---

43   Cicero and Quintilian have laid down rules how far, and in what instances, this liberty was allowable, and both agree it ought to be used with great sagacity and judgment. The latter of these excellent critics mentions a witticism of Flavius Virginius, who asked one of these orators, "Quot nillia assuum deciamassett." How many miles he had declaimed. M.

be proportionably the more favourable in the judgments they pass upon them. I shall endeavour, therefore, if you persist in my reciting it, to collect as learned an audience as I can. But before you determine this point, do weigh impartially the different considerations I have laid before you, and then decide as reason shall direct; for it is reason that must justify you; obedience to your commands will be a sufficient apology for me. Farewell.

TO CALVISIUS

GIVE ME A PENNY, and I will tell you a story "worth gold," or, rather, you shall hear two or three; for one brings to my mind another. It makes no difference with which I begin. Verania, the widow of Piso, the Piso, I mean, whom Galba adopted, lay extremely ill, and Regulus paid her a visit. By the way, mark the assurance of the man, visiting a lady who detested him herself, and to whose husband he was a declared enemy! Even barely to enter her house would have been bad enough, but he actually went and seated himself by her bed-side and began enquiring on what day and hour she was born. Being informed of these important particulars, he composes his countenance, fixes his eyes, mutters something to himself, counts upon his fingers, and all this merely to keep the poor sick lady in suspense. When he had finished, "You are," he says, "in one of your climacterics; however, you will get over it. But for your greater satisfaction, I will consult with a certain diviner, whose skill I have frequently experienced." Accordingly off he goes, performs a sacrifice, and returns with the strongest assurances that the omens confirmed what he had promised on the part of the stars. Upon this the good woman, whose danger made her credulous, calls for her will and gives Regulus a legacy. She grew worse shortly after this; and in her last moments exclaimed against this wicked, treacherous, and worse than perjured wretch, who had sworn falsely to her by his own son's life. But imprecations of this sort are as common with Regulus as they are impious; and he continually devotes that unhappy youth to the curse of those gods whose vengeance his own frauds every day provoke.

Velleius Blaesus, a man of consular rank, and remarkable for his immense wealth, in his last illness was anxious to make some alterations in his will. Regulus, who had lately endeavoured to insinuate himself into his good graces, hoped to get something from the new will, and accordingly addresses himself to his physicians, and conjures them to exert all their skill to prolong the poor man's life. But after the will was signed, he changes his character, reversing his tone: "How long," says he to these very same physicians, "do you intend keeping this man in misery? Since you cannot preserve his life, why do you grudge him the happy release of death?" Blaesus dies, and, as if he had overheard every word that Regulus had said, has not left him one farthing.—And now have you had enough? or are you for the third, according to rhetorical canon? If so, Regulus will supply you. You must know, then, that Aurelia, a lady of remarkable accomplishments, purposing to execute her will,[44] had put on her smartest dress for the occasion. Regulus, who was present as a witness, turned to the lady, and "Pray," says he, "leave me these fine clothes." Aurelia thought the man was joking: but he insisted upon it perfectly seriously, and, to be brief, obliged her to open her will, and insert the dress she had on as a legacy to him, watching as she wrote, and then looking over it to see that it was all down correctly. Aurelia, however, is still alive: though Regulus, no doubt, when he solicited this bequest, expected to enjoy it pretty soon. The fellow gets estates, he gets legacies, conferred upon him, as if he really deserved them! But why should I go on dwelling upon this in a city where wickedness and knavery have, for this time past, received, the same, do I say, nay, even greater encouragement, than modesty and virtue? Regulus is a glaring instance of this truth, who, from a state of poverty, has by a train of villainies acquired such immense riches that he once told me, upon consulting the omens to know how soon he should be worth sixty millions of sesterces,[45] he found them so favourable as to portend he should possess double that sum. And possibly he may, if he continues to dictate wills for other people in this way: a sort of fraud, in my opinion, the most infamous of any. Farewell.

TO CALVISIUS

I NEVER, I think, spent any time more agreeably than my time lately with Spurinna. So agreeably, indeed, that if ever I should arrive at old age, there is no man whom I would sooner choose for my model, for nothing can be more perfect in arrangement than his mode of life. I look upon order in human actions, especially at that advanced age, with the same sort of pleasure as I behold the settled course of the heavenly bodies. In young men, indeed, a little confusion and disarrangement is

---

44   This was an act of great ceremony; and if Aurelia's dress was of the kind which some of the Roman ladies used, the legacy must have been considerable which Regulus had the impudence to ask. M.
45    $3,350,000.

all well enough: but in age, when business is unseasonable, and ambition indecent, all should be composed and uniform. This rule Spurinna observes with the most religious consistency. Even in those matters which one might call insignificant, were they not of every-day occurrence, he observes a certain periodical season and method. The early morning he passes on his couch; at eight he calls for his slippers, and walks three miles, exercising mind and body together. On his return, if he has any friends in the house with him, he gets upon some entertaining and interesting topic of conversation; if by himself, some book is read to him, sometimes when visitors are there even, if agreeable to the company. Then he has a rest, and after that either takes up a book or resumes his conversation in preference to reading. By-and-by he goes out for a drive in his carriage, either with his wife, a most admirable woman, or with some friend: a happiness which lately was mine.—How agreeable, how delightful it is getting a quiet time alone with him in this way! You could imagine you were listening to some worthy of ancient times! What deeds, what men you hear about, and with what noble precepts you are imbued! Yet all delivered with so modest an air that there is not the least appearance of dictating. When he has gone about seven miles, he gets out of his chariot and walks a mile more, after which he returns home, and either takes a rest or goes back to his couch and writing. For he composes most elegant lyrics both in Greek and Latin. So wonderfully soft, sweet, and gay they are, while the author's own unsullied life lends them additional charm. When the baths are ready, which in winter is about three o'clock, and in summer about two, he undresses himself and, if there happen to be no wind, walks for some time in the sun. After this he has a good brisk game of tennis: for by this sort of exercise too, he combats the effects of old age. When he has bathed, he throws himself upon his couch, but waits a little before he begins eating, and in the meanwhile has some light and entertaining author read to him. In this, as in all the rest, his friends are at full liberty to share; or to employ themselves in any other way, just as they prefer. You sit down to an elegant dinner, without extravagant display, which is served up in antique plate of pure silver. He has another complete service in Corinthian metal, which, though he admires as a curiosity, is far from being his passion. During dinner he is frequently entertained with the recital of some dramatic piece, by way of seasoning his very pleasures with study; and although he continues at the table, even in summer, till the night is somewhat advanced, yet he prolongs the entertainment with so much affability and politeness that none of his guests ever finds it tedious. By this method of living he has preserved all his senses entire, and his body vigorous and active to his seventy-eighth year, without showing any sign of old age except wisdom. This is the sort of life I ardently aspire after; as I purpose enjoying it when I shall arrive at those years which will justify a retreat from active life. Meanwhile I am embarrassed with a thousand affairs, in which Spurinna is at once my support and my example: for he too, so long as it became him, discharged his professional duties, held magistracies, governed provinces, and by toiling hard earned the repose he now enjoys. I propose to myself the same career and the same limits: and I here give it to you under my hand that I do so. If an ill-timed ambition should carry me beyond those bounds, produce this very letter of mine in court against me; and condemn me to repose, whenever I enjoy it without being reproached with indolence. Farewell.

TO BAEBIUS MACER

IT GIVES ME GREAT pleasure to find you such a reader of my uncle's works as to wish to have a complete collection of them, and to ask me for the names of them all. I will act as index then, and you shall know the very order in which they were written, for the studious reader likes to know this. The first work of his was a treatise in one volume, "On the Use of the Dart by Cavalry"; this he wrote when in command of one of the cavalry corps of our allied troops, and is drawn up with great care and ingenuity. "The Life of Pomponius Secundus,"[46] in two volumes. Pomponius had a great affection for him, and he thought he owed this tribute to his memory. "The History of the Wars in Germany," in twenty books, in which he gave an account of all the battles we were engaged in against that nation. A dream he had while serving in the army in Germany first suggested the design of this work to him. He imagined that Drusus Nero[47] (who extended his conquest very far into that country, and there lost his life) appeared to him in his sleep, and entreated him to rescue his memory from oblivion. Next comes a work entitled "The Student," in three parts, which from their length spread into six volumes: a work in which is discussed the earliest training and subsequent education of the orator. "Questions of Grammar and Style," in

---

46   A poet to whom Quintilian assigns the highest rank, as a Writer of tragedies, among his contemporaries (book X. C. I. 98). Tacitus also speaks of him in terms of high appreciation (Annals, v. 8).

47   Stepson of Augustus and brother to Tiberius. An amiable and popular prince. He died at the close of his third campaign, from a fracture received by falling from his horse.

eight books, written in the latter part of Nero's reign, when the tyranny of the times made it dangerous to engage in literary pursuits requiring freedom and elevation of tone. He has completed the history which Aufidius Bassus[48] left unfinished, and has added to it thirty books. And lastly he has left thirty-seven books on Natural History, a work of great compass and learning, and as full of variety as nature herself. You will wonder how a man as busy as he was could find time to compose so many books, and some of them too involving such care and labour. But you will be still more surprised when you hear that he pleaded at the bar for some time, that he died in his sixty-sixth year, that the intervening time was employed partly in the execution of the highest official duties, partly in attendance upon those emperors who honoured him with their friendship. But he had a quick apprehension, marvellous power of application, and was of an exceedingly wakeful temperament. He always began to study at midnight at the time of the feast of Vulcan, not for the sake of good luck, but for learning's sake; in winter generally at one in the morning, but never later than two, and often at twelve.[49] He was a most ready sleeper, insomuch that he would sometimes, whilst in the midst of his studies, fall off and then wake up again. Before day-break he used to wait upon Vespasian' (who also used his nights for transacting business in), and then proceed to execute the orders he had received. As soon as he returned home, he gave what time was left to study. After a short and light refreshment at noon (agreeably to the good old custom of our ancestors) he would frequently in the summer, if he was disengaged from business, lie down and bask in the sun; during which time some author was read to him, while he took notes and made extracts,

---

48   A historian under Augustus and Tiberius. He wrote part of a history of Rome, which was continued by the elder Pliny; also an account of the German war, to which Quintilian makes allusion (Inst. X. 103), pronouncing him, as a historian, "estimable in all respects, yet in some things failing to do himself justice."

49   The distribution of time among the Romans was very different from ours. They divided the night into four equal parts, which they called watches, each three hours in length; and part of these they devoted either to the pleasures of the table or to study. The natural day they divided into twelve hours, the first beginning with sunrise, and the last ending with sunset; by which means their hours were of unequal length, varying according to the different seasons of the year. The time for business began with sunrise, and continued to the fifth hour, being that of dinner, which with them was only a slight repast. From thence to the seventh hour was a time of repose; a custom which still prevails in Italy. The eighth hour was employed in bodily exercises; after which they constantly bathed, and from thence went to supper. M.

for every book he read he made extracts out of, indeed it was a maxim of his, that "no book was so bad but some good might be got out of it." When this was over, he generally took a cold bath, then some light refreshment and a little nap. After this, as if it had been a new day, he studied till supper-time, when a book was again read to him, which he would take down running notes upon. I remember once his reader having mis-pronounced a word, one of my uncle's friends at the table made him go back to where the word was and repeat it again; upon which my uncle said to his friend, "Surely you understood it?" Upon his acknowledging that he did, "Why then," said he, "did you make him go back again? We have lost more than ten lines by this interruption." Such an economist he was of time! In the summer he used to rise from sup-per at daylight, and in winter as soon as it was dark: a rule he observed as strictly as if it had been a law of the state. Such was his manner of life amid the bustle and turmoil of the town: but in the country his whole time was devoted to study, excepting only when he bathed. In this exception I include no more than the time during which he was actually in the bath; for all the while he was being rubbed and wiped, he was employed either in hearing some book read to him or in dictating himself. In going about anywhere, as though he were disengaged from all other business, he applied his mind wholly to that single pursuit. A shorthand writer constantly attended him, with book and tablets, who, in the winter, wore a particular sort of warm gloves, that the sharpness of the weather might not occasion any interruption to my uncle's stud-ies: and for the same reason, when in Rome, he was always carried in a chair. I recollect his once taking me to task for walking. "You need not," he said, "lose these hours." For he thought every hour gone that was not given to study. Through this extraordinary application he found time to compose the several treatises I have mentioned, besides one hundred and sixty volumes of extracts which he left me in his will, consisting of a kind of common-place, written on both sides, in very small hand, so that one might fairly reckon the number considerably more. He used himself to tell us that when he was comptroller of the revenue in Spain, he could have sold these manuscripts to Largius Licinus for four hun-dred thousand sesterces,[50] and then there were not so many of them. When you consider the books he has read, and the volumes he has writ-ten, are you not inclined to suspect that he never was engaged in public duties or was ever in the confidence of his prince? On the other hand, when you are told how indefatigable he was in his studies, are you not

---

50   $16,000.

inclined to wonder that he read and wrote no more than he did? For, on one side, what obstacles would not the business of a court throw in his way? and on the other, what is it that such intense application might not effect? It amuses me then when I hear myself called a studious man, who in comparison with him am the merest idler. But why do I mention myself, who am diverted from these pursuits by numberless affairs both public and private? Who amongst those whose whole lives are devoted to literary pursuits would not blush and feel himself the most confirmed of sluggards by the side of him? I see I have run out my letter farther than I had originally intended, which was only to let you know, as you asked me, what works he had left behind him. But I trust this will be no less acceptable to you than the books themselves, as it may, possibly, not only excite your curiosity to read his works, but also your emulation to copy his example, by some attempts of a similar nature. Farewell.

TO ANNIUS SEVERUS

I HAVE LATELY PURCHASED with a legacy that was left me a small statue of Corinthian brass. It is small indeed, but elegant and life-like, as far as I can form any judgment, which most certainly in matters of this sort, as perhaps in all others, is extremely defective. However, I do see the beauties of this figure: for, as it is naked the faults, if there be any, as well as the perfections, are the more observable. It represents an old man, in an erect attitude. The bones, muscles, veins, and the very wrinkles, give the Impression of breathing life. The hair is thin and failing, the forehead broad, the face shrivelled, the throat lank, the arms loose and hanging, the breast shrunken, and the belly fallen in, as the whole turn and air of the figure behind too is equally expressive of old age. It appears to be true antique, judging from the colour of the brass. In short, it is such a masterpiece as would strike the eyes of a connoisseur, and which cannot fail to charm an ordinary observer: and this induced me, who am an absolute novice in this art, to buy it. But I did so, not with any intention of placing it in my own house (for I have nothing of the kind there), but with a design of fixing it in some conspicuous place in my native province; I should like it best in the temple of Jupiter, for it is a gift well worthy of a temple, well worthy of a god. I desire therefore you would, with that care with which you always perform my requests, undertake this commission and give immediate orders for a pedestal to be made for it, out of what marble you please, but let my name be engraved upon it, and, if you think proper to add these as well, my titles. I will send the statue by the first person I can find who will not mind the trouble of it; or possibly (which I am sure you will like better) I may myself bring it along with me: for I intend, if business can spare me that is to say, to make an excursion over to you. I see joy in your looks when I promise to come; but you will soon change your countenance when I add, only for a few days: for the same business that at present keeps me here will prevent my making a longer stay. Farewell.

TO CANINIUS RUFUS

I HAVE JUST BEEN informed that Silius Italicus[51] has starved himself to death, at his villa near Naples. Ill-health was the cause. Being troubled with an incurable cancerous humour, he grew weary of life and therefore put an end to it with a determination not to be moved. He had been extremely fortunate all through his life with the exception of the death of the younger of his two sons; however, he has left behind him the elder and the worthier man of the two in a position of distinction, having even attained consular rank. His reputation had suffered a little in Nero's time, as he was suspected of having officiously joined in some of the informations in that reign; but he used his interest with Vitellius, with great discretion and humanity. He acquired considerable honour by his administration of the government of Asia, and, by his good conduct after his retirement from business, cleared his character from that stain which his former public exertions had thrown upon it. He lived as a private nobleman, without power, and consequently without envy. Though he was frequently confined to his bed, and always to his room, yet he was highly respected, and much visited; not with an interested view, but on his own account. He employed his time between conversing with literary men and composing verses; which he sometimes read out, by way of testing the public opinion: but they evidence more industry than genius. In the decline of his years he entirely quitted Rome, and lived altogether in Campania, from whence even the accession of the new emperor[52] could not draw him. A circumstance which I mention as much to the honour of Cæsar, who was not displeased with that

---

51   Born about A. D. 25. He acquired some distinction as an advocate. The only poem of his which has come down to us is a heavy prosaic performance in seventeen books, entitled "Tunica," and containing an account of the events of the Second Punic War, from the capture of Saguntum to the triumph of Scipio Africanus. See Smith's Dict. of Gr. and Roin. Biog.

52   Trajan.

liberty, as of Italicus, who was not afraid to make use of it. He was reproached with indulging his taste for the fine arts at an immoderate expense. He had several villas in the same province, and the last purchase was always the especial favourite, to the neglect of all the rest, These residences overflowed with books, statues, and pictures, which he more than enjoyed, he even adored; particularly that of Virgil, of whom he was so passionate an admirer that he celebrated the anniversary of that poet's birthday with more solemnity than his own, at Naples especially where he used to approach his tomb as if it had been a temple. In this tranquillity he passed his seventy-fifth year, with a delicate rather than an infirm constitution.

As he was the last person upon whom Nero conferred the consular office, so he was the last survivor of all those who had been raised by him to that dignity. It is also remarkable that, as he was the last to die of Nero's consuls, so Nero died when he was consul. Recollecting this, a feeling of pity for the transitory condition of mankind comes over me. Is there anything in nature so short and limited as human life, even at its longest? Does it not seem to you but yesterday that Nero was alive? And yet not one of all those who were consuls in his reign now remains! Though why should I wonder at this? Lucius Piso (the father of that Piso who was so infamously assassinated by Valerius Festus in Africa) used to say, he did not see one person in the senate whose opinion he had consulted when he was consul: in so short a space is the very term of life of such a multitude of beings comprised! so that to me those royal tears seem not only worthy of pardon but of praise. For it is said that Xerxes, on surveying his immense army, wept at the reflection that so many thousand lives would in such a short space of time be extinct. The more ardent therefore should be our zeal to lengthen out this frail and transient portion of existence, if not by our deeds (for the opportunities of this are not in our power) yet certainly by our literary accomplishments; and since long life is denied us, let us transmit to posterity some memorial that we have at least LIVED. I well know you need no incitements, but the warmth of my affection for you inclines me to urge you on in the course you are already pursuing, just as you have so often urged me. "Happy rivalry" when two friends strive in this way which of them shall animate the other most in their mutual pursuit of immortal fame. Farewell.

TO SPURINNA AND COTTIA[53]

I DID NOT TELL you, when I paid you my last visit, that I had composed something in praise of your son; because, in the first place, I wrote it not for the sake of talking about my performance, but simply to satisfy my affection, to console my sorrow for the loss of him. Again, as you told me, my dear Spurinna, that you had heard I had been reciting a piece of mine, I imagined you had also heard at the same time what was the subject of the recital, and besides I was afraid of casting a gloom over your cheerfulness in that festive season, by reviving the remembrance of that heavy sorrow. And even now I have hesitated a little whether I should gratify you both, in your joint request, by sending only what I recited, or add to it what I am thinking of keeping back for another essay. It does not satisfy my feelings to devote only one little tract to a memory so dear and sacred to me, and it seemed also more to the interest of his fame to have it thus disseminated by separate pieces. But the consideration, that it will be more open and friendly to send you the whole now, rather than keep back some of it to another time, has determined me to do the former, especially as I have your promise that it shall not be communicated by either of you to anyone else, until I shall think proper to publish it. The only remaining favour I ask is, that you will give me a proof of the same unreserve by pointing out to me what you shall judge would be best altered, omitted, or added. It is difficult for a mind in affliction to concentrate itself upon such little cares. However, as you would direct a painter or sculptor who was representing the figure of your son what parts he should retouch or express, so I hope you will guide and inform my hand in this more durable or (as you are pleased to think it) this immortal likeness which I am endeavouring to execute: for the truer to the original, the more perfect and finished it is, so much the more lasting it is likely to prove. Farewell.

TO JULIUS GENITOR

IT IS JUST LIKE the generous disposition of Artemidorus to magnify the kindnesses of his friends; hence he praises my deserts (though he is really indebted to me) beyond their due. It is true indeed that when the

---

53   Spurinna's wife.

philosophers were expelled from Rome,[54] I visited him at his house near the city, and ran the greater risk in paying him that civility, as it was more noticeable then, I being praetor at the time. I supplied him too with a considerable sum to pay certain debts he had contracted upon very honourable occasions, without charging interest, though obliged to borrow the money myself, while the rest of his rich powerful friends stood by hesitating about giving him assistance. I did this at a time when seven of my friends were either executed or banished; Senecio, Rusticus, and Helvidius having just been put to death, while Mauricus, Gratilla, Arria, and Fannia, were sent into exile; and scorched as it were by so many lightning-bolts of the state thus hurled and flashing round me, I augured by no uncertain tokens my own impending doom. But I do not look upon myself, on that account, as deserving of the high praises my friend bestows upon me: all I pretend to is the being clear of the infamous guilt of abandoning him in his misfortunes. I had, as far as the differences between our ages would admit, a friendship for his father-in-law Musonius, whom I both loved and esteemed, while Artemidorus himself I entered into the closest intimacy with when I was serving as a military tribune in Syria. And I consider as a proof that there is some good in me the fact of my being so early capable of appreciating a man who is either a philosopher or the nearest resemblance to one possible; for I am sure that, amongst all those who at the present day call themselves philosophers, you will find hardly any one of them so full of sincerity and truth as he. I forbear to mention how patient he is of heat and cold alike, how indefatigable in labour, how abstemious in his food, and what an absolute restraint he puts upon all his appetites; for these qualities, considerable as they would certainly be in any other character, are less noticeable by the side of the rest of those virtues of his which recommended him to Musonius for a son-in-law, in preference to so many others of all ranks who paid their addresses to his daughter. And when I think of all these things, I cannot help feeling pleasurably affected by those unqualified terms of praise in which he speaks of me to you as well as to everyone else. I am only apprehensive lest the warmth of his kind feeling carry him beyond the due limits; for he, who is so free from all other errors, is apt to fall into just this one good-natured one, of overrating the merits of his friends. Farewell.

---

54   Domitian banished the philosophers not only from Rome, but Italy,
as Suetonius (Dom. C. X.) and Aulus Gellius (Noct. Att. b. XV. CXI. 3, 4, 5)
Inform us among these was the celebrated Epictetus. M.

TO CATILIUS SEVERUS

I WILL COME TO supper, but must make this agreement beforehand, that I go when I please, that you treat me to nothing expensive, and that our conversation abound only in Socratic discourse, while even that in moderation. There are certain necessary visits of ceremony, bringing people out before daylight, which Cato himself could not safely fall in with; though I must confess that Julius Cæsar reproaches him with that circumstance in such a manner as redounds to his praise; for he tells us that the persons who met him reeling home blushed at the discovery, and adds, "You would have thought that Cato had detected them, and not they Cato." Could he place the dignity of Cato in a stronger light than by representing him thus venerable even in his cups? But let our supper be as moderate in regard to hours as in the preparation and expense: for we are not of such eminent reputation that even our enemies cannot censure our conduct without applauding it at the same time. Farewell.

TO ACILIUS

THE ATROCIOUS TREATMENT THAT Largius Macedo, a man of praetorian rank, lately received at the hands of his slaves is so extremely tragical that it deserves a place rather in public history than in a private letter; though it must at the same time be acknowledged there was a haughtiness and severity in his behaviour towards them which shewed that he little remembered, indeed almost entirely forgot, the fact that his own father had once been in that station of life. He was bathing at his Formian Villa, when he found himself suddenly surrounded by his slaves; one seizes him by the throat, another strikes him on the mouth, whilst others trampled upon his breast, stomach, and even other parts which I need not mention. When they thought the breath must be quite out of his body, they threw him down upon the heated pavement of the bath, to try whether he were still alive, where he lay outstretched and motionless, either really insensible or only feigning to be so, upon which they concluded him to be actually dead. In this condition they brought him out, pretending that he had got suffocated by the heat of the bath. Some of his more trusty servants received him, and his mistresses came about him shrieking and lamenting. The noise of their cries and the fresh air, together, brought him a little to himself; he opened his eyes, moved his body, and shewed them (as he now safely might) that he was not quite dead. The murderers immediately made their escape; but most of them have been caught again, and they are after the rest. He was with great difficulty kept alive for a few days, and then expired, having however the satisfaction of finding himself as amply revenged in his lifetime as he would have been after his death. Thus you see to what affronts, indignities, and dangers we are exposed. Lenity and kind treatment are no safeguard; for it is malice and not reflection that arms such ruffians against their masters. So much for this piece of news. And what else? What else? Nothing else, or you should hear it, for I have still paper, and time too (as it is holiday time with me) to spare for more, and I can tell you one further circumstance relating to Macedo, which now occurs to me. As he was in a public bath once, at Rome, a remarkable, and (judging from the manner of his death) an ominous, accident happened to him. A slave of his, in order to make way for his master, laid his hand gently upon a Roman knight, who, turning suddenly round, struck, not the slave who had touched him, but Macedo, so violent a blow with his open palm that he almost knocked him down. Thus the bath by a kind of gradation proved fatal to him; being first the scene of an indignity he suffered, afterwards the scene of his death. Farewell.

TO NEPOS

I HAVE CONSTANTLY OBSERVED that amongst the deeds and sayings of illustrious persons of either sex, some have made more noise in the world, whilst others have been really greater, although less talked about; and I am confirmed in this opinion by a conversation I had yesterday with Fannia. This lady is a grand-daughter to that celebrated Arria, who animated her husband to meet death, by her own glorious example. She informed me of several particulars relating to Arria, no less heroic than this applauded action of hers, though taken less notice of, and I think you will be as surprised to read the account of them as I was to hear it. Her husband Caecinna Paetus, and her son, were both attacked at the same time with a fatal illness, as was supposed; of which the son died, a youth of remarkable beauty, and as modest as he was comely, endeared indeed to his parents no less by his many graces than from the fact of his being their son. His mother prepared his funeral and conducted the usual ceremonies so privately that Paetus did not know of his death. Whenever she came into his room, she pretended her son was alive and actually better: and as often as he enquired after his health, would answer, "He has had a good rest, and eaten his food with quite an appetite." Then when she found the tears, she had so long kept back, gushing forth in spite of herself, she would leave the room, and having given vent to her grief, return with dry eyes and a serene countenance, as though she had dismissed every feeling of bereavement at the door of her husband's chamber. I must confess it was a brave action[55] in her to draw the steel, plunge it into her breast, pluck out the dagger, and present it to her husband with that ever memorable, I had almost said that divine, expression, "Paetus, it is not painful." But when she spoke and acted thus, she had the prospect of glory and immortality before her; how far greater, without the support of any such animating motives, to hide her tears, to conceal her grief, and cheerfully to act the mother, when a mother no more!

Scribonianus had taken up arms in Illyria against Clatidius, where he lost his life, and Paetus, who was of his party, was brought a prisoner to Rome. When they were going to put him on board ship, Arria besought the soldiers that she might be permitted to attend him: "For surely," she urged, "you will allow a man of consular rank some servants to dress him, attend to him at meals, and put his shoes on for him; but if you will take me, I alone will perform all these offices." Her request was refused; upon which she hired a fishing-boat, and in that small vessel followed the ship. On her return to Rome, meeting the wife of Scribonianus in the emperor's palace, at the time when this woman voluntarily gave evidence against the conspirators—"What," she exclaimed, "shall I hear you even speak to me, you, on whose bosom your husband Scribonianus was murdered, and yet you survive him?"—an expression which plainly shews that the noble manner in which she put an end to her life was no unpremeditated effect of sudden passion. Moreover, when Thrasea, her son-in-law, was endeavouring to dissuade her from her purpose of destroying herself, and, amongst other arguments which he used, said to her, "Would you then advise your daughter to die with me if my life were to be taken from me?" "Most certainly I would," she replied, "if she had lived as long, and in as much harmony with you, as I have with my Paetus." This answer greatly increased the alarm of her family, and made them watch her for the future more narrowly; which, when she perceived, "It is of no use," she said, "you

---

55   The following is the story, as related by several of the ancient historians. Paetus, having joined Scribonianus, who was in arms, in Illyria, against Claudius, was taken after the death of Scribonianus, and condemned to death. Arria having, in vain, solicited his life, persuaded him to destroy himself, rather than suffer the ignominy of falling by the executioner's hands; and, in order to encourage him to an act, to which, it seems, he was not particularly inclined, she set him the example in the manner Pliny relates. M.

may oblige me to effect my death in a more painful way, but it is impossible you should prevent it." Saying this, she sprang from her chair, and running her head with the utmost violence against the wall, fell down, to all appearance, dead; but being brought to herself again, "I told you," she said, "if you would not suffer me to take an easy path to death, I should find a way to it, however hard." Now, is there not, my friend, something much greater in all this than in the so-much-talked-of "Paetus, it is not painful," to which these led the way? And yet this last is the favourite topic of fame, while all the former are passed over in silence. Whence I cannot but infer, what I observed at the beginning of my letter, that some actions are more celebrated, whilst others are really greater. Farewell.

TO SEVERUS

I was obliged by my consular office to compliment the emperor[56] in the name of the republic; but after I had performed that ceremony in the senate in the usual manner, and as fully as the time and place would allow, I thought it agreeable to the affection of a good subject to enlarge those general heads, and expand them into a complete discourse. My principal object in doing so was, to confirm the emperor in his virtues, by paying them that tribute of applause which they so justly deserve; and at the same time to direct future princes, not in the formal way of lecture, but by his more engaging example, to those paths they must pursue if they would attain the same heights of glory. To instruct princes how to form their conduct, is a noble, but difficult task, and may, perhaps, be esteemed an act of presumption: but to applaud the character of an accomplished prince, and to hold out to posterity, by this means, a beacon-light as it were, to guide succeeding monarchs, is a method equally useful, and much more modest. It afforded me a very singular pleasure that when I wished to recite this panegyric in a private assembly, my friends gave me their company, though I did not solicit them in the usual form of notes or circulars, but only desired their attendance, "should it be quite convenient to them," and "if they should happen to have no other engagement." You know the excuses generally made at Rome to avoid invitations of this kind; how prior invitations are usually alleged; yet, in spite of the worst possible weather, they attended the recital for two days together; and when I thought it would be unreasonable to detain them any longer, they insisted upon my going

---

56   Trajan.

through with it the next day. Shall I consider this as an honour done to myself or to literature? Rather let me suppose to the latter, which, though well-nigh extinct, seems to be now again reviving amongst us. Yet what was the subject which raised this uncommon attention? No other than what formerly, even in the senate, where we had to submit to it, we used to grudge even a few moments' attention to. But now, you see, we have patience to recite and to attend to the same topic for three days together; and the reason of this is, not that we have more eloquent writing now than formerly, but we write under a fuller sense of individual freedom, and consequently more genially than we used to. It is an additional glory therefore to our present emperor that this sort of harangue, which was once as disgusting as it was false, is now as pleasing as it is sincere. But it was not only the earnest attention of my audience which afforded me pleasure; I was greatly delighted too with the justness of their taste: for I observed, that the more nervous parts of my discourse gave them peculiar satisfaction. It is true, indeed, this work, which was written for the perusal of the world in general, was read only to a few; however, I would willingly look upon their particular judgment as an earnest of that of the public, and rejoice at their manly taste as if it were universally spread. It was just the same in eloquence as it was in music, the vitiated ears of the audience introduced a depraved style; but now, I am inclined to hope, as a more refined judgment prevails in the public, our compositions of both kinds will improve too; for those authors whose sole object is to please will fashion their works according to the popular taste. I trust, however, in subjects of this nature the florid style is most proper; and am so far from thinking that the vivid colouring I have used will be esteemed foreign and unnatural that I am most apprehensive that censure will fall upon those parts where the diction is most simple and unornate. Nevertheless, I sincerely wish the time may come, and that it now were, when the smooth and luscious, which has affected our style, shall give place, as it ought, to severe and chaste composition. — Thus have I given you an account of my doings of these last three days, that your absence might not entirely deprive you of a pleasure which, from your friendship to me, and the part you take in everything that concerns the interest of literature, I know you would have received, had you been there to hear. Farewell.

TO CALVISIUS RUFUS

I MUST HAVE RECOURSE to you, as usual, in an affair which concerns my finances. An estate adjoining my land, and indeed running into it, is for sale. There are several considerations strongly inclining me to this purchase, while there are others no less weighty deterring me from it. Its first recommendation is, the beauty which will result from uniting this farm to my own lands; next, the advantage as well as pleasure of being able to visit it without additional trouble and expense; to have it superintended by the same steward, and almost by the same sub-agents, and to have one villa to support and embellish, the other just to keep in common repair. I take into this account furniture, housekeepers, fancy-gardeners, artificers, and even hunting-apparatus, as it makes a very great difference whether you get these altogether into one place or scatter them about in several. On the other hand, I don't know whether it is prudent to expose so large a property to the same climate, and the same risks of accident happening; to distribute one's possessions about seems a safer way of meeting the caprice of fortune, besides, there is something extremely pleasant in the change of air and place, and the going about between one's properties. And now, to come to the chief consideration:—the lands are rich, fertile, and well-watered, consist-ing chiefly of meadow-ground, vineyard, and wood, while the supply of building timber and its returns, though moderate, still, keep at the same rate. But the soil, fertile as it is, has been much impoverished by not having been properly looked after. The person last in possession used frequently to seize and sell the stock, by which means, although he lessened his tenants' arrears for the time being, yet he left them noth-ing to go on with and the arrears ran up again in consequence. I shall be obliged, then, to provide them with slaves, which I must buy, and at a higher than the usual price, as these will be good ones; for I keep no fettered slaves[57] myself, and there are none upon the estate. For the rest, the price, you must know, is three millions of sesterces.[58] It has formerly gone over five millions,[59] but owing, partly to the general hardness of the times, and partly to its being thus stripped of tenants, the income of this estate is reduced, and consequently its value. You will be inclined perhaps to enquire whether I can easily raise the purchase-money? My estate, it is true, is almost entirely in land, though I have some money out at interest; but I shall find no difficulty in borrowing any sum I may want. I can get it from my wife's mother, whose purse I may use with the same freedom as my own; so that you need not trouble yourself at

57   The Roman, used to employ their criminals in the lower ones of husbandry, such as ploughing, &c. Pun. H. N. 1. 18, 3. M.
58   About $500,000.
59   About $800,000.

all upon that point, should you have no other objections, which I should like you very carefully to consider: for, as in everything else, so, particularly in matters of economy, no man has more judgment and experience than yourself. Farewell.

TO CORNELIUS PRISCUS

I HAVE JUST HEARD of Valerius Martial's death, which gives me great concern. He was a man of an acute and lively genius, and his writings abound in equal wit, satire, and kindliness. On his leaving Rome I made him a present to defray his travelling expenses, which I gave him, not only as a testimony of friendship, but also in return for the verses with which he had complimented me. It was the custom of the ancients to distinguish those poets with honours or pecuniary rewards, who had celebrated particular individuals or cities in their verses; but this good custom, along with every other fair and noble one, has grown out of fashion now; and in consequence of our having ceased to act laudably, we consider praise a folly and impertinence. You may perhaps be curious to see the verses which merited this acknowledgment from me, and I believe I can, from memory, partly satisfy your curiosity, without referring you to his works: but if you should be pleased with this specimen of them, you must turn to his poems for the rest. He addresses himself to his muse, whom he directs to go to my house upon the Esquiline,[60] but to approach it with respect.

> "Go, wanton muse, but go with care,
> Nor meet, ill-tim'd, my Pliny's ear;
> He, by sage Minerva taught,
> Gives the day to studious thought,
> And plans that eloquence divine,
> Which shall to future ages shine,
> And rival, wondrous Tully! thine.
> Then, cautious, watch the vacant hour,
> When Bacchus reigns in all his pow'r;
> When, crowned with rosy chaplets gay,
> Catos might read my frolic lay."[61]

---

60   One of the famous seven hills upon which Rome was situated.
61   Mart. LX. 19.

Do you not think that the poet who wrote of me in such terms deserved some friendly marks of my bounty then, and of my sorrow now? For he gave me the very best he had to bestow, and would have given more had it been in his power. Though indeed what can a man have conferred on him more valuable than the honour of never-fading praise? But his poems will not long survive their author, at least I think not, though he wrote them in the expectation of their doing so. Farewell.

TO FABATUS (HIS WIFE'S GRANDFATHER)

YOU HAVE LONG DESIRED a visit from your grand-daughter[62] accompanied by me. Nothing, be assured, could be more agreeable to either of us; for we equally wish to see you, and are determined to delay that pleasure no longer. For this purpose we are already packing up, and hastening to you with all the speed the roads will permit of. We shall make only one, short, stoppage, for we intend turning a little out of our way to go into Tuscany: not for the sake of looking upon our estate, and into our family concerns, which we can postpone to another opportunity, but to perform an indispensable duty. There is a town near my estate, called Tifernum-upon-the-Tiber,[63] which, with more affection than wisdom, put itself under my patronage when I was yet a youth. These people celebrate my arrival among them, express the greatest concern when I leave them, and have public rejoicings whenever they hear of my preferments. By way of requiting their kindnesses (for what generous mind can bear to be excelled in acts of friendship?) I have built a temple in this place, at my own expense, and as it is finished, it would be a sort of impiety to put off its dedication any longer. So we shall be there on the day on which that ceremony is to be performed, and I have resolved to celebrate it with a general feast. We may possibly stay on there for all the next day, but shall make so much the greater haste in our journey afterwards. May we have the happiness to find you and your daughter in good health! In good spirits I am sure we shall, should we get to you all safely. Farewell.

TO ATTIUS CLEMENS

62   Calpurnia, Pliny's wife.
63   Now Citta di Castello.

REGULUS HAS LOST HIS son; the only undeserved misfortune which could have befallen him, in that I doubt whether he thinks it a misfortune. The boy had quick parts, but there was no telling how he might turn out; however, he seemed capable enough of going right, were he not to grow up like his father. Regulus gave him his freedom,[64] in order to entitle him to the estate left him by his mother; and when he got into possession of it, (I speak of the current rumours, based upon the character of the man,) fawned upon the lad with a disgusting shew of fond affection which in a parent was utterly out of place. You may hardly think this credible; but then consider what Regulus is. However, he now expresses his concern for the loss of this youth in a most extravagant manner. The boy had a number of ponies for riding and driving, dogs both big and little, together with nightingales, parrots, and blackbirds in abundance. All these Regulus slew round the funeral pile. It was not grief, but an ostentatious parade of grief. He is visited upon this occasion by a surprising number of people, who all hate and detest the man, and yet are as assiduous in their attendance upon him as if they really esteemed and loved him, and, to give you my opinion in a word, in endeavouring to do Regulus a kindness, make themselves exactly like him. He keeps himself in his park on the other side the Tiber, where he has covered a vast extent of ground with his porticoes, and crowded all the shore with his statues; for he unites prodigality with excessive covetousness, and vain-glory with the height of infamy. At this very unhealthy time of year he is boring society, and he feels pleasure and consolation in being a bore. He says he wishes to marry,—a piece of perversity, like all his other conduct. You must expect, therefore, to hear shortly of the marriage of this mourner, the marriage of this old man; too early in the former case, in the latter, too late. You ask me why I conjecture this? Certainly not because he says so himself (for a greater liar never stepped), but because there is no doubt that Regulus will do whatever ought not to be done. Farewell.

TO CATIUS LEPIDUS

I OFTEN TELL YOU that there is a certain force of character about Regulus: it is wonderful how he carries through what he has set his mind to. He chose lately to be extremely concerned for the loss of his son: ac-

---

64   The Romans had an absolute power over their children, of which no age or station of the latter deprived them.

cordingly he mourned for him as never man mourned before. He took it into his head to have an immense number of statues and pictures of him; immediately all the artisans in Rome are set to work. Canvas, wax, brass, silver, gold, ivory, marble, all exhibit the figure of the young Regulus. Not long ago he read, before a numerous audience, a memoir of his son: a memoir of a mere boy! However he read it. He wrote likewise a sort of circular letter to the several Decurii desiring them to choose out one of their order who had a strong clear voice, to read this eulogy to the people; it has been actually done. Now had this force of character or whatever else you may call a fixed determination in obtaining whatever one has a mind for, been rightly applied, what infinite good it might have effected! The misfortune is, there is less of this quality about good people than about bad people, and as ignorance begets rashness, and thoughtfulness produces deliberation, so modesty is apt to cripple the action of virtue, whilst confidence strengthens vice. Regulus is a case in point: he has a weak voice, an awkward delivery, an indistinct utterance, a slow imagination, and no memory; in a word, he possesses nothing but a sort of frantic energy: and yet, by the assistance of a flighty turn and much impudence, he passes as an orator. Herennius Senecio admirably reversed Cato's definition of an orator, and applied it to Regulus: "An orator," he said, "is a bad man, unskilled in the art of speaking." And really Cato's definition is not a more exact description of a true orator than Seneclo's is of the character of this man. Would you make me a suitable return for this letter? Let me know if you, or any of my friends in your town, have, like a stroller in the marketplace, read this doleful production of Regulus's, "raising," as Demosthenes says, "your voice most merrily, and straining every muscle in your throat." For so absurd a performance must excite laughter rather than compassion; and indeed the composition is as puerile as the subject. Farewell.

TO MATURUS ARRIANUS

MY ADVANCEMENT TO THE dignity of augur[65] is an honour that justly indeed merits your congratulations; not only because it is highly honourable to receive, even in the slightest instances, a testimony of the ap-

---

65   Their business was to interpret dreams, oracles, prodigies, &c., and to foretell whether any action should be fortunate or prejudicial, to particular persons, or to the whole commonwealth. Upon this account, they very often occasioned the displacing of magistrates, the deferring of public assemblies, &c. Kennet's Ron,. Antig. M.

probation of so wise and discreet a prince,[66] but because it is moreover an ancient and religious institution, which has this sacred and peculiar privilege annexed to it, that it is for life. Other sacerdotal offices, though they may, perhaps, be almost equal to this one in dignity, yet as they are given so they may be taken away again: but fortune has no further power over this than to bestow it. What recommends this dignity still more highly is, that I have the honour to succeed so illustrious a person as Julius Frontinus. He for many years, upon the nomination-day of proper persons to be received into the sacred college, constantly proposed me, as though he had a view to electing me as his successor; and since it actually proved so in the event, I am willing to look upon it as something more than mere accident. But the circumstance, it seems, that most pleases you in this affair, is, that Cicero enjoyed the same post; and you rejoice (you tell me) to find that I follow his steps as closely in the path of honours as I endeavour to do in that of eloquence. I wish, indeed, that as I had the advantage of being admitted earlier into the same order of priesthood, and into the consular office, than Cicero, that so I might, in my later years, catch some spark, at least, of his divine genius! The former, indeed, being at man's disposal, may be conferred on me and on many others, but the latter it is as presumptuous to hope for as it is difficult to reach, being in the gift of heaven alone. Farewell.

TO STATIUS SABINUS

Your letter informs me that Sabina, who appointed you and me her heirs, though she has nowhere expressly directed that Modestus shall have his freedom, yet has left him a legacy in the following words, "I give, &c.—To Modestus, whom I have ordered to have his freedom": upon which you desire my opinion. I have consulted skilful lawyers upon the point, and they all agree Modestus is not entitled to his liberty, since it is not expressly given, and consequently that the legacy is void, as being bequeathed to a slave.[67] But it evidently appears to be a mistake in the testatrix; and therefore I think we ought to act in this case as though Sabina had directed, in so many words, what, it is clear, she had ordered. I am persuaded you will go with me in this opinion, who so religiously regard the will of the deceased, which indeed where

---

66   Trajan.

67   A slave was incapable of property; and, therefore, whatever he acquired became the right of his master. M.

it can be discovered will always be law to honest heirs. Honour is to you and me as strong an obligation as the compulsion of law is to others. Let Modestus then enjoy his freedom and his legacy as fully as if Sabina had observed all the requisite forms, as indeed they effectually do who make a judicious choice of their heirs. Farewell.

TO CORNELIUS MINICIANUS[68]

HAVE YOU HEARD—I suppose, not yet, for the news has but just arrived — that Valerius Licinianus has become a professor in Sicily? This unfortunate person, who lately enjoyed the dignity of praetor, and was esteemed the most eloquent of our advocates, is now fallen from a senator to an exile, from an orator to a teacher of rhetoric. Accordingly in his inaugural speech he uttered, sorrowfully and solemnly, the following words: "Oh! Fortune, how capriciously dost thou sport with mankind! Thou makest rhetoricians of senators, and senators of rhetoricians!" A sarcasm so poignant and full of gall that one might almost imagine he fixed upon this profession merely for the sake of an opportunity of applying it. And having made his first appearance in school, clad in the Greek cloak (for exiles have no right to wear the toga), after arranging himself and looking down upon his attire, "I am, however," he said, "going to declaim in Latin." You will think, perhaps, this situation, wretched and deplorable as it is, is what he well deserves for having stained the honourable profession of an orator with the crime of incest. It is true, indeed, he pleaded guilty to the charge; but whether from a consciousness of his guilt, or from an apprehension of worse consequences if he denied it, is not clear; for Domitian generally raged most

---

68   "Their office was to attend upon the rites of Vests, the chief part of which was the preservation of the holy fire. If this fire happened to go out, it was considered impiety to light it at any common flame, but they made use of the pure and unpolluted rays of the sun for that purpose. There were various other duties besides connected with their office. The chief rules prescribed them were, to vow the strictest chastity, for the space of thirty years. After this term was completed, they had liberty to leave the order. If they broke their vow of virginity, they were buried alive in a place allotted to that peculiar use." Kennet's Antiq. Their reputation for sanctity was so high that Livy mentions the fact of two of those virgins having violated their vows, as a prodigy that, threatened destruction to the Roman state. Lib. XXII. C. 57. And Suetonius inform, us that Augiastus had so high an opinion of this religious order, that he consigned the care of his will to the Vestal Virgins. Suet, in vit. Aug. C. XCI. M.

furiously where his evidence failed him most hopelessly. That emperor had determined that Cornelia, chief of the Vestal Virgins, should be buried alive, from an extravagant notion that exemplary severities of this kind conferred lustre upon his reign. Accordingly, by virtue of his office as supreme pontiff, or, rather, in the exercise of a tyrant's cruelty, a despot's lawlessness, he convened the sacred college, not in the pontifical court where they usually assemble, but at his villa near Alba; and there, with a guilt no less heinous than that which he professed to be punishing, he condemned her, when she was not present to defend herself, on the charge of incest, while he himself had been guilty, not only of debauching his own brother's daughter, but was also accessory to her death: for that lady, being a widow, in order to conceal her shame, endeavoured to procure an abortion, and by that means lost her life. However, the priests were directed to see the sentence immediately executed upon Cornelia. As they were leading her to the place of execution, she called upon Vesta, and the rest of the gods, to attest her innocence; and, amongst other exclamations, frequently cried out, "Is it possible that Cæsar can think me polluted, under the influence of whose sacred functions he has conquered and triumphed?"[69] Whether she said this in flattery or derision; whether it proceeded from a consciousness of her innocence, or contempt of the emperor, is uncertain; but she continued exclaiming in this manner, till she came to the place of execution, to which she was led, whether innocent or guilty I cannot say, at all events with every appearance and demonstration of innocence. As she was being lowered down into the subterranean vault, her robe happening to catch upon something in the descent, she turned round and disengaged it, when, the executioner offering his assistance, she drew herself back with horror, refusing to be so much as touched by him, as though it were a defilement to her pure and unspotted chastity: still preserving the appearance of sanctity up to the last moment; and, among all the other instances of her modesty,

"She took great care to fall with decency."[70]

Celer likewise, a Roman knight, who was accused of an intrigue with her, while they were scourging him with rods[71] in the Forum, persisted in

---

69   It was usual with Domitian to triumph, not only without a victory, but even after a defeat, M.

70   Euripides' Hecuba,

71   The punishment inflicted upon the violators of Vestal chastity was to be scourged to death. M.

exclaiming, "What have I done?—I have done nothing." These declarations of innocence had exasperated Domitian exceedingly, as imputing to him acts of cruelty and injustice, accordingly Licinianus being seized by the emperor's orders for having concealed a freedwoman of Cornelia's in one of his estates, was advised, by those who took him in charge, to confess the fact, if he hoped to obtain a remission of his punishment, circumstance to add further, that a young nobleman, having had his tunic torn, an ordinary occurrence in a crowd, stood with his gown thrown over him, to hear me, and that during the seven hours I was speaking, whilst my success more than counterbalanced the fatigue of so long a speech. So let us set to and not screen our own indolence under pretence of that of the public. Never, be very sure of that, will there be wanting hearers and readers, so long as we can only supply them with speakers and writers worth their attention. Farewell.

TO ASINIUS

You ADVISE ME, nay you entreat me, to undertake, in her absence, the cause of Corellia, against C. Caecilius, consul elect. For your advice I am grateful, of your entreaty I really must complain; without the first, indeed, I should have been ignorant of this affair, but the last was unnecessary, as I need no solicitations to comply, where it would be ungenerous in me to refuse; for can I hesitate a moment to take upon myself the protection of a daughter of Corellius? It is true, indeed, though there is no particular intimacy between her adversary and myself, still we are upon good enough terms. It is also true that he is a person of rank, and one who has a high claim upon my especial regard, as destined to enter upon an office which I have had the honour to fill; and it is natural for a man to be desirous those dignities should be held in the highest esteem which he himself once possessed. Yet all these considerations appear indifferent and trifling when I reflect that it is the daughter of Corellius whom I am to defend. The memory of that excellent person, than whom this age has not produced a man of greater dignity, rectitude, and acuteness, is indelibly imprinted upon my mind. My regard for him sprang from my admiration of the man, and contrary to what is usually the case, my admiration increased upon a thorough knowledge of him, and indeed I did know him thoroughly, for he kept nothing back from me, whether gay or serious, sad or joyous. When he was but a youth, he esteemed, and (I will even venture to say) revered, me as if I had been his equal. When I solicited any post of honour, he supported me with his interest, and recommended me with his testimony; when I entered upon it, he was my introducer and my companion; when I exercised it, he was my guide and my counsellor. In a word, whenever my interest was concerned, he exerted himself, in spite of his weakness and declining years, with as much alacrity as though he were still young and lusty. In private, in public, and at court, how often has he advanced and supported my credit and interest! It happened once that the conversation, in the presence of the emperor Nerva, turned upon the promising young men of that time, and several of the company present were pleased to mention me with applause; he sat for a little while silent, which gave what he said the greater weight; and then, with that air of dignity, to which you are no stranger, "I must be reserved," said he, "in my praises of Pliny, because he does nothing without advice." By which single sentence he bestowed upon me more than my most extravagant wishes could aspire to, as he represented my conduct to be always such as wisdom must approve, since it was wholly under the direction of one of the wisest of men. Even in his last moments he said to his daughter (as she often mentions), "I have in the course of a long life raised up many friends to you, but there are none in whom you may more assuredly confide than Pliny and Cornutus." A circumstance I cannot reflect upon without being deeply sensible how incumbent it is upon me to endeavour not to disappoint the confidence so excellent a judge of human nature reposed in me. I shall therefore most readily give my assistance to Corellia in this affair, and willingly risk any displeasure I may incur by appearing in her behalf. Though I should imagine, if in the course of my pleadings I should find an opportunity to explain and enforce more fully and at large than the limits of a letter allow of the reasons I have here mentioned, upon which I rest at once my apology and my glory; her adversary (whose suit may perhaps, as you say, be entirely without precedent, as it is against a woman) will not only excuse, but approve, my conduct. Farewell.

TO HISPULLA

As YOU ARE A model of all virtue, and loved your late excellent brother, who had such a fondness for you, with an affection equal to his own; regarding too his daughter[72] as your child, not only shewing her an aunt's tenderness but supplying the place of the parent she had lost; I know it will give you the greatest pleasure and joy to hear that she proves

---

72   Calpurnia, Pliny's wife.

worthy of her father, her grandfather, and yourself. She possesses an excellent understanding together with a consummate prudence, and gives the strongest evidence of the purity of her heart by her fondness of her husband. Her affection for me, moreover, has given her a taste for books, and my productions, which she takes a pleasure in reading, and even in getting by heart, are continually in her hands. How full of tender anxiety is she when I am going to speak in any case, how rejoiced she feels when it is got through. While I am pleading, she stations persons to inform her from time to time how I am heard, what applauses I receive, and what success attends the case. When I recite my works at any time, she conceals herself behind some curtain, and drinks in my praises with greedy ears. She sings my verses too, adapting them to her lyre, with no other master but love, that best of instructors, for her guide. From these happy circumstances I derive my surest hopes, that the harmony between us will increase with our days, and be as lasting as our lives. For it is not my youth or person, which time gradually impairs; it is my honour and glory that she cares for. But what less could be expected from one who was trained by your hands, and formed by your instructions; who was early familiarized under your roof with all that is pure and virtuous, and who learnt to love me first through your praises? And as you revered my mother with all the respect due even to a parent, so you kindly directed and encouraged my tender years, presaging from that early period all that my wife now fondly imagines I really am. Accept therefore of our mutual thanks, mine, for your giving me her, hers for your giving her me; for you have chosen us out, as it were, for each other. Farewell.

TO ROMATIUS FIASIUS

LOOK HERE! The next time the court sits, you must, at all events, take your place there. In vain would your indolence repose itself under my protection, for there is no absenting oneself with impunity. Look at that severe, determined, praetor, Licinius Nepos, who fined even a senator for the same neglect! The senator pleaded his cause in person, but in supplicant tone. The fine, it is true, was remitted, but sore was his dismay, humble his intercession, and he had to ask pardon. "All praetors are not so severe as that," you will reply; you are mistaken — for though indeed to be the author and reviver of an example of this kind may be an act of severity, yet, once introduced, even lenity herself may follow the precedent. Farewell.

TO LICINIUS SURA

I HAVE BROUGHT YOU as a little present out of the country a query which well deserves the consideration of your extensive knowledge. There is a spring which rises in a neighbouring mountain, and running among the rocks is received into a little banqueting-room, artificially formed for that purpose, from whence, after being detained a short time, it falls into the Larian lake. The nature of this spring is extremely curious; it ebbs and flows regularly three times a day. The increase and decrease is plainly visible, and exceedingly interesting to observe. You sit down by the side of the fountain, and while you are taking a repast and drinking its water, which is extremely cool, you see it gradually rise and fall. If you place a ring, or anything else at the bottom, when it is dry, the water creeps gradually up, first gently washing, finally covering it entirely, and then little by little subsides again. If you wait long enough, you may see it thus alternately advance and recede three successive times. Shall we say that some secret current of air stops and opens the fountain-head, first rushing in and checking the flow and then, driven back by the counter-resistance of the water, escaping again; as we see in bottles, and other vessels of that nature, where, there not being a free and open passage, though you turn their necks perpendicularly or obliquely downwards, yet, the outward air obstructing the vent, they discharge their contents as it were by starts? Or, may not this small collection of water be successively contracted and enlarged upon the same principle as the ebb and flow of the sea? Or, again, as those rivers which discharge themselves into the sea, meeting with contrary winds and the swell of the ocean, are forced back in their channels, so, in the same way, may there not be something that checks this fountain, for a time, in its progress? Or is there rather a certain reservoir that contains these waters in the bowels of the earth, and while it is recruiting its discharges, the stream in consequence flows more slowly and in less quantity, but, when it has collected its due measure, runs on again in its usual strength and fulness? Or lastly, is there I know not what kind of subterranean counterpoise, that throws up the water when the fountain is dry, and keeps it back when it is full? You, who are so well qualified for the enquiry, will examine into the causes of this wonderful phenomenon; it will be sufficient for me if I have given you an adequate description of it. Farewell.

TO ANNIUS SEVERUS

A SMALL LEGACY WAS lately left me, yet one more acceptable than a far larger bequest would have been. How more acceptable than a far larger one? In this way. Pomponia Gratilla, having disinherited her son Assidius Curianus, appointed me of one of her heirs, and Sertorius Severus, of pretorian rank, together with several eminent Roman knights, co-heirs along with me. The son applied to me to give him my share of the inheritance, in order to use my name as an example to the rest of the joint-heirs, but offered at the same time to enter into a secret agreement to return me my proportion. I told him, it was by no means agreeable to my character to seem to act one way while in reality I was acting another, besides it was not quite honourable making presents to a man of his fortune, who had no children; in a word, this would not at all answer the purpose at which he was aiming, whereas, if I were to withdraw my claim, it might be of some service to him, and this I was ready and willing to do, if he could clearly prove to me that he was unjustly disinherited.

"Do then," he said, "be my arbitrator in this case." After a short pause I answered him, "I will, for I don't see why I should not have as good an opinion of my own impartial disinterestedness as you seem to have. But, mind, I am not to be prevailed upon to decide the point in question against your mother, if it should appear she had just reason for what she has done." "As you please," he replied, "which I am sure is always to act according to justice." I called in, as my assistants, Corellius and Frontinus, two of the very best lawyers Rome at that time afforded. With these in attendance, I heard the case in my own chamber. Curianus said everything which he thought would favour his pretensions, to whom (there being nobody but myself to defend the character of the deceased) I made a short reply; after which I retired with my friends to deliberate, and, being agreed upon our verdict, I said to him, "Curianus, it is our opinion that your conduct has justly drawn upon you your mother's displeasure." Sometime afterwards, Curianus commenced a suit in the Court of the Hundred against all the co-heirs except myself. The day appointed for the trial approaching, the rest of the co-heirs were anxious to compromise the affair and have done with it, not out of any diffidence of their cause, but from a distrust of the times. They were apprehensive of what had happened to many others, happening to them, and that from a civil suit it might end in a criminal one, as there were some among them to whom the friendship of Gratilla and Rusticus[73] might be extremely prejudicial: they therefore desired me to go and talk with Curianus. We met in the temple of Concord; "Now supposing," I said, "your mother had left you the fourth part of her estate, or even suppose she had made you sole heir, but had exhausted so much of the estate in legacies that there would not be more than a fourth part remaining to you, could you justly complain? You ought to be content, therefore, if, being absolutely disinherited as you are, the heirs are willing to relinquish to you a fourth part, which however I will increase by contributing my proportion. You know you did not commence any suit against me, and two years have now elapsed, which gives me legal and indisputable possession. But to induce you to agree to the proposals on the part of the other co-heirs, and that you may be no sufferer by the peculiar respect you shew me, I offer to advance my proportion with them." The silent approval of my own conscience is not the only result out of this transaction; it has contributed also to the honour of my character. For it is this same Cunianus who has left me the legacy I have mentioned in the beginning of my letter, and I received it as a very notable mark of his approbation of my conduct, if I do not flatter myself. I have written and told you all this, because in all my joys and sorrows I am wont to look upon you as myself, and I thought it would be unkind not to communicate to so tender a friend whatever occasions me a sensible gratification; for I am not philosopher enough to be indifferent, when I think I have acted like an honour-able man, whether my actions meet with that approval which is in some sort their due. Farewell.

TO TITIUS ARISTO

AMONG THE MANY AGREEABLE and obliging instances I have received of your friendship, your not concealing from me the long conversations which lately took place at your house concerning my verses, and the various judgments passed upon them (which served to prolong the talk,) is by no means the least. There were some, it seems, who did not disapprove of my poems in themselves, but at the same time censured me in a free and friendly way, for employing myself in composing and reciting them. I am so far, however, from desiring to extenuate

---

73   Gratilla was the wife of Rusticus: Rusticus was put to death by Domitian, and Gratilla banished. It was sufficient crime in the reign of that execrable prince to be even a friend of those who were obnoxious to him. M.

the charge that I willingly acknowledge myself still more deserving of it, and confess that I sometimes amuse myself with writing verses of the gayer sort. I compose comedies, divert myself with pantomimes, read the lyric poets, and enter into the spirit of the most wanton muse, besides that, I indulge myself sometimes in laughter, mirth, and frolic, and, to sum up every kind of innocent relaxation in one word, I am a man. I am not in the least offended, though, at their low opinion of my morals, and that those who are ignorant of the fact that the most learned, the wisest, and the best of men have employed themselves in the same way, should be surprised at the tone of my writings: but from those who know what noble and numerous examples I follow, I shall, I am confident, easily obtain permission to err with those whom it is an honour to imitate, not only in their most serious occupations but their lightest triflings. Is it unbecoming me (I will not name any living example, lest I should seem to flatter), but is it unbecoming me to practise what became Tully, Calvus, Pollio, Messala, Hortensius, Brutus, Sulla, Catulus, Scaevola, Sulpitius, Varro, the Torquati, Memmius, Gaetulicus, Seneca, Lucceius, and, within our own memory, Verginius Rufus? But if the examples of private men are not sufficient to justify me, I can cite Julius Casar, Augustus, Nerva, and Tiberius Casar. I forbear to add Nero to the catalogue, though I am aware that what is practised by the worst of men does not therefore degenerate into wrong: on the contrary, it still maintains its credit, if frequently countenanced by the best. In that number, Virgil, Cornelius Nepos, and prior to these, Ennius and Attius, justly deserve the most distinguished place. These last indeed were not senators, but goodness knows no distinction of rank or title. I recite my works, it is true, and in this instance I am not sure I can support myself by their examples. They, perhaps, might be satisfied with their own judgment, but I have too humble an opinion of mine to suppose my compositions perfect, because they appear so to my own mind. My reason then for reciting are, that, for one thing, there is a certain deference for one's audience, which excites a somewhat more vigorous application, and then again, I have by this means an opportunity of settling any doubts I may have concerning my performance, by observing the general opinion of the audience. In a word, I have the advantage of receiving different hints from different persons: and although they should not declare their meaning in express terms, yet the expression of the countenance, the movement of the head, the eyes, the motion of a hand, a whisper, or even silence itself will easily distinguish their real opinion from the language of politeness. And so if any one of my audience should have the curiosity to read over the same performance which he heard me read, he may find several things altered or omitted, and perhaps too upon his particular judgment, though he did not say a single word to me. But I am not defending my conduct in this particular, as if I had actually recited my works in public, and not in my own house before my friends, a numerous appearance of whom has upon many occasions been held an honour, but never, surely, a reproach. Farewell.

TO NONIUS MAXIMUS

I AM DEEPLY AFFLICTED with the news I have received of the death of Fannius; in the first place, because I loved one so eloquent and refined, in the next, because I was accustomed to be guided by his judgment—and indeed he possessed great natural acuteness, improved by practice, rendering him able to see a thing in an instant. There are some circumstances about his death, which aggravate my concern. He left behind him a will which had been made a considerable time before his decease, by which it happens that his estate is fallen into the hands of those who had incurred his displeasure, whilst his greatest favourites are excluded. But what I particularly regret is, that he has left unfinished a very noble work in which he was employed. Notwithstanding his full practice at the bar, he had begun a history of those persons who were put to death or banished by Nero, and completed three books of it. They are written with great elegance and precision, the style is pure, and preserves a proper medium between the plain narrative and the historical: and as they were very favourably received by the public, he was the more desirous of being able to finish the rest. The hand of death is ever, in my opinion, too untimely and sudden when it falls upon such as are employed in some immortal work. The sons of sensuality, who have no outlook beyond the present hour, put an end every day to all motives for living, but those who look forward to posterity, and endeavour to transmit their names with honour to future generations by their works—to such, death is always immature, as it still snatches them from amidst some unfinished design. Fannius, long before his death, had a presentiment of what has happened: he dreamed one night that as he was lying on his couch, in an undress, all ready for his work, and with his desk,[74] as usual, in front of him, Nero entered, and placing himself by his side, took up the three first books of this history, which he read through and then departed.

74   In the original, scrinium, box for holding MSS.

This dream greatly alarmed him, and he regarded it as an intimation, that he should not carry on his history any farther than Nero had read, and so the event has proved. I cannot reflect upon this accident without lamenting that he was prevented from accomplishing a work which had cost him so many toilsome vigils, as it suggests to me, at the same time, reflections on my own mortality, and the fate of my writings: and I am persuaded the same apprehensions alarm you for those in which you are at present employed. Let us then, my friend, while life permits, exert all our endeavours, that death, whenever it arrives, may find as little as possible to destroy. Farewell.

TO DOMITIUS APOLLINARIS

THE KIND CONCERN YOU expressed on hearing of my design to pass the summer at my villa in Tuscany, and your obliging endeavours to dissuade me from going to a place which you think unhealthy, are extremely pleasing to me. It is quite true indeed that the air of that part of Tuscany which lies towards the coast is thick and unwholesome: but my house stands at a good distance from the sea, under one of the Apennines which are singularly healthy. But, to relieve you from all anxiety on my account, I will give you a description of the temperature of the climate, the situation of the country, and the beauty of my villa, which, I am persuaded, you will hear with as much pleasure as I shall take in giving it. The air in winter is sharp and frosty, so that myrtles, olives, and trees of that kind which delight in constant warmth, will not flourish here: but the laurel thrives, and is remarkably beautiful, though now and then the cold kills it—though not oftener than it does in the neighbourhood of Rome. The summers are extraordinarily mild, and there is always a refreshing breeze, seldom high winds. This accounts for the number of old men we have about, you would see grandfathers and great-grandfathers of those now grown up to be young men, hear old stories and the dialect of our ancestors, and fancy yourself born in some former age were you to come here. The character of the country is exceedingly beautiful. Picture to yourself an immense amphitheatre, such as nature only could create. Before you lies a broad, extended plain bounded by a range of mountains, whose summits are covered with tall and ancient woods, which are stocked with all kinds of game.

The descending slopes of the mountains are planted with underwood, among which are a number of little risings with a rich soil, on which hardly a stone is to be found. In fruitfulness they are quite equal to a valley, and though their harvest is rather later, their crops are just as good. At the foot of these, on the mountain-side, the eye, wherever it turns, runs along one unbroken stretch of vineyards terminated by a belt of shrubs. Next you have meadows and the open plain. The arable land is so stiff that it is necessary to go over it nine times with the biggest oxen and the strongest ploughs. The meadows are bright with flowers, and produce trefoil and other kinds of herbage as fine and tender as if it were but just sprung up, for all the soil is refreshed by never failing streams. But though there is plenty of water, there are no marshes; for the ground being on a slope, whatever water it receives without absorbing runs off into the Tiber. This river, which winds through the middle of the meadows, is navigable only in the winter and spring, at which seasons it transports the produce of the lands to Rome: but in summer it sinks below its banks, leaving the name of a great river to an almost empty channel: towards the autumn, however, it begins again to renew its claim to that title. You would be charmed by taking a view of this country from the top of one of our neighbouring mountains, and would fancy that not a real, but some imaginary landscape, painted by the most exquisite pencil, lay before you, such an harmonious variety of beautiful objects meets the eye, whichever way it turns. My house, although at the foot of a hill, commands as good a view as if it stood on its brow, yet you approach by so gentle and gradual a rise that you find yourself on high ground without perceiving you have been making an ascent. Behind, but at a great distance, is the Apennine range. In the calmest days we get cool breezes from that quarter, not sharp and cutting at all, being spent and broken by the long distance they have travelled. The greater part of the house has a southern aspect, and seems to invite the afternoon sun in summer (but rather earlier in the winter) into a broad and proportionately long portico, consisting of several rooms, particularly a court of antique fashion. In front of the portico is a sort of terrace, edged with box and shrubs cut into different shapes. You descend, from the terrace, by an easy slope adorned with the figures of animals in box, facing each other, to a lawn overspread with the soft, I had almost said the liquid, Acanthus: this is surrounded by a walk enclosed with evergreens, shaped into a variety of forms. Beyond it is the gestation laid out in the form of a circus running round the multiform box-hedge and the dwarf-trees, which are cut quite close. The whole is fenced in with a wall completely covered by box cut into steps all the way up to the top. On the outside of the wall lies a meadow that owes as many beauties to nature as all I have been describing within does to art; at the end of which are open plain and numerous other meadows and copses. From the extremity of the portico a large dining-room runs out, opening upon one end of the terrace, while from the windows there is a very extensive view over the meadows up into the country, and from these you also see the terrace and the projecting wing of the house together with the woods enclosing the adjacent hippo-drome. Almost opposite the centre of the portico, and rather to the back, stands a summer-house, enclosing a small area shaded by four plane-trees, in the midst of which rises a marble fountain which gently plays upon the roots of the plane-trees and upon the grass-plots under-neath them. This summer-house has a bed-room in it free from every sort of noise, and which the light itself cannot penetrate, together with a common dining-room I use when I have none but intimate friends with me. A second portico looks upon this little area, and has the same view as the other I have just been describing. There is, besides, another room, which, being situate close to the nearest plane-tree, enjoys a con-stant shade and green. Its sides are encrusted with carved marble up to the ceiling, while above the marble a foliage is painted with birds among the branches, which has an effect altogether as agreeable as that of the carving, at the foot of which a little fountain, playing through several small pipes into a vase it encloses, produces a most pleasing murmur. From a corner of the portico you enter a very large bed-chamber op-posite the large dining-room, which from some of its windows has a view of the terrace, and from others, of the meadow, as those in the front look upon a cascade, which entertains at once both the eye and the ear; for the water, dashing from a great height, foams over the mar-ble basin which receives it below. This room is extremely warm in win-ter, lying much exposed to the sun, and on a cloudy day the heat of an adjoining stove very well supplies his absence. Leaving this room, you pass through a good-sized, pleasant, undressing-room into the cold-bath-room, in which is a large gloomy bath: but if you are inclined to swim more at large, or in warmer water, in the middle of the area stands a wide basin for that purpose, and near it a reservoir from which you may be supplied with cold water to brace yourself again, if you should find you are too much relaxed by the warm. Adjoining the cold bath is one of a medium degree of heat, which enjoys the kindly warmth of the sun, but not so intensely as the hot bath, which projects farther. This last consists of three several compartments, each of different degrees of heat; the two former lie open to the full sun, the latter, though not much exposed to its heat, receives an equal share of its light. Over the undressing-room is built the tennis-court, which admits of different kinds of games and different sets of players. Not far from the baths is the staircase leading to the enclosed portico, three rooms intervening. One of these looks out upon the little area with the four plane-trees round it, the other upon the meadows, and from the third you have a view of several vineyards, so that each has a different one, and looks towards a different point of the heavens. At the upper end of the enclosed portico, and indeed taken off from it, is a room that looks out upon the hippodrome, the vineyards, and the mountains; adjoining is a room which has a full exposure to the sun, especially in winter, and out of which runs another connecting the hippodrome with the house. This forms the front. On the side rises an enclosed portico, which not only looks out upon the vineyards, but seems almost to touch them. From the middle of this portico you enter a dining-room cooled by the wholesome breezes from the Apennine valleys: from the windows behind, which are extremely large, there is a close view of the vineyards, and from the folding doors through the summer portico. Along that side of the dining-room where there are no windows runs a private staircase for greater convenience in serving up when I give an entertainment; at the farther end is a sleeping-room with a look-out upon the vineyards, and (what is equally agreeable) the portico. Underneath this room is an enclosed portico resembling a grotto, which, enjoying in the midst of summer heats its own natural coolness, neither admits nor wants external air. After you have passed both these porticoes, at the end of the dining-room stands a third, which according as the day is more or less advanced, serves either for Winter or summer use. It leads to two different apartments, one containing four chambers, the other, three, which enjoy by turns both sun and shade. This arrangement of the different parts of my house is exceedingly pleasant, though it is not to be compared with the beauty of the hippodrome,' lying entirely open in the middle of the grounds, so that the eye, upon your first entrance, takes it in entire in one view. It is set round with plane-trees covered with ivy, so that, while their tops flourish with their own green, towards the roots their verdure is borrowed from the ivy that twines round the trunk and branches, spreads from tree to tree, and connects them together. Between each plane-tree are planted box-trees, and behind these stands a grove of laurels which blend their shade with that of the planes. This straight boundary to the hippodrome[75] alters its shape at

---

75   The hippodromus, in its proper signification, was a place, among the Grecians, set apart for horse-racing and other exercises of that kind. But it seems here to be nothing more than a particular walk, to which Pliny perhaps gave that name, from its bearing some resemblance in its form to the public places so called. M.

the farther end, bending into a semicircle, which is planted round, shut in with cypresses, and casts a deeper and gloomier shade, while the inner circular walks (for there are several), enjoying an open exposure, are filled with plenty of roses, and correct, by a very pleasant contrast, the coolness of the shade with the warmth of the sun. Having passed through these several winding alleys, you enter a straight walk, which breaks out into a variety of others, partitioned off by box-row hedges. In one place you have a little meadow, in another the box is cut in a thousand different forms, sometimes into letters, expressing the master's name, sometimes the artificer's, whilst here and there rise little obelisks with fruit-trees alternately intermixed, and then on a sudden, in the midst of this elegant regularity, you are surprised with an imitation of the negligent beauties of rural nature. In the centre of this lies a spot adorned with a knot of dwarf plane-trees. Beyond these stands an acacia, smooth and bending in places, then again various other shapes and names. At the upper end is an alcove of white marble, shaded with vines and supported by four small Carystian columns. From this semicircular couch, the water, gushing up through several little pipes, as though pressed out by the weight of the persons who recline themselves upon it, falls into a stone cistern underneath, from whence it is received into a fine polished marble basin, so skilfully contrived that it is always full without ever overflowing. When I sup here, this basin serves as a table, the larger sort of dishes being placed round the margin, while the smaller ones swim about in the form of vessels and water-fowl. Opposite this is a fountain which is incessantly emptying and filling, for the water which it throws up to a great height, falling back again into it, is by means of consecutive apertures returned as fast as it is received. Facing the alcove (and reflecting upon it as great an ornament as it borrows from it) stands a summer-house of exquisite marble, the doors of which project and open into a green enclosure, while from its upper and lower windows the eye falls upon a variety of different greens. Next to this is a little private closet (which, though it seems distinct, may form part of the same room), furnished with a couch, and notwithstanding it has windows on every side, yet it enjoys a very agreeable gloom, by means of a spreading vine which climbs to the top, and entirely overshadows it. Here you may lie and fancy yourself in a wood, with this only difference, that you are not exposed to the weather as you would be there. Here too a fountain rises and instantly disappears—several marble seats are set in different places, which are as pleasant as the summer-house itself after one is tired out with walking. Near each is a little fountain, and throughout the whole hippodrome several small rills run murmuring along through pipes, wherever the hand of art has thought proper to conduct them, watering here and there different plots of green, and sometimes all parts at once. I should have ended before now, for fear of being too chatty, had I not proposed in this letter to lead you into every corner of my house and gardens. Nor did I apprehend your thinking it a trouble to read the description of a place which I feel sure would please you were you to see it; especially as you can stop just when you please, and by throwing aside my letter, sit down as it were, and give yourself a rest as often as you think proper. Besides, I gave my little passion indulgence, for I have a passion for what I have built, or finished, myself. In a word, (for why should I conceal from my friend either my deliberate opinion or my prejudice?) I look upon it as the first duty of every writer to frequently glance over his title-page and consider well the subject he has proposed to himself; and he may be sure, if he dwells on his subject, he cannot justly be thought tedious, whereas if, on the contrary, he introduces and drags in anything irrelevant, he will be thought exceedingly so. Homer, you know, has employed many verses in the description of the arms of Achilles, as Virgil has also in those of Aeneas, yet neither 'of them is prolix, because they each keep within the limits of their original design. Aratus, you observe, is not considered too circumstantial, though he traces and enumerates the minutest stars, for he does not go out of his way for that purpose, but only follows where his subject leads him. In the same way (to compare small things with great), so long as, in endeavouring to give you an idea of my house, I have not introduced anything irrelevant or superfluous, it is not my letter which describes, but my villa which is described, that is to be considered large. But to return to where I began, lest I should justly be condemned by my own law, if I continue longer in this digression, you see now the reasons why I prefer my Tuscan villa to those which I possess at Tusculum, Tiber, and Praeneste.[76] Besides the advantages already mentioned, I enjoy here a cozier, more profound and undisturbed retirement than anywhere else, as I am at a greater distance from the business of the town and the interruption of troublesome clients. All is calm and composed; which circumstances contribute no less than its clear air and unclouded sky to that health of body and mind I particularly enjoy in this place, both of which I keep in full swing by study and hunting. And indeed there is no place which agrees better with my family, at least I am sure I have not yet lost one (may the expression be

---

76   Now called Frascati, Tivoli, and Palestrina, all of them situated in the Campagna di Roma, and at no great distance from Rome. M.

allowed![77]) of all those I brought here with me. And may the gods continue that happiness to me, and that honour to my villa. Farewell.

TO CALVISIUS

IT IS CERTAIN THE law does not allow a corporate city to inherit any estate by will, or to receive a legacy. Saturninus, however, who has appointed me his heir, had left a fourth part of his estate to our corporation of Comum; afterwards, instead of a fourth part, he bequeathed four hundred thousand sesterces.[78] This bequest, in the eye of the law, is null and void, but, considered as the clear and express will of the deceased, ought to stand firm and valid. Myself, I consider the will of the dead (though I am afraid what I say will not please the lawyers) of higher authority than the law, especially when the interest of one's native country is concerned. Ought I, who made them a present of eleven hundred thousand sesterces[79] out of my own patrimony, to withhold a benefaction of little more than a third part of that sum out of an estate which has come quite by a chance into my hands? You, who like a true patriot have the same affection for this our common country, will agree with me in opinion, I feel sure. I wish therefore you would, at the next meeting of the Decurii, acquaint them, just briefly and respectfully, as to how the law stands in this case, and then add that I offer them four hundred thousand sesterces according to the direction in Saturninus' will. You will represent this donation as his present and his liberality; I only claim the merit of complying with his request. I did not trouble to write to their senate about this, fully relying as I do upon our intimate friendship and your wise discretion, and being quite satisfied that you are both able and willing to act for me upon this occasion as I would for myself; besides, I was afraid I should not seem to have so cautiously guarded my expressions in a letter as you will be able to do in a speech. The countenance, the gesture, and even the tone of voice govern and determine the sense of the speaker, whereas a letter, being without these advantages, is more liable to malignant misinterpretation. Farewell.

---

77   "This is said in allusion to the idea of Nemesis supposed to threaten excessive prosperity." (Church and Brodribb.)
78   About $15,000.
79   About $42,000.

TO MARCELLINUS

I WRITE THIS TO you in the deepest sorrow: the youngest daughter of my friend Fundanus is dead! I have never seen a more cheerful and more lovable girl, or one who better deserved to have enjoyed a long, I had almost said an immortal, life! She was scarcely fourteen, and yet there was in her a wisdom far beyond her years, a matronly gravity united with girlish sweetness and virgin bashfulness. With what an endearing fondness did she hang on her father's neck! How affectionately and modestly she used to greet us his friends! With what a tender and deferential regard she used to treat her nurses, tutors, teachers, each in their respective offices! What an eager, industrious, intelligent, reader she was! She took few amusements, and those with caution. How self-controlled, how patient, how brave, she was, under her last illness! She complied with all the directions of her physicians; she spoke cheerful, comforting words to her sister and her father; and when all her bodily strength was exhausted, the vigour of her mind sustained her. That indeed continued even to her last moments, unbroken by the pain of a long illness, or the terrors of approaching death; and it is a reflection which makes us miss her, and grieve that she has gone from us, the more. 0 melancholy, untimely, loss, too truly! She was engaged to an excellent young man; the wedding-day was fixed, and we were all invited. How our joy has been turned into sorrow! I cannot express in words the inward pain I felt when I heard Fundanus himself (as grief is ever finding out fresh circumstances to aggravate its affliction) ordering the money he had intended laying out upon clothes, pearls, and jewels for her marriage, to be employed in frankincense, ointments, and perfumes for her funeral. He is a man of great learning and good sense, who has applied himself from his earliest youth to the deeper studies and the fine arts, but all the maxims of fortitude which he has received from books, or advanced himself, he now absolutely rejects, and every other virtue of his heart gives place to all a parent's tenderness. You will excuse, you will even approve, his grief, when you consider what he has lost. He has lost a daughter who resembled him in his manners, as well as his person, and exactly copied out all her father. So, if you should think proper to write to him upon the subject of so reasonable a grief, let me remind you not to use the rougher arguments of consolation, and such as seem to carry a sort of reproof with them, but those of kind and sympathizing humanity. Time will render him more open to the dictates of reason: for as a fresh wound shrinks back from the hand of the surgeon, but by degrees submits to, and even seeks of its own accord the means of its cure, so a mind under the first impression of a misfortune shuns and rejects all consolations, but at length desires and is lulled by their gentle application. Farewell.

TO SPURINNA

KNOWING, AS I DO, how much you admire the polite arts, and what satisfaction you take in seeing young men of quality pursue the steps of their ancestors, I seize this earliest opportunity of informing you that I went to-day to hear Calpurnius Piso read a beautiful and scholarly production of his, entitled the Sports of Love. His numbers, which were elegiac, were tender, sweet, and flowing, at the same time that they occasionally rose to all the sublimity of diction which the nature of his subject required. He varied his style from the lofty to the simple, from the close to the copious, from the grave to the florid, with equal genius and judgment. These beauties were further recommended by a most harmonious voice; which a very becoming modesty rendered still more pleasing. A confusion and concern in the countenance of a speaker imparts a grace to all he utters; for diffidence, I know not how, is infinitely more engaging than assurance and self-sufficiency. I might mention several other circumstances to his advantage, which I am the more inclined to point out, as they are exceedingly striking in one of his age, and are most uncommon in a youth of his quality: but not to enter into a farther detail of his merit, I will only add that, when he had finished his poem, I embraced him very heartily, and being persuaded that nothing is a greater encouragement than applause, I exhorted him to go on as he had begun, and to shine out to posterity with the same glorious lustre, which was reflected upon him from his ancestors. I congratulated his excellent mother, and particularly his brother, who gained as much honour by the generous affection he manifested upon this occasion as Calpurnius did by his eloquence; so remarkable a solicitude he showed for him when he began to recite his poem, and so much pleasure in his success. May the gods grant me frequent occasions of giving you accounts of this nature! for I have a partiality to the age in which I live, and should rejoice to find it not barren of merit. I ardently wish, therefore, our young men of quality would have something else to show of honourable memorial in their houses than the images[80] of their ancestors. As for those which are

---

80   None had the right of using family pictures or statues but those whose ancestors or themselves had borne some of the highest dignities. So that the jus

placed in the mansion of these excellent youths, I now figure them to myself as silently applauding and encouraging their pursuits, and (what is a sufficient degree of honour to both brothers) as recognizing their kindred. Farewell.

TO PAULINUS

As I KNOW THE humanity with which you treat your own servants, I have less reserve in confessing to you the indulgence I shew to mine. I have ever in my mind that line of Homer's —
"Who swayed his people with a father's love":
and this expression of ours, "father of a family." But were I harsher and harder than I really am by nature, the ill state of health of my freedman Zosimus (who has the stronger claim upon my tenderness, in that he now stands in more especial need of it) would be sufficient to soften me. He is a good, honest fellow, attentive in his services, and well-read; but his chief talent, and indeed his distinguishing qualification, is that of a comedian, in which he highly excels. His pronunciation is distinct, correct in emphasis, pure, and graceful: he has a very skilled touch, too, upon the lyre, and performs with better execution than is necessary for one of his profession. To this I must add, he reads history, oratory, and poetry, as well as if these had been the sole objects of his study. I am the more particular in enumerating his qualifications, to let you see how many agreeable services I receive from this one servant alone. He is indeed endeared to me by the ties of a long affection, which are strengthened by the danger he is now in. For nature has so formed our hearts that nothing contributes more to incite and kindle affection than the fear of losing the object of it: a fear which I have suffered more than once on his account. Some years ago he strained himself so much by too strong an exertion of his voice, that he spit blood, upon which account I sent him into Egypt;[81] from whence, after a long absence, belately returned with great benefit to his health. But having again exerted himself for several days together beyond his strength, he was reminded of his former malady by a slight return of his cough, and a spitting of blood. For this reason I intend to send him to your farm at Forum-Julii,[82] having frequently heard you mention it as

imaginis was much the same thing among the Romans as the right of bearing a coat of arms among us. Ken. Antiq. M.
81   The Roman physicians used to send their patients in consumptive cases into Egypt, particularly to Alexandria. M.
82   Frejus, in Provence, the southern part of France. M.

a healthy air, and recommend the milk of that place as very salutary in disorders of his nature. I beg you would give directions to your people to receive him into your house, and to supply him with whatever he may have occasion for: which will not be much, for he is so sparing and abstemious as not only to abstain from delicacies, but even to deny himself the necessaries his ill state of health requires. I shall furnish him towards his journey with what will be sufficient for one of his moderate requirements, who is coming under your roof. Farewell.

TO RUFUS

I WENT INTO THE Julian[83] court to hear those lawyers to whom, according to the last adjournment, I was to reply. The judges had taken their seats, the decemviri[84] were arrived, the eyes of the audience were fixed upon the counsel, and all was hushed silence and expectation, when a messenger arrived from the praetor, and the Hundred are at once dismissed, and the case postponed: an accident extremely agreeable to me, who am never so well prepared but that I am glad of gaining further time. The occasion of the court's rising thus abruptly was a short edict of Nepos, the praetor for criminal causes, in which he directed all persons concerned as plaintiffs or defendants in any cause before him to take notice that he designed strictly to put in force the decree of the senate annexed to his edict. Which decree was expressed in the following words:

ALL PERSONS WHOSOEVER THAT HAVE ANY LAW-SUITS DEPENDING ARE HEREBY REQUIRED AND COMMANDED, BEFORE ANY PROCEEDINGS BE HAD THEREON, TO TAKE AN OATH THAT THEY HAVE NOT GIVEN, PROMISED, OR ENGAGED TO GIVE, ANY FEE OR REWARD TO ANY ADVOCATE, UPON ACCOUNT OF HIS UNDERTAKING THEIR CAUSE.

In these terms, and many others equally full and express, the lawyers were prohibited to make their professions venal. However, after the case

83   A court of justice erected by Julius Cæsar in the forum, and opposite to the basilica Aemilia.
84   The deceniviri seem to have been magistrates for the administration of justice, subordinate to the praetors, who (to give the English reader a general notion of their office) may be termed lords chief justices, as the judges here mentioned were something in the nature of our juries. M.

is decided, they are permitted to accept a gratuity of ten thousand sesterces.[85] The praetor for civil causes, being alarmed at this order of Nepos,
gave us this unexpected holiday in order to take time to consider whether
he should follow the example. Meanwhile the whole town is talking, and
either approving or condemning this edict of Nepos. We have got then at
last (say the latter with a sneer) a redressor of abuses. But pray was there
never a praetor before this man? Who is he then who sets up in this way
for a public reformer? Others, on the contrary, say, "He has done perfectly
right upon his entry into office; he has paid obedience to the laws; considered the decrees of the senate, repressed most indecent contracts, and
will not suffer the most honourable of all professions to be debased into
a sordid lucre traffic." This is what one hears all around one; but which
side may prevail, the event will shew. It is the usual method of the world
(though a very unequitable rule of estimation) to pronounce an action
either right or wrong, according as it is attended with good or ill success;
in consequence of which you may hear the very same conduct attributed
to zeal or folly, to liberty or licentiousness, upon different several occasions. Farewell.

TO ARRIANUS

SOMETIMES I MISS REGULUS in our courts. I cannot say I deplore his
loss. The man, it must be owned, highly respected his profession, grew
pale with study and anxiety over it, and used to write out his speeches
though he could not get them by heart. There was a practice he had
of painting round his right or left eye,[86] and wearing a white patch[87]
over one side or the other of his forehead, according as he was to
plead either for the plaintiff or defendant; of consulting the soothsay-
ers upon the issue of an action; still, all this excessive superstition was
really due to his extreme earnestness in his profession. And it was
acceptable enough being concerned in the same cause with him, as

---

85   About $400.

86   This silly piece of superstition seems to have been peculiar to Regulus,
and not of any general practice; at least it is a custom of which we find no other
mention in antiquity. M.

87   "We gather from Martial that the wearing of these was not an unusual
practice with fops and dandies." See Epig. II. 29, in which he ridicules a certain
Rufus, and hints that if you were to "strip off the 'splenia (plasters)' from his
face, you would find out that he was a branded runaway slave." (Church and
Brodribb.)

he always obtained full indulgence in point of time, and never failed to get an audience together; for what could be more convenient than, under the protection of a liberty which you did not ask yourself, and all the odium of the arrangement resting with another, and before an audience which you had not the trouble of collecting, to speak on at your ease, and as long as you thought proper? Nevertheless Regulus did well in departing this life, though he would have done much better had he made his exit sooner. He might really have lived now without any danger to the public, in the reign of a prince under whom he would have had no opportunity of doing any harm. I need not scruple therefore, I think, to say I sometimes miss him: for since his death the custom has prevailed of not allowing, nor indeed of asking more than an hour or two to plead in, and sometimes not above half that time. The truth is, our advocates take more pleasure in finishing a cause than in defending it; and our judges had rather rise from the bench than sit upon it: such is their indolence, and such their indifference to the honour of eloquence and the interest of justice! But are we wiser than our ancestors? are we more equitable than the laws which grant so many hours and days of adjournments to a case? were our forefathers slow of apprehension, and dull beyond measure? and are we clearer of speech, quicker in our conceptions, or more scrupulous in our decisions, because we get over our causes in fewer hours than they took days? O Regulus! it was by zeal in your profession that you secured an advantage which is but rarely given to the highest integrity. As for myself, whenever I sit upon the bench (which is much oftener than I appear at the bar), I always give the advocates as much time as they require: for I look upon it as highly presuming to pretend to guess, before a case is heard, what time it will require, and to set limits to an affair before one is acquainted with its extent; especially as the first and most sacred duty of a judge is patience, which constitutes an important part of justice. But this, it is objected, would give an opening to much superfluous matter: I grant it may; yet is it not better to hear too much than not to hear enough? Besides, how shall you know that what an advocate has farther to offer will be superfluous, until you have heard him? But this, and many other public abuses, will be best reserved for a conversation when we meet; for I know your affection to the commonwealth inclines you to wish that some means might be found out to check at least those grievances, which would now be very difficult absolutely to remove. But to return to affairs of private concern: I hope all goes well in your family; mine remains in its usual situation. The good which I enjoy grows more acceptable to me by its continuance; as habit renders me less sensible of the evils I suffer. Farewell.

TO CALPURNIA[88]

NEVER WAS BUSINESS MORE disagreeable to me than when it prevented me not only from accompanying you when you went into Campania for your health, but from following you there soon after; for I want particularly to be with you now, that I may learn from my own eyes whether you are growing stronger and stouter, and whether the tranquillity, the amusements, and plenty of that charming country really agree with you. Were you in perfect health, yet I could ill support your absence; for even a moment's uncertainty of the welfare of those we tenderly love causes a feeling of suspense and anxiety: but now your sickness conspires with your absence to trouble me grievously with vague and various anxieties. I dread everything, fancy everything, and, as is natural to those who fear, conjure up the very things I most dread. Let me the more earnestly entreat you then to think of my anxiety, and write to me every day, and even twice a day: I shall be more easy, at least while I am reading your letters, though when I have read them, I shall immediately feel my fears again. Farewell.

TO CALPURNIA

YOU KINDLY TELL ME my absence very sensibly affects you, and that your only consolation is in conversing with my works, which you frequently substitute in my stead. I am glad that you miss me; I am glad that you find some rest in these alleviations. In return, I read over your letters again and again, and am continually taking them up, as if I had just received them; but, alas! this only stirs in me a keener longing for you; for how sweet must her conversation be whose letters have so many charms? Let me receive them, however, as often as possible, notwithstanding there is still a mixture of pain in the pleasure they afford me. Farewell.

---

88   His wife.

TO PRISCUS

YOU KNOW ATTILIUS CRESCENS, and you love him; who is there, indeed, of any rank or worth, that does not? For myself, I profess to have a friendship for him far exceeding ordinary attachments of the world. Our native towns are separated only by a day's journey; and we got to care for each other when we were very young; the season for passionate friendships. Ours improved by years; and so far from being chilled, it was confirmed by our riper judgments, as those who know us best can witness. He takes pleasure in boasting everywhere of my friendship; as I do to let the world know that his reputation, his ease, and his interest are my peculiar concern. Insomuch that upon his expressing to me some apprehension of insolent treatment from a certain person who was entering upon the tribuneship of the people, I could not forbear answering, —

> *"Long as Achilles breathes this vital air,*
> *To touch thy head no impious hand shall dare."*[89]

What is my object in telling you these things? Why, to shew you that I look upon every injury offered to Attilius as done to myself. "But what is the object of all this?" you repeat. You must know then, Valerius Varus, at his death, owed Attilius a sum of money. Though I am on friendly terms with Maximus, his heir, yet there is a closer friendship between him and you. I beg therefore, and entreat you by the affection you have for me, to take care that Attilius is not only paid the capital which is due to him, but all the long arrears of interest too. He neither covets the property of others nor neglects the care of his own; and as he is not engaged in any lucrative profession, he has nothing to depend upon but his own frugality: for as to literature, in which he greatly distinguishes himself, he pursues this merely from motives of pleasure and ambition. In such a situation, the slightest loss presses hard upon a man, and the more so because he has no opportunities of repairing any injury done to his fortune. Remove then, I entreat you, our uneasiness, and suffer me still to enjoy the pleasure of his wit and bonhommie; for I cannot bear to see the cheerfulness of my friend over-clouded, whose mirth and good humour dissipates every gloom of melancholy in myself. In short, you know what a pleasant entertaining fellow he is, and I hope you will not suffer any injury to engloom and embitter his disposition. You may

---

89   Hom. II. lib, I. V. 88.

judge by the warmth of his affection how severe his resentments would prove; for a generous and great mind can ill brook an injury when coupled with contempt. But though he could pass it over, yet cannot I: on the contrary, I shall regard it as a wrong and indignity done to myself, and resent it as one offered to my friend; that is, with double warmth. But, after all, why this air of threatening? rather let me end in the same style in which I began, namely, by begging, entreating you so to act in this affair that neither Attilius may have reason to imagine (which I am exceedingly anxious he should not) that I neglect his interest, nor that I may have occasion to charge you with carelessness of mine: as undoubtedly I shall not if you have the same regard for the latter as I have for the former. Farewell.

TO ALBINUS

I WAS LATELY AT Alsium,[90] where my mother-in-law has a villa which once belonged to Verginius Rufus. The place renewed in my mind the sorrowful remembrance of that-great and excellent man. He was extremely fond of this retirement, and used to call it the nest of his old age. Whichever way I looked, I missed him, I felt his absence. I had an inclination to visit his monument; but I repented having seen it, afterwards: for I found it still unfinished, and this, not from any difficulty residing in the work itself, for it is very plain, or rather indeed slight; but through the neglect of him to whose care it was entrusted. I could not see without a concern, mixed with indignation, the remains of a man, whose fame filled the whole world, lie for ten years after his death without an inscription, or a name. He had however directed that the divine and immortal action of his life should be recorded upon his tomb in the following lines:

> *"Here Rufus lies, who Vindex' arms withstood,*
> *Not for himself, but for his country's good."*

But faithful friends are so rare, and the dead so soon forgotten, that we shall be obliged ourselves to build even our very tombs, and anticipate the office of our heirs. For who is there that has no reason to fear for himself what we see has happened to Verginius, whose eminence and distinction, while rendering such treatment more shameful, so, in

---

90   Now Alzia, not far from Corno.

the same way, make it more notorious? Farewell.

TO MAXIMUS

O WHAT A HAPPY day I lately spent! I was called by the prefect of Rome, to assist him in a certain case, and had the pleasure of hearing two excellent young men, Fuscus Salinator and Numidius Quadratus, plead on the opposite sides: their worth is equal, and each of them will one day, I am persuaded, prove an ornament not only to the present age, but to literature itself. They evinced upon this occasion an admirable probity, supported by inflexible courage: their dress was decent, their elocution distinct, their tones were manly, their memory retentive, their genius elevated, and guided by an equal solidity of judgment. I took infinite pleasure in observing them display these noble qualities; particularly as I had the satisfaction to see that, while they looked upon me as their guide and model, they appeared to the audience as my imitators and rivals. It was a day (I cannot but repeat it again) which afforded me the most exquisite happiness, and which I shall ever distinguish with the fairest mark. For what indeed could be either more pleasing to me on the public account than to observe two such noble youths building their fame and glory upon the polite arts; or more desirable upon my own than to be marked out as a worthy example to them in their pursuits of virtue? May the gods still grant me the continuance of that pleasure! And I implore the same gods, you are my witness, to make all these who think me deserving of imitation far better than I am, Farewell.

TO ROMANUS

YOU WERE NOT PRESENT at a very singular occurrence here lately: neither was I, but the story reached me just after it had happened. Passienus Paulus, a Roman knight, of good family, and a man of peculiar learning and culture besides, composes elegies, a talent which runs in the family, for Propertius is reckoned by him amongst his ancestors, as well as being his countryman. He was lately reciting a poem which began thus:

"Priscus, at thy command"—

Whereupon Javolenus Priscus, who happened to be present as a particular friend of the poet's, cried out—"But he is mistaken, I did not command him." Think what laughter and merriment this occasioned. Priscus's wits, you must know, are reckoned rather unsound,[91] though he takes a share in public business, is summoned to consultations, and even publicly acts as a lawyer, so that this behaviour of his was the more remarkable and ridiculous: meanwhile Paulus was a good deal disconcerted by his friend's absurdity. You see how necessary it is for those who are anxious to recite their works in public to take care that the audience as well as the author are perfectly sane. Farewell.

TO TACITUS

YOUR REQUEST THAT I would send you an account of my uncle's death, in order to transmit a more exact relation of it to posterity, deserves my acknowledgments; for, if this accident shall be celebrated by your pen, the glory of it, I am well assured, will be rendered forever illustrious. And notwithstanding he perished by a misfortune, which, as it involved at the same time a most beautiful country in ruins, and destroyed so many populous cities, seems to promise him an everlasting remembrance; notwithstanding he has himself composed many and lasting works; yet I am persuaded, the mentioning of him in your immortal writings, will greatly contribute to render his name immortal. Happy I esteem those to be to whom by provision of the gods has been granted the ability either to do such actions as are worthy of being related or to relate them in a manner worthy of being read; but peculiarly happy are they who are blessed with both these uncommon talents: in the number of which my uncle, as his own writings and your history will evidently prove, may justly be ranked. It is with extreme willingness, therefore, that I execute your commands; and should indeed have claimed the task if you had not enjoined it. He was at that time with the fleet under his command at Misenum.[92] On the 24th of August, about one in the afternoon, my mother desired him to observe a cloud which appeared of a very unusual size and shape. He had just taken a turn in the sun[93]

---

91   Nevertheless, Javolentis Priscus was one of the most eminent lawyers of his time, and is frequently quoted in the Digesta of Justinian.
92   In the Bay of Naples.
93   The Romans used to lie or walk naked in the sun, after anointing their bodies with oil, which was esteemed as greatly contributing to health, and therefore daily practised by them. This custom, however, of anointing

and, after bathing himself in cold water, and making a light luncheon, gone back to his books: he immediately arose and went out upon a rising ground from whence he might get a better sight of this very uncommon appearance. A cloud, from which mountain was uncertain, at this distance (but it was found afterwards to come from Mount Vesuvius), was ascending, the appearance of which I cannot give you a more exact description of than by likening it to that of a pine tree, for it shot up to a great height in the form of a very tall trunk, which spread itself out at the top into a sort of branches; occasioned, I imagine, either by a sudden gust of air that impelled it, the force of which decreased as it advanced upwards, or the cloud itself being pressed back again by its own weight, expanded in the manner I have mentioned; it appeared sometimes bright and sometimes dark and spotted, according as it was either more or less impregnated with earth and cinders. This phenomenon seemed to a man of such learning and research as my uncle extraordinary and worth further looking into. He ordered a light vessel to be got ready, and gave me leave, if I liked, to accompany him. I said I had rather go on with my work; and it so happened, he had himself given me something to write out. As he was coming out of the house, he received a note from Rectina, the wife of Bassus, who was in the utmost alarm at the imminent danger which threatened her; for her villa lying at the foot of Mount Vesuvius, there was no way of escape but by sea; she earnestly entreated him therefore to come to her assistance. He accordingly changed his first intention, and what he had begun from a philosophical, he now carries out in a noble and generous spirit. He ordered the galleys to be put to sea, and went himself on board with an intention of assisting not only Rectina, but the several other towns which lay thickly strewn along that beautiful coast. Hastening then to the place from whence others fled with the utmost terror, he steered his course direct to the point of danger, and with so much calmness and presence of mind as to be able to make and dictate his observations upon the motion and all the phenomena of that dreadful scene. He was now so close to the mountain that the cinders, which grew thicker and hotter the nearer he approached, fell into the ships, together with pumice-stones, and black pieces of burning rock: they were in danger too not only of being aground by the sudden retreat of

themselves, is inveighed against by the Satirists as in the number of their luxurious indulgences: but since we find the elder Pliny here, and the amiable Spurinna in a former letter, practising this method, we can not suppose the thing itself was esteemed unmanly, but only when it was attended with some particular circumstances of an over-refined delicacy. M.

the sea, but also from the vast fragments which rolled down from the mountain, and obstructed all the shore. Here he stopped to consider whether he should turn back again; to which the pilot advising him, "Fortune," said he, "favours the brave; steer to where Pomponianus is." Pomponianus was then at Stabiae,[94] separated by a bay, which the sea, after several insensible windings, forms with the shore. He had already sent his baggage on board; for though he was not at that time in actual danger, yet being within sight of it, and indeed extremely near, if it should in the least increase, he was determined to put to sea as soon as the wind, which was blowing dead in-shore, should go down. It was favourable, however, for carrying my uncle to Pomponianus, whom he found in the greatest consternation: he embraced him tenderly, encouraging and urging him to keep up his spirits, and, the more effectually to soothe his fears by seeming unconcerned himself, ordered a bath to be got ready, and then, after having bathed, sat down to supper with great cheerfulness, or at least (what is just as heroic) with every appearance of it. Meanwhile broad flames shone out in several places from Mount Vesuvius, which the darkness of the night contributed to render still brighter and clearer. But my uncle, in order to soothe the apprehensions of his friend, assured him it was only the burning of the villages, which the country people had abandoned to the flames: after this he retired to rest, and it is most certain he was so little disquieted as to fall into a sound sleep: for his breathing, which, on account of his corpulence, was rather heavy and sonorous, was heard by the attendants outside. The court which led to his apartment being now almost filled with stones and ashes, if he had continued there any time longer, it would have been impossible for him to have made his way out. So he was awoke and got up, and went to Pomponianus and the rest of his company, who were feeling too anxious to think of going to bed. They consulted together whether it would be most prudent to trust to the houses, which now rocked from side to side with frequent and violent concussions as though shaken from their very foundations; or fly to the open fields, where the calcined stones and cinders, though light indeed, yet fell in large showers, and threatened destruction. In this choice of dangers they resolved for the fields: a resolution which, while the rest of the company were hurried into by their fears, my uncle embraced upon cool and deliberate consideration. They went out then, having pillows tied upon their heads with napkins; and this was their whole defence against the storm of stones that fell round them. It was now day everywhere

94   Now called Castelamare, in the Bay of Naples. M.

else, but there a deeper darkness prevailed than in the thickest night; which however was in some degree alleviated by torches and other lights of various kinds. They thought proper to go farther down upon the shore to see if they might safely put out to sea, but found the waves still running extremely high, and boisterous. There my uncle, laying himself down upon a sail cloth, which was spread for him, called twice for some cold water, which he drank, when immediately the flames, preceded by a strong whiff of sulphur, dispersed the rest of the party, and obliged him to rise. He raised himself up with the assistance of two of his servants, and instantly fell down dead; suffocated, as I conjecture, by some gross and noxious vapour, having always had a weak throat, which was often inflamed. As soon as it was light again, which was not till the third day after this melancholy accident, his body was found entire, and without any marks of violence upon it, in the dress in which he fell, and looking more like a man asleep than dead. During all this time my mother and I, who were at Miscnum—but this has no connection with your history, and you did not desire any particulars besides those of my uncle's death; so I will end here, only adding that I have faithfully related to you what I was either an eye-witness of myself or received immediately after the accident happened, and before there was time to vary the truth. You will pick out of this narrative whatever is most important: for a letter is one thing, a history another; it is one thing writing to a friend, another thing writing to the public. Farewell.

TO CORNELIUS TACITUS

THE LETTER WHICH, in compliance with your request, I wrote to you concerning the death of my uncle has raised, it seems, your curiosity to know what terrors and dangers attended me while I continued at Misenum; for there, I think, my account broke off:

> *"Though my shock'd soul recoils, my tongue shall tell."*

My uncle having left us, I spent such time as was left on my studies (it was on their account indeed that I had stopped behind), till it was time for my bath. After which I went to supper, and then fell into a short and uneasy sleep. There had been noticed for many days before a trembling of the earth, which did not alarm us much, as this is quite an ordinary occurrence in Campania; but it was so particularly violent that night that it not only shook but actually overturned, as it would seem, everything about us. My mother rushed into my chamber, where she found me rising, in order to awaken her. We sat down in the open court of the house, which occupied a small space between the buildings and the sea. As I was at that time but eighteen years of age, I know not whether I should call my behaviour, in this dangerous juncture, courage or folly; but I took up Livy, and amused myself with turning over that author, and even making extracts from him, as if I had been perfectly at my leisure. Just then, a friend of my uncle's, who had lately come to him from Spain, joined us, and observing me sitting by my mother with a book in my hand, reproved her for her calmness, and me at the same time for my careless security: nevertheless I went on with my author. Though it was now morning, the light was still exceedingly faint and doubtful; the buildings all around us tottered, and though we stood upon open ground, yet as the place was narrow and confined, there was no remaining without imminent danger: we therefore resolved to quit the town. A panic-stricken crowd followed us, and (as to a mind distracted with terror every suggestion seems more prudent than its own) pressed on us in dense array to drive us forward as we came out. Being at a convenient distance from the houses, we stood still, in the midst of a most dangerous and dreadful scene. The chariots, which we had ordered to be drawn out, were so agitated backwards and forwards, though upon the most level ground, that we could not keep them steady, even by supporting them with large stones. The sea seemed to roll back upon itself, and to be driven from its banks by the convulsive motion of the earth; it is certain at least the shore was considerably enlarged, and several sea animals were left upon it. On the other side, a black and dreadful cloud, broken with rapid, zigzag flashes, revealed behind it variously shaped masses of flame: these last were like sheet-lightning, but much larger. Upon this our Spanish friend, whom I mentioned above, addressing himself to my mother and me with great energy and urgency: "If your brother," he said, "if your uncle be safe, he certainly wishes you may be so too; but if he perished, it was his desire, no doubt, that you might both survive him: why therefore do you delay your escape a moment?" We could never think of our own safety, we said, while we were uncertain of his. Upon this our friend left us, and withdrew from the danger with the utmost precipitation. Soon afterwards, the cloud began to descend, and cover the sea. It had already surrounded and concealed the island of Capreae and the promontory of Misenum. My mother now besought, urged, even commanded me to make my escape at any rate, which, as I was young, I might easily do; as for herself, she said, her age and corpulency rendered all attempts of that sort impossible; however, she would willingly meet death if she could have the satisfaction of seeing that she was not the occasion of mine. But I absolutely refused to leave her, and, taking her by the hand, compelled her to go with me. She complied with great reluctance, and not without many reproaches to herself for retarding my flight. The ashes now began to fall upon us, though in no great quantity. I looked back; a dense dark mist seemed to be following us, spreading itself over the country like a cloud. "Let us turn out of the high-road," I said, "while we can still see, for fear that, should we fall in the road, we should be pressed to death in the dark, by the crowds that are following us." We had scarcely sat down when night came upon us, not such as we have when the sky is cloudy, or when there is no moon, but that of a room when it is shut up, and all the lights put out. You might hear the shrieks of women, the screams of children, and the shouts of men; some calling for their children, others for their parents, others for their husbands, and seeking to recognise each other by the voices that replied; one lamenting his own fate, another that of his family; some wishing to die, from the very fear of dying; some lifting their hands to the gods; but the greater part convinced that there were now no gods at all, and that the final endless night of which we have heard had come upon the world.[95] Among these there were some who augmented the real terrors by others imaginary or wilfully invented. I remember some who declared that one part of Misenum had fallen, that another was on fire; it was false, but they found people to believe them. It now grew rather lighter, which we imagined to be rather the forerunner of an approaching burst of flames (as in truth it was) than the return of day: however, the fire fell at a distance from us: then again we were immersed in thick darkness, and a heavy shower of ashes rained upon us, which we were obliged every now and then to stand up to shake off, otherwise we should have been crushed and buried in the heap. I might boast that, during all this scene of horror, not a sigh, or expression of fear, escaped me, had not my support been grounded in that miserable, though mighty, consolation, that all mankind were involved in the same calamity, and that I was perishing with the world itself. At last this dreadful darkness was dissipated by degrees, like a cloud or smoke; the real day returned, and even the sun shone out, though with a lurid light, like when an eclipse is coming on. Every object that presented itself to our eyes (which were extremely weakened) seemed changed, being cov-

---

95   The Stoic and Epicurean philosophers held that the world was to be destroyed by fire, and all things fall again into original chaos; not excepting even the national gods themselves from the destruction of this general conflagration. M.

ered deep with ashes as if with snow. We returned to Misenum, where we refreshed ourselves as well as we could, and passed an anxious night between hope and fear; though, indeed, with a much larger share of the latter: for the earthquake still continued, while many frenzied persons ran up and down heightening their own and their friends' calamities by terrible predictions. However, my mother and I, notwithstanding the danger we had passed, and that which still threatened us, had no thoughts of leaving the place, till we could receive some news of my uncle.

And now, you will read this narrative without any view of inserting it in your history, of which it is not in the least worthy; and indeed you must put it down to your own request if it should appear not worth even the trouble of a letter. Farewell.

TO MACER

How much does the fame of human actions depend upon the station of those who perform them! The very same conduct shall be either applauded to the skies or entirely overlooked, just as it may happen to proceed from a person of conspicuous or obscure rank. I was sailing lately upon our lake,[96] with an old man of my acquaintance, who desired me to observe a villa situated upon its banks, which had a chamber overhanging the water. "From that room," said he, "a woman of our city threw herself and her husband." Upon enquiring into the cause, he informed me, "That her husband having been long afflicted with an ulcer in those parts which modesty conceals, she prevailed with him at last to let her inspect the sore, assuring him at the same time that she would most sincerely give her opinion whether there was a possibility of its being cured. Accordingly, upon viewing the ulcer, she found the case hopeless, and therefore advised him to put an end to his life: she herself accompanying him, even leading the way by her example, and being actually the means of his death; for tying herself to her husband, she plunged with him into the lake." Though this happened in the very city where I was born, I never heard it mentioned before; and yet that this action is taken less notice of than that famous one of Arria's, is not because it was less remarkable, but because the person who performed it was more obscure. Farewell.

---

96   The lake Larius.

TO SERVIANUS

I AM EXTREMELY GLAD to hear that you intend your daughter for Fuscus Salinator, and congratulate you upon it. His family is patrician,[97] and both his father and mother are persons of the most distinguished merit. As for himself, he is studious, learned, and eloquent, and, with all the innocence of a child, unites the sprightliness of youth and the wisdom of age. I am not, believe me, deceived by my affection, when I give him this character; for though I love him, I confess, beyond measure (as his friendship and esteem for me well deserve), yet partiality has no share in my judgment: on the contrary, the stronger my affection for him, the more exactingly I weigh his merit. I will venture, then, to assure you (and I speak it upon my own experience) you could not have, formed to your wishes, a more accomplished son-in-law. May he soon present you with a grandson, who shall be the exact copy of his father! and with what pleasure shall I receive from the arms of two such friends their children or grand-children, whom I shall claim a sort of right to embrace as my own! Farewell.

TO SEVERUS

YOU DESIRE ME TO consider what turn you should give to your speech in honour of the emperor,[98] upon your being appointed consul elect.[99] It is easy to find copies, not so easy to choose out of them; for his virtues afford such abundant material. However, I will write and give you my opinion, or (what I should prefer) I will let you have it in person, after having laid before you the difficulties which occur to me. I am doubtful, then, whether I should advise you to pursue the method which I observed myself on the same occasion. When I was consul elect, I avoided running into the usual strain of compliment, which, however far from adulation, might yet look like it. Not that I affected

---

97   Those families were styled patrician whose ancestors had been members of the senate in the earliest times of the regal or consular government. M.
98   Trajan
99   The consuls, though they were chosen in August, did not enter upon their office till the first of January, during which interval they were styled consules designati, consuls elect. It was usual for them upon that occasion to compliment the emperor, by whose appointment, after the dissolution of the republican government, they were chosen. M.

firmness and independence; but, as well knowing the sentiments of our amiable prince, and being thoroughly persuaded that the highest praise I could offer to him would be to show the world I was under no necessity of paying him any. When I reflected what profusion of honours had been heaped upon the very worst of his predecessors, nothing, I imagined, could more distinguish a prince of his real virtues from those infamous emperors than to address him in a different manner. And this I thought proper to observe in my speech, lest it might be suspected I passed over his glorious acts, not out of judgment, but inattention. Such was the method I then observed; but I am sensible the same measures are neither agreeable nor indeed suitable to all alike. Besides the propriety of doing or omitting a thing depends not only upon persons, but time and circumstances; and as the late actions of our illustrious prince afford materials for panegyric, no less just than recent and glorious, I doubt (as I said before) whether I should persuade you in the present instance to adopt the same plan as I did myself. In this, however, I am clear, that it was proper to offer you by way of advice the method I pursued. Farewell.

TO FABATUS

I HAVE THE BEST reason, certainly, for celebrating your birthday as my own, since all the happiness of mine arises from yours, to whose care and diligence it is owing that I am gay here and at my ease in town. — Your Camillian villa[100] in Campania has suffered by the injuries of time, and is falling into decay; however, the most valuable parts of the building either remain entire or are but slightly damaged, and it shall be my care to see it put into thorough repair. — Though I flatter myself I have many friends, yet I have scarcely any of the sort you enquire after, and which the affair you mention demands. All mine lie among those whose employments engage them in town; whereas the conduct of country business requires a person of a robust constitution, and bred up to the country, to whom the work may not seem hard, nor the office beneath him, and who does not feel a solitary life depressing. You think most highly of Rufus, for he was a great friend of your son's; but of what use he can be to us upon this occasion, I cannot conceive; though I am sure he will be glad to do all he can for us. Farewell.

TO CORNELIANUS

I RECEIVED LATELY THE most exquisite satisfaction at Centumcellae[101] (as it is now called), being summoned thither by Cæsar[102] to attend a council. Could anything indeed afford a higher pleasure than to see the emperor exercising his justice, his wisdom, and his affability, even in retirement, where those virtues are most observable? Various were the points brought in judgment before him, and which proved, in so many different instances, the excellence of the judge. The cause of Claudius Ariston came on first. He is an Ephesian nobleman, of great munificence and unambitious popularity, whose virtues have rendered him obnoxious to a set of people of far different characters; they had instigated an informer against him, of the same infamous stamp with themselves; but he was honourably acquitted. The next day, the case of Galitta, accused of adultery, was heard. Her husband, who is a military tribune, was

---

100   So called, because it formerly belonged to Camillus. M.
101   Civita Vecchia.
102   Trajan.

upon the point of offering himself as a candidate for certain honours at Rome, but she had stained her own good name and his by an intrigue with a centurion.[103] The husband informed the consul's lieutenant, who wrote to the emperor about it. Cæsar, having thoroughly sifted the evidence, cashiered the centurion, and sentenced him to banishment. It remained that some penalty should be inflicted likewise upon the other party, as it is a crime of which both must necessarily be equally guilty. But the husband's affection for his wife inclined him to drop that part of the prosecution, not without some reflections on his forbearance; for he continued to live with her even after he had commenced this prosecution, content, it would seem, with having removed his rival. But he was ordered to proceed in the suit: and, though he complied with great reluctance, it was necessary, nevertheless, that she should be condemned. Accordingly, she was sentenced to the punishment directed by the Julian law.[104] The emperor thought proper to specify, in his decree, the name and office of the centurion, that it might appear he passed it in virtue of military discipline; lest it should be imagined he claimed a particular cognizance in every cause of the same nature. The third day was employed in examining into an affair which had occasioned a good deal of talk and various reports; it was concerning the codicils of Julius Tiro, part of which was plainly genuine, while the other part, it was alleged, was forged. The persons accused of this fraud were Sempronius Senecio, a Roman knight, and Eurythmus, Cæsar's freedman and procurator.[105] The heirs jointly petitioned the emperor, when he was in Dacia,[106] that he would reserve to himself the trial of this cause; to which he consented. On his return from that expedition, he appointed a day for the hearing; and when some of the heirs, as though out of respect to Eurythmus, offered to withdraw the suit, the emperor nobly replied, "He is not Polycletus,[107] nor am I Nero." However, he indulged the petitioners with an adjournment, and the time being expired, he now sat to hear the cause. Two of the heirs appeared, and desired that either their whole number might be compelled to plead, as they had all joined in the information, or that they also might have leave to withdraw. Cæsar delivered

---

103   An officer in the Roman legions, answering in some sort to a captain In our companies. M.

104   This law was made by Augustus Cæsar; but it nowhere clearly appears what was the peculiar punishment it inflicted. M.

105   An officer employed by the emperor to receive and regulate the public revenue in the provinces. M.

106   Comprehending Transylvania, Moldavia, and Walaehia. M.

107   Polycletus was a freedman, and great favourite of Nero. M.

his opinion with great dignity and moderation; and when the counsel on the part of Senecio and Eurythmus had represented that unless their clients were heard, they would remain under the suspicion of guilt,—"I am not concerned," said the emperor, "what suspicions they may lie under, it is I that am suspected;" and then turning to us, "Advise me," said he, "how to act in this affair, for you see they complain when allowed to withdraw their suit." At length, by the advice of the counsel, he 'ordered notice to be given to the heirs that they should either proceed with the case or each of them justify their reasons for not doing so; otherwise that he would pass sentence upon them as calumniators.[108] Thus you see how usefully and seriously we spent our time, which however was diversified with amusements of the most agreeable kind. We were every day invited to Cæsar's table, which, for so great a prince, was spread with much plainness and simplicity. There we were either entertained with interludes or passed the night in the most pleasing conversation. When we took our leave of him the last day, he made each of us presents; so studiously polite is Cæsar! As for myself, I was not only charmed with the dignity and wisdom of the judge, the honour done to the assessors, the ease and unreserved freedom of our social intercourse, but with the exquisite situation of the place itself. This delightful villa is surrounded by the greenest meadows, and overlooks the shore, which bends inwards, forming a complete harbour. The left arm of this port is defended by exceedingly strong works, while the right is in process of completion. An artificial island, which rises at the mouth of the harbour, breaks the force of the waves, and affords a safe passage to ships on either side. This island is formed by a process worth seeing: stones of a most enormous size are transported hither in a large sort of pontoons, and being piled one upon the other, are fixed by their own weight, gradually accumulating in the manner, as it were, of a natural mound. It already lifts its rocky back above the ocean, while the waves which beat upon it, being broken and tossed to an immense height, foam with a prodigious noise, and whiten all the surrounding sea. To these stones are added wooden piers, which in process of time will give it the appearance of a natural island. This haven is to be called by the name of its great author,[109] and

---

108   Memmius, or Rhemmius (the critics are not agreed which), was author of a law by which it was enacted that whosoever was convicted of calumny and false accusation should be stigmatised with a mark in his forehead; and by the law of the twelve tables, false accusers were to suffer the same punishment as would have been inflicted upon the person unjustly accused if the crime had been proved. M.
109   Trajan.

will prove of infinite benefit, by affording a secure retreat to ships on that extensive and dangerous coast. Farewell.

TO MAXIMUS

YOU DID PERFECTLY RIGHT in promising a gladiatorial combat to our good friends the citizens of Verona, who have long loved, looked up to, and honoured, you; while it was from that city too you received that amiable object of your most tender affection, your late excellent wife. And since you owed some monument or public representation to her memory, what other spectacle could you have exhibited more appropriate to the occasion? Besides, you were so unanimously pressed to do so that to have refused would have looked more like hardness than resolution. The readiness too with which you granted their petition, and the magnificent manner in which you performed it, is very much to your honour; for a greatness of soul is seen in these smaller instances, as well as in matters of higher moment. I wish the African panthers, which you had largely provided for this purpose, had arrived on the day appointed, but though they were delayed by the stormy weather, the obligation to you is equally the same, since it was not your fault that they were not exhibited. Farewell.

TO RESTITUTUS

THIS OBSTINATE ILLNESS OF yours alarms me; and though I know how extremely temperate you are, yet I fear lest your disease should get the better of your moderation. Let me entreat you then to resist it with a determined abstemiousness: a remedy, be assured, of all others the most laudable as well as the most salutary. Human nature itself admits the practicability of what I recommend: it is a rule, at least, which I always enjoin my family to observe with respect to myself. "I hope," I say to them, "that should I be attacked with any disorder, I shall desire nothing of which I ought either to be ashamed or have reason to repent; however, if my distemper should prevail over my resolution, I forbid that anything be given me but by the consent of my physicians; and I shall resent your compliance with me in things improper as much as another man would their refusal." I once had a most violent fever; when the fit was a little abated, and I had been anointed,[110] my physician offered me something to drink; I held out my hand, desiring he would first feel my pulse, and upon his not seeming quite satisfied, I instantly returned the cup, though it was just at my lips. Afterwards, when I was preparing to go into the bath, twenty days from the first attack of my illness, perceiving the physicians whispering together, I enquired what they were saying. They replied they were of opinion I may possibly bathe with safety, however that they were not without some suspicion of risk. "What need is there," said I, "of my taking a bath at all?" And so, with perfect calmness and tranquillity, I gave up a pleasure I was upon the point of enjoying, and abstained from the bath as serenely and composedly as though I were going into it. I mention this, not only by way of enforcing my advice by example, but also that this letter may be a sort of tie upon me to persevere in the same resolute abstinence for the future. Farewell.

TO CALPURNIA[111]

YOU WILL NOT BELIEVE what a longing for you possesses me. The chief cause of this is my love; and then we have not grown used to be apart. So it comes to pass that I lie awake a great part of the night, thinking of you; and that by day, when the hours return at which I was wont to visit you, my feet take me, as it is so truly said, to your chamber, but not finding you there, I return, sick and sad at heart, like an excluded lover. The only time that is free from these torments is when I am being worn out at the bar, and in the suits of my friends. Judge you what must be my life when I find my repose in toil, my solace in wretchedness and anxiety. Farewell.

TO MACRINUS

A VERY SINGULAR AND remarkable accident has happened in the affair of Varenus,[112] the result of which is yet doubtful. The Bithynians, it is said, have dropped their prosecution of him being convinced at

---

110 Unction was much esteemed and prescribed by the ancients. Celsus expressly recommends it in the remission of acute distempers: "ungi leniterque pertractari corpus, etiam in acutic et recentibus niorbis opartet; us rernissione fumen," &c. Celsi Med. ed. Aliucloveen, p. 88. M.
111 His wife.
112 See book V. letter XX.

last that it was rashly undertaken. A deputy from that province is arrived, who has brought with him a decree of their assembly; copies of which he has delivered to Cæsar,[113] and to several of the leading men in Rome, and also to us, the advocates for Varenus. Magnus,[114] nevertheless, whom I mentioned in my last letter to you, persists in his charge, to support which he is incessantly teasing the worthy Nigrinus. This excellent person was counsel for him in his former petition to the consuls, that Varenus might be compelled to produce his accounts. Upon this occasion, as I attended Varenus merely as a friend, I determined to be silent. I thought it highly imprudent for me, as I was appointed his counsel by the senate, to attempt to defend him as an accused person, when it was his business to insist that there was actually no charge subsisting against him. However, when Nigrinus had finished his speech, the consuls turning their eyes upon me, I rose up, and, "When you shall hear," I said, "what the real deputies from the province have to object against the motion of Nigrinus, you will see that my silence was not without just reason." Upon this Nigrinus asked me, "To whom are these deputies sent?" I replied, "To me among others; I have the decree of the province in my hands." He returned, "That is a point which, though it may be clear to you, I am not so well satisfied of." To this I answered, "Though it may not be so evident to you, who are concerned to support the accusation, it may be perfectly clear to me, who am on the more favourable side." Then Polyaenus, the deputy from the province, acquainted the senate with the reasons for superseding the prosecution, but desired it might be without prejudice to Cæsar's determination. Magnus answered him; Polyaenus replied; as for myself, I only now and then threw in a word, observing in general a complete silence. For I have learned that upon some occasions it is as much an orator's business to be silent as to speak, and I remember, in some criminal cases, to have done even more service to my clients by a discreet silence than I could have expected from the most carefully prepared speech. To enter into the subject of eloquence is indeed very foreign to the purpose of my letter, yet allow me to give you one instance in proof of my last observation. A certain lady having lost her son suspected that his freedmen, whom he had appointed coheirs with her, were guilty of forging the will and poisoning him. Accordingly she charged them with the fact before the emperor, who directed Julianus Suburanus to try the cause. I was counsel for the defendants,

---

113   Trajan.
114   One of the Bithynians employed to manage the trial. M.

and the case being exceedingly remarkable, and the counsel engaged on both sides of eminent ability, it drew together a very numerous audience. The issue was, the servants being put to the torture, my clients were acquitted. But the mother applied a second time to the emperor, pretending she had discovered some new evidence. Suburanus was therefore directed to hear the cause, and see if she could produce any fresh proofs. Julius Africanus was counsel for the mother, a young man of good parts, but slender experience. He is grandson to the famous orator of that name, of whom it is reported that Passienus Crispus, hearing him one day plead, archly said, "Very fine, I must confess, very fine; but is all this fine speaking to the purpose?" Julius Africanus, I say, having made a long harangue, and exhausted the portion of time allotted to him, said, "I beg you, Suburanus, to allow me to add one word more." When he had concluded, and the eyes of the whole assembly had been fixed a considerable time upon me, I rose up. "I would have answered Africanus," said I, "if he had added that one word he begged leave to do, in which I doubt not he would have told us all that we had not heard before." I do not remember to have gained so much applause by any speech that I ever made as I did in this instance by making none. Thus the little that I had hitherto said for Varenus was received with the same general approbation. The consuls, agreeably to the request of Polyaenus, reserved the whole affair for the determination of the emperor, whose resolution I impatiently wait for; as that will decide whether I may be entirely secure and easy with respect to Varenus, or must again renew all my trouble and anxiety upon his account. Farewell.

TO TUSCUS

YOU DESIRE MY OPINION as to the method of study you should pursue, in that retirement to which you have long since withdrawn. In the first place, then, I look upon it as a very advantageous practice (and it is what many recommend) to translate either from Greek into Latin or from Latin into Greek. By this means you acquire propriety and dignity of expression, and a variety of beautiful figures, and an ease and strength of exposition, and in the imitation of the best models a facility of creating such models for yourself. Besides, those things which you may possibly have overlooked in an ordinary reading over cannot escape you in translating: and this method will also enlarge your knowledge, and improve your judgment. It may not be amiss, after you have read an author, to turn, as it were, to his rival, and attempt something ol your own upon the same topic, and then make a careful comparison between your performance and his, in order to see in what points either you or he may be the happier. You may congratulate yourself indeed if you shall find in some things that you have the advantage of him, while it will be a great mortification if he is always superior. You may sometimes select very famous passages and compete with what you select. The competition is daring enough, but, as it is private, cannot be called impudent. Not but that we have seen instances of persons who have publicly entered this sort of lists with great credit to themselves, and, while they did not despair of overtaking, have gloriously outstripped those whom they thought it sufficient honour to follow. A speech no longer fresh in your memory, you may take up again. You will find plenty in it to leave unaltered, but still more to reject; you will add a new thought here, and alter another there. It is a laborious and tedious task, I own, thus to re-enflame the mind after the first heat is over, to recover an impulse when its force has been checked and spent, and, worse than all, to put new limbs into a body already complete without disturbing the old; but the advantage attending this method will overbalance the difficulty. I know the bent of your present attention is directed towards the eloquence of the bar; but I would not for that reason advise you never to quit the polemic, if I may so call it, and contentious style. As land is improved by sowing it with various seeds, constantly changed, so is the mind by exercising it now with this subject of study, now with that. I would recommend you, therefore, sometimes to take a subject from history, and you might give more care to the composition of your letters. For it frequently happens that in pleading one has occasion to make use not only of historical, but even poetical, styles of description; and then from letters you acquire a concise and simple mode of expression. You will do quite right again in refreshing yourself with poetry: when I say so, I do not mean that species of poetry which turns upon subjects of great length and continuity (such being suitable only for persons of leisure), but those little pieces of the sprightly kind of poesy, which serve as proper reliefs to, and are consistent with, employments of every sort. They commonly go under the title of poetical amusements; but these amusements have sometimes gained their authors as much reputation as works of a more serious nature; and thus (for while I am exhorting you to poetry, why should I not turn poet myself?)

    "As yielding wax the artist's skill commands,

Submissive shap'd beneath his forming hands;
Now dreadful stands in arms a Mars confest;
Or now with Venus's softer air imprest;
A wanton Cupid now the mould belies;
Now shines, severely chaste, a Pallas wife:
As not alone to quench the raging flame,
The sacred fountain pours her friendly stream;
But sweetly gliding through the flow'ry green,
Spreads glad refreshment o'er the smiling scene:
So, form'd by science, should the ductile mind
Receive, distinct, each various art refin'd."

In this manner the greatest men, as well as the greatest orators, used either to exercise or amuse themselves, or rather indeed did both. It is surprising how much the mind is enlivened and refreshed by these little poetical compositions, as they turn upon love, hatred, satire, tenderness, politeness, and everything, in short, that concerns life and the affairs of the world. Besides, the same advantage attends these, as every other sort of poems, that we turn from them to prose with so much the more pleasure after having experienced the difficulty of being constrained and fettered by metre. And now, perhaps, I have troubled you upon this subject longer than you desired; however, there is one thing I have left out: I have not told you what kind of authors you should read; though indeed that was sufficiently implied when I told you on what you should write. Remember to be careful in your choice of authors of every kind: for, as it has been well observed, "though we should read much, we should not read many books." Who those authors are, is so clearly settled, and so generally known, that I need not particularly specify them; besides, I have already extended this letter to such an immoderate length that, while suggesting how you ought to study, I have, I fear, been actually interrupting your studies. I will here resign you therefore to your tablets, either to resume the studies in which you were before engaged or to enter upon some of those I have recommended. Farewell.

TO FABATUS (HIS WIFE'S GRANDFATHER)

YOU ARE SURPRISED, I find, that my share of five-twelfths of the estate which lately fell to me, and which I had directed to be sold to the best bidder, should have been disposed of by my freedman Hermes to

Corellia (without putting it up to auction) at the rate of seven hundred thousand sesterces[115] for the whole. And as you think it might have fetched nine hundred thousand,[116] you are so much the more desirous to know whether I am inclined to ratify what he has done. I am; and listen, while I tell you why, for I hope that not only you will approve, but also that my fellow-coheirs will excuse me for having, upon a motive of superior obligation, separated my interest from theirs. I have the highest esteem for Corellia, both as the sister of Rufus, whose memory will always be a sacred one to me, and as my mother's intimate friend. Besides, that excellent man Minutius Tuscus, her husband, has every claim to my affection that a long friendship can give him; as there was likewise the closest intimacy between her son and me, so much so indeed that I fixed upon him to preside at the games which I exhibited when I was elected praetor. This lady, when I was last in the country, expressed a strong desire for some place upon the borders of our lake of Comum; I therefore made her an offer, at her own price, of any part of my land there, except what came to me from my father and mother; for that I could not consent to part with, even to Corellia, and accordingly when the inheritance in question fell to me, I wrote to let her know it was to be sold. This letter I sent by Hermes, who, upon her requesting him that he would immediately make over to her my proportion of it, consented. Am I not then obliged to confirm what my freedman has thus done in pursuance of my inclinations? I have only to entreat my fellow-coheirs that they will not take it ill at my hands that I have made a separate sale of what I had certainly a right to dispose of. They are not bound in any way to follow my example, since they have not the same connections with Corellia. They are at full liberty therefore to be guided by interest, which in my own case I chose to sacrifice to friendship. Farewell.

TO CORELLIA

YOU ARE TRULY GENEROUS to desire and insist that I take for my share of the estate you purchased of me, not after the rate of seven hundred thousand sesterces for the whole, as my freedman sold it to you; but in the proportion of nine hundred thousand, agreeably to what you gave to the farmers of the twentieths for their part. But I must desire and insist

---

115   About $28,000.
116   About $26,000.

in my turn that you would consider not only what is suitable to your character, but what is worthy of mine; and that you would suffer me to oppose your inclination in this single instance, with the same warmth that I obey it in all others. Farewell.

TO CELER

EVERY AUTHOR HAS HIS particular reasons for reciting his works; mine, I have often said, are, in order, if any error should have escaped my own observation (as no doubt they do escape it sometimes), to have it pointed out to me. I cannot therefore but be surprised to find (what your letter assures me) that there are some who blame me for reciting my speeches: unless, perhaps, they are of opinion that this is the single species of composition that ought to be held exempt from any correction. If so, I would willingly ask them why they allow (if indeed they do allow) that history may be recited, since it is a work which ought to be devoted to truth, not ostentation? or why tragedy, as it is composed for action and the stage, not for being read to a private audience? or lyric poetry, as it is not a reader, but a chorus of voices and instruments that it requires? They will reply, perhaps, that in the instances referred to custom has made the practice in question usual: I should be glad to know, then, if they think the person who first introduced this practice is to be condemned? Besides the rehearsal of speeches is no unprecedented thing either with us or the Grecians. Still, perhaps, they will insist that it can answer no purpose to recite a speech which has already been delivered. True; if one were immediately to repeat the very same speech word for word, and to the very same audience; but if you make several additions and alterations; if your audience is composed partly of the same, and partly of different persons, and the recital is at some distance of time, why is there less propriety in rehearsing your speech than in publishing it? "But it is difficult," the objectors urge, "to give satisfaction to an audience by the mere recital of a speech;" that is a consideration which concerns the particular skill and pains of the person who rehearses, but by no means holds good against recitation in general. The truth is, it is not whilst I am reading, but when I am read, that I aim at approbation; and upon this principle I omit no sort of correction. In the first place, I frequently go carefully over what I have written, by myself, after this I read it out to two or three friends, and then give it to others to make their remarks. If after this I have any doubt concerning the justness of their observations, I carefully weigh them again with a friend or two; and, last of all, I recite them to a larger audience, then is the time, believe me, when I correct most energetically and unsparingly; for my care and attention rise in proportion to my anxiety; as nothing renders the judgment so acute to detect error as that deference, modesty, and diffidence one feels upon those occasions. For tell me, would you not be infinitely less affected were you to speak before a single person only, though ever so learned, than before a numerous assembly, even though composed of none but illiterate people? When you rise up to plead, are you not at that juncture, above all others, most self-distrustful? and do you not wish, I will not say some particular parts only, but that the whole arrangement of your intended speech were altered? especially if the concourse should be large in which you are to speak? for there is something even in a low and vulgar audience that strikes one with awe. And if you suspect you are not well received at the first opening of your speech, do you not find all your energy relaxed, and feel yourself ready to give way? The reason I imagine to be that there is a certain weight of collective opinion in a multitude, and although each individual judgment is, perhaps, of little value, yet when united it becomes considerable. Accordingly, Pomponius Secundus, the famous tragic poet, whenever some very intimate friend and he differed about the retaining or rejecting anything in his writings, used to say, "I appeal[117] to the people"; and thus, by their silence or applause, adopted either his own or his friend's opinion; such was the deference he paid to the popular judgment! Whether justly or not, is no concern of mine, as I am not in the habit of reciting my works publicly, but only to a select circle, whose presence I respect, and whose judgment I value; in a word, whose opinions I attend to as if they were so many individuals I had separately consulted, at the same time that I stand in as much awe before them as I should before the most numerous assembly. What Cicero says of composing will, in my opinion, hold true of the dread we have of the public: "Fear is the most rigid critic imaginable." The very thought of reciting, the very entrance into an assembly, and the agitated concern when one is there; each of these circumstances tends to improve and perfect an author's performance. Upon the whole, therefore, I cannot repent of a practice which I have found by experience so exceedingly useful; and am so far from being discouraged by the trifling objections

---

117   There is a kind of witticism in this expression, which will be lost to the mere English reader unless he be informed that the Romans had a privilege, confirmed to them by several laws which passed in the earlier ages of the republic, of appealing from the decisions of the magistrates to the general assembly of the people: and they did so in the form of words which Pomponius here applies to a different purpose. M.

of these censors that I request you would point out to me if there is yet any other kind of correction, that I may also adopt it; for nothing can sufficiently satisfy my anxiety to render my compositions perfect. I reflect what an undertaking it is resigning any work into the hands of the public; and I cannot but be persuaded that frequent revisals, and many consultations, must go to the perfecting of a performance, which one desires should universally and forever please. Farewell.

TO PRISCUS

THE ILLNESS OF MY friend Fannia gives me great concern. She contracted it during her attendance on Junia, one of the Vestal virgins, engaging in this good office at first voluntarily, Junia being her relation, and afterwards being appointed to it by an order from the college of priests: for these virgins, when excessive ill-health renders it necessary to remove them from the temple of Vesta, are always delivered over to the care and custody of some venerable matron. It was owing to her assiduity in the execution of this charge that she contracted her present dangerous disorder, which is a continual fever, attended with a cough that increases daily. She is extremely emaciated, and every part of her seems in a total decay except her spirits: those, indeed, she fully keeps up; and in a way altogether worthy the wife of Helvidius, and the daughter of Thrasea. In all other respects there is such a falling away that I am more than apprehensive upon her account; I am deeply afflicted. I grieve, my friend, that so excellent a woman is going to be removed from the eyes of the world, which will never, perhaps, again behold her equal. So pure she is, so pious, so wise and prudent, so brave and steadfast! Twice she followed her husband into exile, and the third time she was banished herself upon his account. For Senecio, when arraigned for writing the life of Helvidius, having said in his defence that he composed that work at the request of Fannia, Metius Carus, with a stern and threatening air, asked her whether she had made that request, and she replied, "I made it." Did she supply him likewise with materials for the purpose? "I did." Was her mother privy to this transaction? "She was not." In short, throughout her whole examination, not a word escaped her which betrayed the smallest fear. On the contrary, she had preserved a copy of those very books which the senate, over-awed by the tyranny of the times, had ordered to be suppressed, and at the same time the effects of the author to be confiscated, and carried with her into exile the very cause of her exile. How pleasing she is, how courteous, and (what is granted to few) no less lovable than worthy of all esteem and admiration! Will she hereafter be pointed out as a model to all wives; and perhaps be esteemed worthy of being set forth as an example of fortitude even to our sex; since, while we still have the pleasure of seeing and conversing with her, we contemplate her with the same admiration, as those heroines who are celebrated in ancient story? For myself, I confess, I cannot but tremble for this illustrious house, which seems shaken to its very foundations, and ready to fall; for though she will leave descendants behind her, yet what a height of virtue must they attain, what glorious deeds must they perform, ere the world will be persuaded that she was not the last of her family! It is an additional affliction and anguish to me that by her death I seem to lose her mother a second time; that worthy mother (and what can I say higher in her praise?) of so noble a woman! who, as she was restored to me in her daughter, so she will now again be taken from me, and the loss of Fannia will thus pierce my heart at once with a fresh, and at the same time re-opened, wound. I so truly loved and honoured them both, that I know not which I loved the best; a point they desired might ever remain undetermined. In their prosperity and their adversity I did them every kindness in my power, and was their comforter in exile, as well as their avenger at their return. But I have not yet paid them what I owe, and am so much the more solicitous for the recovery of this lady, that I may have time to discharge my debt to her. Such is the anxiety and sorrow under which I write this letter! But if some divine power should happily turn it into joy, I shall not complain of the alarms I now suffer. Farewell.

TO GEMINIUS

NUMIDIA QUADRATILLA IS DEAD, having almost reached her eightieth year. She enjoyed, up to her last illness, uninterrupted good health, and was unusually stout and robust for one of her sex. She has left a very prudent will, having disposed of two-thirds of her estate to her grandson, and the rest to her grand-daughter. The young lady I know very slightly, but the grandson is one of my most intimate friends. He is a remarkable young man, and his merit entitles him to the affection of a relation, even where his blood does not. Notwithstanding his remarkable personal beauty, he escaped every malicious imputation both whilst a boy and when a youth: he was a husband at four-and-twenty, and would have been a father if Providence had not disappointed his hopes. He lived in the family with his grandmother, who was exceedingly devoted to the pleasures of the town, yet observed great severity of conduct himself, while always perfectly deferential and submissive to her. She retained a set of pantomimes, and was an encourager of this class of people to a degree inconsistent with one of her sex and rank. But Quadratus never appeared at these entertainments, whether she exhibited them in the theatre or in her own house; nor indeed did she require him to be present. I once heard her say, when she was recommending to me the supervision of her grandson's studies, that it was her custom, in order to pass away some of those unemployed hours with which female life abounds, to amuse herself with playing at chess, or seeing the mimicry of her pantomimes; but that, whenever she engaged in either of those amusements, she constantly sent away her grandson to his studies: she appeared to me to act thus as much out of reverence for the youth as from affection. I was a good deal surprised, as I am sure you will be too, at what he told me the last time the Pontifical games[118] were exhibited. As we were coming out of the theatre together, where we had been entertained with a show of these pantomimes, "Do you know," said he, "to-day is the first time I ever saw my grandmother's freedman dance?" Such was the grandson's speech! while a set of men of a far different stamp, in order to do honour to Quadratilla (am ashamed to call it honour), were running up and down the theatre, pretending to be struck with the utmost admiration and rapture at the performances of those pantomimes, and then imitating in musical chant the mien and manner of their lady patroness. But now all the reward they have got, in return for their theatrical performances, is just a few trivial legacies, which they have the mortification to receive from an heir who was never so much as present at these shows.—I send you this account, knowing you do not dislike hearing town news, and because, too, when any occurrence has given me pleasure, I love to renew it again by relating it. And indeed this instance of affection in Quadratilla, and the honour done therein to that excellent youth her grandson, has afforded me a very sensible satisfaction; as I extremely rejoice that the house which once belonged to Cassius,[119] the founder and chief of the Cassian school, is come into the possession of one no less considerable than its former master. For my friend will fill it and become it as he ought, and its ancient dignity, lustre, and glory will again revive under Quadratus, who, I am persuaded, will prove as eminent an orator as Cassius was a

118   The priests, as well as other magistrates, exhibited public games to the people when they entered upon their office. M.

119   A famous lawyer who flourished in the reign of the emperor Claudius: those who followed his opinions were said to be Cassians, or of the school of Cassius. M.

lawyer. Farewell.

TO MAXIMUS

THE LINGERING DISORDER OF a friend of mine gave me occasion lately to reflect that we are never so good as when oppressed with illness. Where is the sick man who is either solicited by avarice or inflamed with lust? At such a season he is neither a slave of love nor the fool of ambition; wealth he utterly disregards, and is content with ever so small a portion of it, as being upon the point of leaving even that little. It is then he recollects there are gods, and that he himself is but a man: no mortal is then the object of his envy, his admiration, or his contempt; and the tales of slander neither raise his attention nor feed his curiosity: his dreams are only of baths and fountains. These are the supreme objects of his cares and wishes, while he resolves, if he should recover, to pass the remainder of his days in ease and tranquillity, that is, to live innocently and happily. I may therefore lay down to you and myself a short rule, which the philosophers have endeavoured to inculcate at the expense of many words, and even many volumes; that "we should try and realise in health those resolutions we form in sickness." Farewell.

TO SURA

THE PRESENT RECESS FROM business we are now enjoying affords you leisure to give, and me to receive, instruction. I am extremely desirous therefore to know whether you believe in the existence of ghosts, and that they have a real form, and are a sort of divinities, or only the visionary impressions of a terrified imagination. What particularly inclines me to believe in their existence is a story which I heard of Curtius Rufus. When he was in low circumstances and unknown in the world, he attended the governor of Africa into that province. One evening, as he was walking in the public portico, there appeared to him the figure of a woman, of unusual size and of beauty more than human. And as he stood there, terrified and astonished, she told him she was the tutelary power that presided over Africa, and was come to inform him of the future events of his life: that he should go back to Rome, to enjoy high honours there, and return to that province invested with the pro-consular dignity, and there should die. Every circumstance of this prediction actually came to pass. It is said farther that upon his arrival at Carthage, as he was coming out of the ship, the same figure met him upon the shore. It is certain, at least, that being seized with a fit of illness, though there were no symptoms in his case that led those about him to despair, he instantly gave up all hope of recovery; judging, apparently, of the truth of the future part of the prediction by what had already been fulfilled, and of the approaching misfortune from his former prosperity. Now the following story, which I am going to tell you just as I heard it, is it not more terrible than the former, while quite as wonderful? There was at Athens a large and roomy house, which had a bad name, so that no one could live there. In the dead of the night a noise, resembling the clashing of iron, was frequently heard, which, if you listened more attentively, sounded like the rattling of chains, distant at first, but approaching nearer by degrees: immediately afterwards a spectre appeared in the form of an old man, of extremely emaciated and squalid appearance, with a long beard and dishevelled hair, rattling the chains on his feet and hands. The distressed occupants meanwhile passed their wakeful nights under the most dreadful terrors imaginable. This, as it broke their rest, ruined their health, and brought on distempers, their terror grew upon them, and death ensued. Even in the day time, though the spirit did not appear, yet the impression remained so strong upon their imaginations that it still seemed before their eyes, and kept them in perpetual alarm, Consequently the house was at length deserted, as being deemed absolutely uninhabitable; so that it was now entirely abandoned to the ghost. However, in hopes that some tenant might be found who was ignorant of this very alarming circumstance, a bill was put up, giving notice that it was either to be let or sold. It happened that Athenodorus[120] the philosopher came to Athens at this time, and, reading the bill, enquired the price. The extraordinary cheapness raised his suspicion; nevertheless, when he heard the whole story, he was so far from being discouraged that he was more strongly inclined to hire it, and, in short, actually did so. When it grew towards evening, he ordered a couch to be prepared for him in the front part of the house, and, after calling for a light, together with his pencil and tablets, directed all his people to retire. But that his mind might not, for want of employment, be open to the vain terrors of imaginary noises and spirits, he applied himself to writing with the utmost attention. The first part of the night passed in entire silence, as usual; at length a clanking of iron and rattling of chains was heard: however, he neither

---

120   A Stoic philosopher and native of Tarsus. He was tutor for some time to Octavius, afterwards Augustus, Cæsar.

lifted up his eyes nor laid down his pen, but in order to keep calm and collected tried to pass the sounds off to himself as something else. The noise increased and advanced nearer, till it seemed at the door, and at last in the chamber. He looked up, saw, and recognized the ghost exactly as it had been described to him: it stood before him, beckoning with the finger, like a person who calls another. Athenodorus in reply made a sign with his hand that it should wait a little, and threw his eyes again upon his papers; the ghost then rattled its chains over the head of the philosopher, who looked up upon this, and seeing it beckoning as before, immediately arose, and, light in hand, followed it. The ghost slowly stalked along, as if encumbered with its chains, and, turning into the area of the house, suddenly vanished. Athenodorus, being thus deserted, made a mark with some grass and leaves on the spot where the spirit left him. The next day he gave information to the magistrates, and advised them to order that spot to be dug up. This was accordingly done, and the skeleton of a man in chains was found there; for the body, having lain a considerable time in the ground, was putrefied and mouldered away from the fetters. The bones being collected together were publicly buried, and thus after the ghost was appeased by the proper ceremonies, the house was haunted no more. This story I believe upon the credit of others; what I am going to mention, I give you upon my own. I have a freedman named Marcus, who is by no means illiterate. One night, as he and his younger brother were lying together, he fancied he saw somebody upon his bed, who took out a pair of scissors, and cut off the hair from the top part of his own head, and in the morning, it appeared his hair was actually cut, and the clippings lay scattered about the floor. A short time after this, an event of a similar nature contributed to give credit to the former story. A young lad of my family was sleeping in his apartment with the rest of his companions, when two persons clad in white came in, as he says, through the windows, cut off his hair as he lay, and then returned the same way they entered. The next morning it was found that this boy had been served just as the other, and there was the hair again, spread about the room. Nothing remarkable indeed followed these events, unless perhaps that I escaped a prosecution, in which, if Domitian (during whose reign this happened) had lived some time longer, I should certainly have been involved. For after the death of that emperor, articles of impeachment against me were found in his scrutore, which had been exhibited by Carus. It may therefore be conjectured, since it is customary for persons under any public accusation to let their hair grow, this cutting off the hair of my servants was a sign I should escape the imminent danger that threatened me. Let me desire you then to give this question your mature consideration. The subject deserves your examination; as, I trust, I am not myself altogether unworthy a participation in the abundance of your superior knowledge. And though you should, as usual, balance between two opinions, yet I hope you will lean more on one side than on the other, lest, whilst I consult you in order to have my doubt settled, you should dismiss me in the same suspense and indecision that occasioned you the present application. Farewell.

TO SEPTITIUS

YOU TELL ME CERTAIN persons have blamed me in your company, as being upon all occasions too lavish in the praise I give my friends. I not only acknowledge the charge, but glory in it; for can there be a nobler error than an overflowing benevolence? But still, who are these, let me ask, that are better acquainted with my friends than I am myself? Yet grant there are any such, why will they deny me the satisfaction of so pleasing a mistake? For supposing my friends not to deserve the highest encomiums I give them, yet I am happy in believing they do. Let them recommend then this malignant zeal to those (and their number is not inconsiderable) who imagine they show their judgment when they indulge their censure upon their friends. As for myself, they will never be able to persuade me I can be guilty of an excess[121] in friendship, Farewell.

TO TACITUS

I PREDICT (and I am persuaded I shall not be deceived) that your histories will be immortal. I frankly own therefore I so much the more earnestly wish to find a place in them. If we are generally careful to have our faces taken by the best artists, ought we not to desire that our actions may be celebrated by an author of your distinguished abilities? I therefore call your attention to the following matter, which, though it cannot have escaped your notice, as it is mentioned in the public journals, still I call your attention to, that you may the more readily believe how agreeable

---

121   Balzac very prettily observes: "Il y a des riviere: qui ne font jamais tact de bien que quand elles se dibordent; de eneme, l'amitie n'a mealleur quo l'exces." M.

it will be to me that this action, greatly heightened by the risk which attended it, should receive additional lustre from the testimony of a man of your powers. The senate appointed Herennius Senecio, and myself, counsel for the province of Baetica, in their impeachment of Boebius Massa. He was condemned, and the house ordered his effects to be seized into the hands of the public officer. Shortly after, Senecio, having learnt that the consuls intended to sit to hear petitions, came and said to me, "Let us go together, and petition them with the same unanimity in which we executed the office which had been enjoined us, not to suffer Massa's effects to be dissipated by those who were appointed to preserve them." I answered, "As we were counsel in this affair by order of the senate, I recommend it to your consideration whether it would be proper for us, after sentence passed, to interpose any farther." "You are at liberty," said he, "to prescribe what bounds you please to yourself, who have no particular connections with the province, except what arise from your late services to them; but then I was born there, and enjoyed the post of quaestor among them." "If such," I replied, "is your determined resolution, I am ready to accompany you, that whatever resentment may be the consequence of this affair, it may not fall singly upon yourself." We accordingly proceeded to the consuls, where Senecio said what was pertinent to the affair, and I added a few words to the same effect. Scarcely had we ended when Massa, complaining that Senecio had not acted against him with the fidelity of an advocate, but the bitterness of an enemy, desired he might be at liberty to prosecute him for treason. This occasioned general consternation. Whereupon I rose up; "Most noble consuls," said I, "I am afraid it should seem that Massa has tacitly charged me with having favoured him in this cause, since he did not think proper to join me with Senecio in the desired prosecution." This short speech was immediately received with applause, and afterwards got much talked about everywhere. The late emperor Nerva (who, though at that time in a private station, yet interested himself in every meritorious action performed in public) wrote a most impressive letter to me upon the occasion, in which he not only congratulated me, but the age which had produced an example so much in the spirit (as he was pleased to call it) of the good old days. But, whatever be the actual fact, it lies in your power to raise it into a grander and more conspicuously illustrious position, though I am far from desiring you in the least to exceed the bounds of reality. History ought to be guided by strict truth, and worthy actions require nothing more. Farewell.

TO SEPTITIUS

I HAD A GOOD journey here, excepting only that some of my servants were upset by the excessive heat. Poor Encolpius, my reader,[122] who is so indispensable to me in my studies and amusements, was so affected with the dust that it brought on a spitting of blood: an accident which will prove no less unpleasant to me than unfortunate to himself, should he be thereby rendered unfit for the literary work in which he so greatly excels. If that should unhappily result, where shall I find one who will read my works so well, or appreciate them so thoroughly as he? Whose tones will my ears drink in as they do his? But the gods seem to favour our better hopes, as the bleeding is stopped, and the pain abated. Besides, he is extremely temperate; while no concern is wanting on my part or care on his physician's. This, together with the wholesomeness of the air, and the quiet of retirement, gives us reason to expect that the country will contribute as much to the restoration of his health as to his rest. Farewell.

TO CALVISIUS

OTHER PEOPLE VISIT THEIR estates in order to recruit their purses; whilst I go to mine only to return so much the poorer. I had sold my vintage to the merchants, who were extremely eager to purchase it, encouraged by the price it then bore, and what it was probable it would rise to: however they were disappointed in their expectations. Upon this occasion to have made the same general abatement to all would have been much the easiest, though not so equitable a method. Now I hold it particularly worthy of a man of honour to be governed by principles of strict equity in his domestic as well as public conduct; in little matters as in great ones; in his own concerns as well as in those of others. And if every deviation from rectitude is equally criminal,[123] every approach to it must be equally praiseworthy. So accordingly I remitted to all in general one-eighth part of the price they had agreed to give me, that none might go away without some compensation: next, I particularly considered those who had advanced the largest sums towards their purchase, and done me so much the more service, and been greater sufferers themselves. To

---

122   Persons of rank and literature among the Romans retained in their families a domestic whose sole business was to read to them. M.
123   It was a doctrine maintained by the Stoics that all crimes are equal M.

those, therefore, whose purchase amounted to more than ten thousand sesterces,[124] I returned (over and above that which I may call the general and common eighth) a tenth part of what they had paid beyond that sum. I fear I do not express myself sufficiently clearly; I will endeavour to explain my meaning more fully: for instance, suppose a man had purchased of me to the value of fifteen thousand sesterces,[125] I remitted to him one-eighth part of that whole sum, and likewise one-tenth of five thousand.[126] Besides this, as several had deposited, in different proportions, part of the price they had agreed to pay, whilst others had advanced nothing, I thought it would not be at all fair that all these should be favoured with the same undistinguished remission. To those, therefore, who had made any payments, I returned a tenth part upon the sums so paid. By this means I made a proper acknowledgment to each, according to their respective deserts, and likewise encouraged them, not only to deal with me for the future, but to be prompt in their payments. This instance of my good-nature or my judgment (call it which you please) was a considerable expense to me. However, I found my account in it; for all the country greatly approved both of the novelty of these abatements and the manner in which I regulated them. Even those whom I did not "mete" (as they say) "by the same measure," but distinguished according to their several degrees, thought themselves obliged to me, in proportion to the probity of their principles, and went away pleased with having experienced that not with me

"The brave and mean an equal honour find."[127]

Farewell.

TO ROMANUS

HAVE YOU EVER SEEN the source of the river Clitumnus? If you have not (and I hardly think you can have seen it yet, or you would have told me), go there as soon as possible. I saw it yesterday, and I blame myself for not having seen it sooner. At the foot of a little hill, well wooded with old cypress trees, a spring gushes out, which, breaking up into different and unequal streams, forms itself, after several windings, into a

124   About $400.
125   About $600.
126   About $93.
127   Hom. II. lib. IX. V. 319.

large, broad basin of water, so transparently clear that you may count the shining pebbles, and the little pieces of money thrown into it, as they lie at the bottom. From thence it is carried off not so much by the declivity of the ground as by its own weight and exuberance. A mere stream at its source, immediately, on quitting this, you find it expanded into a broad river, fit for large vessels even, allowing a free passage by each other, according as they sail with or against the stream. The current runs so strong, though the ground is level, that the large barges going down the river have no occasion to make use of their oars; while those going up find it difficult to make headway even with the assistance of oars and poles: and this alternate interchange of ease and toil, according as you turn, is exceedingly amusing when one sails up and down merely for pleasure. The banks are well covered with ash and poplar, the shape and colour of the trees being as clearly and distinctly reflected in the stream as if they were actually sunk in it. The water is cold as snow, and as white too. Near it stands an ancient and venerable temple, in which is placed the river-god Clitumnus clothed in the usual robe of state; and indeed the prophetic oracles here delivered sufficiently testify the immediate presence of that divinity. Several little chapels are scattered round, dedicated to particular gods, distinguished each by his own peculiar name and form of worship, and some of them, too, presiding over different fountains. For, besides the principal spring, which is, as it were, the parent of all the rest, there are several other lesser streams, which, taking their rise from various sources, lose themselves in the river; over which a bridge is built that separates the sacred part from that which lies open to common use. Vessels are allowed to come above this bridge, but no person is permitted to swim except below it. The Hispellates, to whom Augustus gave this place, furnish a public bath, and likewise entertain all strangers, at their own expense. Several villas, attracted by the beauty of this river, stand about on its borders. In short, every surrounding object will afford you entertainment. You may also amuse yourself with numberless inscriptions upon the pillars and walls, by different persons, celebrating the virtues of the fountain, and the divinity that presides over it. Many of them you will admire, while some will make you laugh; but I must correct myself when I say so; you are too humane, I know, to laugh upon such an occasion. Farewell.

TO ARISTO

As you are no less acquainted with the political laws of your country (which include the customs and usages of the senate) than with the civil, I am particularly desirous to have your opinion whether I was mistaken in an affair which lately came before the house, or not. This I request, not with a view of being directed in my judgment as to what is passed (for that is now too late), but in order to know how to act in any possible future case of the kind. You will, ask, perhaps, "Why do you apply for information concerning a point on which you ought to be well instructed?" Because the tyranny of former reigns,[128] as it introduced a neglect and ignorance of all other parts of useful knowledge, so particularly of what relates to the customs of the senate; for who is there so tamely industrious as to desire to learn what he can never have an opportunity of putting in practice? Besides, it is not very easy to retain even the knowledge one has acquired where no opportunity of employing it occurs. Hence it was that Liberty, on her return[129] found us totally ignorant and inexperienced; and thus in the warmth of our eagerness to taste her sweets, we are sometimes hurried off to action, ere we are well instructed how we ought to act. But by the institution of our ancestors, it was wisely provided that the young should learn from the old, not only by precept, but by their own observation, how to behave in that sphere in which they were one day themselves to move; while these, again, in their turn, transmitted the same mode of instruction to their children. Upon this principle it was that the youth were sent early into the army, that by being taught to obey they might learn to command, and, whilst they followed others, might be trained by degrees to become leaders themselves. On the same principle, when they were candidates for any office, they were obliged to stand at the door of the senate-house, and were spectators of the public council before they became members of it. The father of each youth was his instructor upon these occasions, or if he had none, some person of years and dignity supplied the place of a father. Thus they were taught by that surest method of discipline, Example; how far the right of proposing any law to the senate extended; what privileges a senator had in delivering his opinion in the house; the power of the magistrates in that assembly, and the rights of the rest of the members; where it is proper to yield, and where to insist; when and how long to speak, and when to be silent; how to make necessary distinctions between contrary opinions, and how to improve upon a former motion: in a word, they learnt by this means every senatorial usage. As for myself, it is true indeed, I served in the army when I was a youth; but it was at a time when courage was

---

128 Those of Nero and Domitian. M.
129 When Nerva and Trajan received the empire. M.

suspected, and want of spirit rewarded; when generals were without authority, and soldiers without modesty; when there was neither discipline nor obedience, but all was riot, disorder, and confusion; in short, when it was happier to forget than to remember what one learnt. I attended likewise in my youth the senate, but a senate shrinking and speechless; where it was dangerous to utter one's opinion, and mean and pitiable to be silent. What pleasure was there in learning, or indeed what could be learnt, when the senate was convened either to do nothing whatever or to give their sanction to some consummate infamy! when they were assembled either for cruel or ridiculous purposes, and when their deliberations were never serious, though often sad! But I was not only a witness to this scene of wretchedness, as a spectator; I bore my share of it too as a senator, and both saw and suffered under it for many years; which so broke and damped my spirits that they have not even yet been able fully to recover themselves. It is within quite recently (for all time seems short in proportion to its happiness) that we could take any pleasure in knowing what relates to or in setting about the duties of our station. Upon these considerations, therefore, I may the more reasonably entreat you, in the first place, to pardon my error (if I have been guilty of one), and, in the next, to lead me out of it by your superior knowledge: for you have always been diligent to examine into the constitution of your country, both with respect to its public and private, its ancient and modern, its general and special laws. I am persuaded indeed the point upon which I am going to consult you is such an unusual one that even those whose great experience in public business must have made them, one would have naturally supposed, acquainted with everything were either doubtful or absolutely ignorant upon it. I shall be more excusable, therefore, if I happen to have been mistaken; as you will earn the higher praise if you can set me right in an affair which it is not clear has ever yet fallen within your observation. The enquiry then before the house was concerning the freedmen of Afranius Dexter, who being found murdered, it was uncertain whether he fell by his own hands, or by those of his household; and if the latter, whether they committed the fact in obedience to the commands of Afranius, or were prompted to it by their own villainy. After they had been put to the question, a certain senator (it is of no importance to mention his name, but if you are desirous to know, it was myself) was for acquitting them; another proposed that they should be banished for a limited time; and a third that they should suffer death.

These several opinions were so extremely different that it was impossible either of them could stand with the other. For what have death and banishment in common with one another? Why, no more than banishment and acquittal have together. Though an acquittal approaches rather nearer a sentence of exile than a sentence of death does: for both the former agree at least in this that they spare life, whereas the latter takes it away. In the meanwhile, those senators who were for punishing with death, and those who proposed banishment, sat together on the same side of the house: and thus by a present appearance of unanimity suspended their real disagreement. I moved, therefore, that the votes for each of the three opinions should be separately taken, and that two of them should not, under favour of a short truce between themselves, join against the third. I insisted that such of the members who were for capital punishment should divide from the others who voted for banishment; and that these two distinct parties should not be permitted to form themselves into a body, in opposition to those who declared for acquittal, when they would immediately after disunite again: for it was not material that they agreed in disliking one proposal, since they differed with respect to the other two. It seemed very extraordinary that he who moved the freedmen should be banished, and the slaves suffer death, should not be allowed to join these two in one motion, but that each question should be ordered to be put to the house separately; and yet that the votes of one who was for inflicting capital punishment upon the freedmen should be taken together with that of one who was for banishing them. For if, in the former instance, it was reasonable that the motion should be divided, because it comprehended two distinct propositions, I could not see why, in the latter case, suffrages so extremely different should be thrown into the same scale. Permit me, then, notwithstanding the point is already settled, to go over it again as if it were still undecided, and to lay before you those reasons at my ease, which I offered to the house in the midst of much interruption and clamour. Let us suppose there had been only three judges appointed to hear this cause, one of whom was of opinion that the parties in question deserved death; the other that they should only be banished; and the third that they ought to be acquitted: should the two former unite their weight to overpower the latter, or should each be separately balanced? For the first and second are no more compatible than the second and third. They ought therefore in the same manner to be counted in the senate as contrary opinions, since they were delivered as different ones. Suppose the same person had moved that they should both have been banished and put to death, could they possibly, in pursuance of this opinion, have suffered both punishments? Or could it have been looked upon as one consistent motion when it united two such different decisions? Why then should the same opinion, when delivered by distinct persons, be considered as one and entire, which would not be deemed so if it were proposed by a single man? Does not the law manifestly imply that a distinction is to be made between those who are for a capital conviction, and those who are for banishment, in the very form of words made use of when the house is ordered to divide? You who are of such an opinion, come to this side; you who are of any other, go over to the side of him whose opinion you follow. Let us examine this form, and weigh every sentence: You who are of this opinion: that is, for instance, you who are for banishment, come on this side; namely, on the side of him who moved for banishment. From whence it is clear he cannot remain on this side of those who are for death. You who are for any other: observe, the law is not content with barely saying another, but it adds any. Now can there be a doubt as to whether they who declare for a capital conviction are of any other opinion than those who propose exile! Go over to the side of him whose opinion you follow: does not the law seem, as it were, to call, compel, drive over, those who are of different opinions, to contrary sides? Does not the consul himself point out, not only by this solemn form of words, but by his hand and gesture, the place in which every man is to remain, or to which he is to go over? "But," it is objected, "if this separation is made between those who vote for inflicting death, and those who are on the side of exile, the opinion for acquitting the prisoners must necessarily prevail." But how does that affect the parties who vote? Certainly it does not become them to contend by every art, and urge every expedient, that the milder sentence may not take place. "Still," say they, "those who are for condemning the accused either capitally or to banishment should be first set in opposition to those who are for acquitting them, and afterwards weighed against each other." Thus, as, in certain public games, some particular combatant is set apart by lot and kept to engage with the conqueror; so, it seems, in the senate there is a first and second combat, and of two different opinions, the prevailing one has still a third to contend with. What? when any particular opinion is received, do not all the rest fall of course? Is it reasonable, then, that one should be thrown into the scale merely to weigh down another? To express my meaning more plainly: unless the two parties who are respectively for capital punishment and exile immediately separate upon the first division of the house it would be to no purpose afterwards to dissent from those with whom they joined before. But I am dictating instead of receiving instruction. — Tell me then whether you think these votes should have been taken separately? My motion, it is true, prevailed; nevertheless I am desirous to know whether you think I ought to have insisted upon this point, or have yielded as that member did who declared for capital punishment? For convinced, I will not say of the legality, but at least of the equity of my proposal, he receded from his opinion, and went over to the party for exile: fearing perhaps, if the votes were taken separately (which he saw would be the case), the freedmen would be acquitted: for the numbers were far greater on that side than on either of the other two, separately counted. The consequence was that those who had been influenced by his authority, when they saw themselves forsaken by his going over to the other party, gave up a motion which they found abandoned by the first proposer, and deserted, as it were, with their leader. Thus the three opinions were resolved at length into two; and of those two, one prevailed, and the other was rejected; while the third, as it was not powerful enough to conquer both the others, had only to choose to which of the two it would yield. Farewell.

TO PATERNUS

THE SICKNESS LATELY IN my family, which has carried off several of my servants, some of them, too, in the prime of their years, has been a great affliction to me. I have two consolations, however, which, though by no means equivalent to such a grief, still are consolations. One is, that as I have always readily manumitted my slaves, their death does not seem altogether immature, if they lived long enough to receive their freedom: the other, that I have allowed them to make a kind of will,[130] which I observe as religiously as if they were legally entitled to that privilege. I receive and obey their last requests and injunctions as so many authoritative commands, suffering them to dispose of their effects to whom they please; with this single restriction, that they leave them to some one in my household, for to slaves the house they are in is a kind of state and commonwealth, so to speak. But though I endeavor to acquiesce under these reflections, yet the same tenderness which led me to show them these indulgences weakens and gets the better of me. However, I would not wish on that account to become harder: though the generality of the world, I know, look upon losses of this kind in no other view than as a diminution of their property, and fancy, by cherishing such an unfeeling temper, they show a superior fortitude and philosophy. Their fortitude and philosophy I will not dispute. But humane,

---

130   A slave could acquire no property, and consequently was incapable bylaw of making a will. M.

I am sure, they are not; for it is the very criterion of true manhood to feel those impressions of sorrow which it endeavors to resist, and to admit not to be above the want of consolation. But perhaps I have detained you too long upon this subject, though not so long as I would. There is a certain pleasure even in giving vent to one's grief; especially when we weep on the bosom of a friend who will approve, or, at least, pardon, our tears. Farewell.

TO MACRINUS

Is THE WEATHER WITH you as rude and boisterous as it is with us? All here is in tempest and inundation. The Tiber has swelled its channel, and overflowed its banks far and wide. Though the wise precaution of the emperor had guarded against this evil, by cutting several outlets to the river, it has nevertheless flooded all the fields and valleys and entirely overspread the whole face of the flat country. It seems to have gone out to meet those rivers which it used to receive and carry off in one united stream, and has driven them back to deluge those countries it could not reach itself. That most delightful of rivers, the Anio, which seems invited and detained in its course by the villas built along its banks, has almost entirely rooted up and carried away the woods which shaded its borders. It has overthrown whole mountains, and, in endeavouring to find a passage through the mass of ruins that obstructed its way, has forced down houses, and risen and spread over the desolation it has occasioned. The inhabitants of the hill countries, who are situated above the reach of this inundation, have been the melancholy spectators of its dreadful effects, having seen costly furniture, instruments of husbandry, ploughs, and oxen with their drivers, whole herds of cattle, together with the trunks of trees, and beams of the neighbouring villas, floating about in different parts. Nor indeed have these higher places themselves, to which the waters could not reach up, escaped the calamity. A continued heavy rain and tempestuous hurricane, as destructive as the river itself, poured down upon them, and has destroyed all the enclosures which divided that fertile country. It has damaged likewise, and even overturned, some of the public buildings, by the fall of which great numbers have been maimed, smothered, bruised. And thus lamentation over the fate of friends has been added to losses. I am extremely uneasy lest this extensive ruin should have spread to you: I beg therefore, if it has not, you will immediately relieve my anxiety; and indeed I desire you would inform me though it should have done so; for the difference is not great between fearing a danger, and feeling it; except that the evil one feels has some bounds, whereas one's apprehensions have none. For we can suffer no more than what actually has happened but we fear all that possibly could happen. Farewell.

TO RUFINUS

THE COMMON NOTION IS certainly quite a false one, that a man's will is a kind of mirror in which we may clearly discern his real character, for Domitius Tullus appears a much better man since his death than he did during his lifetime. After having artfully encouraged the expectations of those who paid court to him, with a view to being his heirs, he has left his estate to his niece whom he adopted. He has given likewise several very considerable legacies among his grandchildren, and also to his great-grandson. In a word, he has shown himself a most kind relation throughout his whole will; which is so much the more to be admired as it was not expected of him. This affair has been very much talked about, and various opinions expressed: some call him false, ungrateful, and forgetful, and, while thus railing at him in this way as if they were actually disinherited kindred, betray their own dishonest designs: others, on the contrary, applaud him extremely for having disappointed the hopes of this infamous tribe of men, whom, considering the disposition of the times, it is but prudence to deceive. They add that he was not at liberty to make any other will, and that he cannot so properly be said to have bequeathed, as returned, his estate to his adopted daughter, since it was by her means it came to him. For Curtilius Mancia, whose daughter Domitius Lucanus, brother to this Tullus, married, having taken a dislike to his son-in-law, made this young lady (who was the issue of that marriage) his heiress, upon condition that Lucanus her father would emancipate her. He accordingly did so, but she being afterwards adopted by Tullus, her uncle, the design of Mancia's will was entirely frustrated. For these two brothers having never divided their patrimony, but living together as joint-tenants of one common estate, the daughter of Lucanus, notwithstanding the act of emancipation, returned back again, together with her large fortune, under the dominion of her father, by means of this fraudulent adoption. It seems indeed to have been the fate of these two brothers to be enriched by those who had the greatest aversion to them. For Domitius Afer, by whom they were adopted, left a will in their favour, which he had made eighteen years before his death; though it was plain he had since altered his opinion with regard to the family, because he was instrumental in procuring the confiscation of their father's estate. There is something extremely singular in the resentment of Afer, and the good fortune of the other two; as it was very extraordinary, on the one hand, that Domitius should endeavour to extirpate from the privileges of society a man whose children he had adopted, and, on the other, that these brothers should find a parent in the very person that ruined their father. But Tullus acted justly, after having been appointed sole heir by his brother, in prejudice to his own daughter, to make her amends by transferring to her this estate, which came to him from Afer, as well as all the rest which he had gained in partnership with his brother. His will therefore deserves the higher praise, having been dictated by nature, justice, and sense of honour; in which he has returned his obligations to his several relations, according to their respective good offices towards him, not forgetting his wife, having bequeathed to that excellent woman, who patiently endured much for his sake, several delightful villas, besides a large sum of money. And indeed she deserved so much the more at his hands, in proportion to the displeasure she incurred on her marriage with him. It was thought unworthy a person of her birth and repute, so long left a widow by her former husband, by whom she had issue, to marry, in the decline of her life, an old man, merely for his wealth, and who was so sickly and infirm that, even had he passed the best years of his youth and health with her, she might well have been heartily tired of him. He had so entirely lost the use of all his limbs that he could not move himself in bed without assistance; and the only enjoyment he had of his riches was to contemplate them. He was even (sad and disgusting to relate) reduced to the necessity of having his teeth washed and scrubbed by others: in allusion to which he used frequently to say, when he was complaining of the indignities which his infirmities obliged him to suffer, that he was every day compelled to lick his servant's fingers. Still, however, he lived on, and was willing to accept of life upon such terms. That he lived so long as he did was particularly owing, indeed, to the care of his wife, who, whatever reputation she might lose at first by her marriage, acquired great honour by her unwearied devotion as his wife. — Thus I have given you all the news of the town, where nothing is talked of but Tullus. It is expected his curiosities will shortly be sold by auction. He had such an abundant collection of very old statues that he actually filled an extensive garden with them, the very same day he purchased it; not to mention numberless other antiques, lying neglected in his lumber-room. If you have anything worth telling me in return, I hope you will not refuse the trouble of writing to me: not only as we are all of us naturally fond, you know, of news, but because example has a very beneficial influence upon our own conduct. Farewell.

TO GALLUS

THOSE WORKS OF ART or nature which are usually the motives of our travels are often overlooked and neglected if they lie within our reach: whether it be that we are naturally less inquisitive concerning those things which are near us, while our curiosity is excited by remote objects; or because the easiness of gratifying a desire is always sure to damp it; or, perhaps, that we put off from time to time going and seeing what we know we have an opportunity of seeing when we please. Whatever the reason be, it is certain there are numberless curiosities in and near Rome which we have not only never seen, but even never so much as heard of: and yet had they been the produce of Greece, or Egypt, or Asia, or any other country which we admire as fertile and productive of belief in wonders, we should long since have heard of them, read of them, and enquired into them. For myself at least, I confess, I have lately been entertained with one of these curiosities, to which I was an entire stranger before. My wife's grandfather desired I would look over his estate near Ameria.[131] As I was walking over his grounds, 1 was shown a lake that lies below them, called Vadirnon,[132] about which several very extraordinary things are told. I went up to this lake. It is perfectly circular in form, like a wheel lying on the ground; there is not the least curve or projection of the shore, but all is regular, even, and just as if it had been hollowed and cut out by the hand of art. The water is of a clear sky-blue, though with somewhat of a greenish tinge; its smell is sulphurous, and its flavour has medicinal properties, and is deemed of great efficacy in all fractures of the limbs, which it is supposed to heal. Though of but moderate extent, yet the winds have a great effect upon it, throwing it into violent agitation. No vessels are suffered to sail here, as its waters are held sacred; but several floating islands swim about it, covered with reeds and rushes, and with whatever other plants the surrounding marshy ground and the edge itself of the lake produce in greater abundance. Each island has its peculiar shape and size, but the edges of all of them are worn away by their frequent collision with the shore and one another. They are all of the same

---

131   Now called Amelia, a town in Ombria. M.
132   Now Laghetto di Bassano. M.

height and motion; as their respective roots, which are formed like the keel of a boat, may be seen hanging not very far down in the water, and at an equal depth, on whichever side you stand. Sometimes they move in a cluster, and seem to form one entire little continent; sometimes they are dispersed into different quarters by the wind; at other times, when it is calm, they float up and down separately. You may frequently see one of the larger islands sailing along with a lesser joined to it, like a ship with its long boat; or, perhaps, seeming to strive which shall out-swim the other: then again they are all driven to the same spot, and by joining themselves to the shore, sometimes on one side and sometimes on the other, lessen or restore the size of the lake in this part or that, accordingly, till at last uniting in the centre they restore it to its usual size. The sheep which graze upon the borders of this lake frequently go upon these islands to feed, without perceiving that they have left the shore, until they are alarmed by finding themselves surrounded with water; as though they had been forcibly conveyed and placed there. Afterwards, when the wind drives them back again, they as little per-ceive their return as their departure. This lake empties itself into a river, which, after running a little way, sinks under ground, and, if anything is thrown in, it brings it up again where the stream emerges.—I have given you this account because I imagined it would not be less new, nor less agreeable, to you than it was to me; as I know you take the same pleasure as myself in contemplating the works of nature. Farewell.

TO ARRIANUS

NOTHING, IN MY OPINION, gives a more amiable and becoming grace to our studies, as well as manners, than to temper the serious with the gay, lest the former should degenerate into melancholy, and the latter run up into levity. Upon this plan it is that I diversify my graver works with compositions of a lighter nature. I had chosen a conve-nient place and season for some productions of that sort to make their appearance in; and designing to accustom them early to the tables of the idle, I fixed upon the month of July, which is usually a time of vacation to the courts of justice, in order to read them to some of my friends I had collected together; and accordingly I placed a desk before each couch. But as I happened that morning to be un-expectedly called away to attend a cause, I took occasion to preface my recital with an apology. I entreated my audience not to impute it to me as any want of due regard for the business to which I had invited them that on the very day I had appointed for reading my performances to a small circle of my friends I did not refuse my services to others in their law affairs. I assured them I would observe the same rule in my writings, and should always give the preference to business, before pleasure; to serious engagements before amusing ones; and to my friends before myself. The poems I recited consisted of a variety of subjects in different metres. It is thus that we who dare not rely for much upon our abilities endeavour to avoid satiating our readers. In compliance with the earnest solicitation of my audience, I recited for two days successively; but not in the manner that several practise, by passing over the feebler passages, and making a merit of so doing: on the contrary, I omitted nothing, and freely confessed it. I read the whole, that I might correct the whole; which it is impossible those who only select particular passages can do. The latter method, indeed, may have more the appearance of modesty, and perhaps respect; but the former shows greater simplicity, as well as a more affectionate disposition towards the audience. For the belief that a man's friends have so much regard for him as not to be weary on these occasions, is a sure indication of the love he bears them. Otherwise, what good do friends do you who assemble merely for their own amusement? He who had rather find his friend's performance correct, than make it so, is to be regarded as a stranger, or one who is too lackadaisical to give himself any trouble. Your affection for me leaves me no room to doubt that you are impatient to read my book, even in its present very imperfect condition. And so you shall, but not until I have made those corrections which were the principal inducement of my recital. You are already acquainted with some parts of it; but even those, after they have been improved (or perhaps spoiled, as is sometimes the case by the delay of excessive revision) will seem quite new to you. For when a piece has undergone various changes, it gets to look new, even in those very parts which remain unaltered. Farewell.

TO MAXIMUS

MY AFFECTION FOR YOU obliges me, not indeed to direct you (for you are far above the want of a guide), but to admonish you carefully to observe and resolutely to put in practice what you already know, that is, in other words, to know it to better purpose. Consider that you are sent to that noble province, Achaia, the real and genuine Greece, where politeness, learning, and even agriculture itself, are supposed to have taken their first rise; sent to regulate the condition of free cities; sent, that is, to a society of men who breathe the spirit of true manhood and liberty; who have maintained the rights they received from Nature, by courage, by virtue, by alliances; in a word, by civil and religious faith. Revere the gods their founders; their ancient glory, and even that very antiquity itself which, venerable in men, is sacred in states. Honour them therefore for their deeds of old renown, nay, their very legendary traditions. Grant to every one his full dignity, privileges, yes, and the indulgence of his very vanity. Remember it was from this nation we derived our laws; that she did not receive ours by conquest, but gave us hers by favour. Remember, it is Athens to which you go; it is Lacedaemon you govern; and to deprive such a people of the declining shadow, the remaining name of liberty, would be cruel, inhuman, barbarous. Physicians, you see, though in sickness there is no difference between freedom and slavery, yet treat persons of the former rank with more tenderness than those of the latter. Reflect what these cities once were; but so reflect as not to despise them for what they are now. Far be pride and asperity from my friend; nor fear, by a proper condescension, to lay yourself open to contempt. Can he who is vested with the power and bears the ensigns of authority, can he fail of meeting with respect, unless by pursuing base and sordid measures, and first breaking through that reverence he owes to himself? Ill, believe me, is power proved by insult; ill can terror command veneration, and far more effectual is affection in obtaining one's purpose than fear. For terror operates no longer than its object is present, but love produces its effects with its object at a distance: and as absence changes the former into hatred, it raises the latter into respect. And therefore you ought (and I cannot but repeat it too often), you ought to well consider the nature of your office, and to represent to yourself how great and important the task is of governing a free state. For what can be better for society than such government, what can be more precious than freedom? How ignominious then must his conduct be who turns good government into anarchy, and liberty into slavery? To these considerations let me add, that you have an established reputation to maintain: the fame you acquired by the administration of the quaestorship in Bithynia,[133] the good opinion of the emperor, the credit you obtained when you were tribune and praetor, in a word, this very government, which may be looked upon as the reward of your former services, are all so many glorious weights which are incumbent upon you to support with suitable dignity. The more

---

133   A province in Anatolia, or Asia Minor. M.

strenuously therefore you ought to endeavour that it may not be said you showed greater urbanity, integrity, and ability in a province remote from Rome, than in one which lies so much nearer the capital; in the midst of a nation of slaves, than among a free people; that it may not be remarked, that it was chance, and not judgment, appointed you to this office; that your character was unknown and unexperienced, not tried and approved. For (and it is a maxim which your reading and conversation must have often suggested to you) it is a far greater disgrace losing the name one has once acquired than never to have attained it. I again beg you to be persuaded that I did not write this letter with a design of instruction, but of reminder. Though indeed, if I had, it would have only been in consequence of the great affection I bear you: a sentiment which I am in no fear of carrying beyond its just bounds: for there can be no danger of excess where one cannot love too well. Farewell.

TO PAULINUS

OTHERS MAY THINK AS they please; but the happiest man, in my opinion, is he who lives in the conscious anticipation of an honest and enduring name, and secure of future glory in the eyes of posterity. I confess, if I had not the reward of an immortal reputation in view, I should prefer a life of uninterrupted ease and indolent retirement to any other. There seems to be two points worthy every man's attention: endless fame, or the short duration of life. Those who are actuated by the former motive ought to exert themselves to the very utmost of their power; while such as are influenced by the latter should quietly resign themselves to repose, and not wear out a short life in perishable pursuits, as we see so many doing—and then sink at last into utter self-contempt, in the midst of a wretched and fruitless course of false industry. These are my daily reflections, which I communicate to you, in order to renounce them if you do not agree with them; as undoubtedly you will, who are for ever meditating some glorious and immortal enterprise. Farewell.

TO CALVISIUS

I HAVE SPENT THESE several days past, in reading and writing, with the most pleasing tranquillity imaginable. You will ask, "How that can possibly be in the midst of Rome?" It was the time of celebrating the Circensian games; an entertainment for which I have not the least taste. They have no novelty, no variety to recommend them, nothing, in short, one would wish to see twice. It does the more surprise me therefore that so many thousand people should be possessed with the childish passion of desiring so often to see a parcel of horses gallop, and men standing upright in their chariots. If, indeed, it were the swiftness of the horses, or the skill of the men that attracted them, there might be some pretence of reason for it. But it is the dress[134] they like; it is the dress that takes their fancy. And if, in the midst of the course and contest, the different parties were to change colours, their different partisans would change sides, and instantly desert the very same men and horses whom just before they were eagerly following with their eyes, as far as they could see, and shouting out their names with all their might. Such mighty charms, such wondrous power reside in the colour of a paltry tunic! And this not only with the common crowd (more contemptible than the dress they espouse), but even with serious-thinking people. When I observe such men thus insatiably fond of so silly, so low, so uninteresting, so common an entertainment, I congratulate myself on my indifference to these pleasures: and am glad to employ the leisure of this season upon my books, which others throw away upon the most idle occupations. Farewell.

TO ROMANUS

I AM PLEASED TO find by your letter that you are engaged in building; for I may now defend my own conduct by your example. I am myself employed in the same sort of work; and since I have you, who shall deny I have reason on my side? Our situations too are not dissimilar; your buildings are carried on upon the sea-coast, mine are rising upon the side of the Larian lake. I have several villas upon the borders of this lake, but

---

134   The performers at these games were divided into companies, distinguished by the particular colour of their habits; the principal of which were the white, the red, the blue, and the green. Accordingly the spectators favoured one or the other colour, as humour and caprice inclined them. In the reign of Justinian a tumult arose in Constantinople, occasioned merely by a contention among the partisans of these several colours, wherein no less than 30,000 men lost their lives. M.

there are two particularly in which, as I take most delight, so they give me most employment. They are both situated like those at Baiae:[135] one of them stands upon a rock, and overlooks the lake; the other actually touches it. The first, supported as it were by the lofty buskin,[136] I call my tragic; the other, as resting upon the humble rock, my comic villa. Each has its own peculiar charm, recommending it to its possessor so much more on account of this very difference. The former commands a wider, the latter enjoys a nearer view of the lake. One, by a gentle curve, embraces a little bay; the other, being built upon a greater height, forms two. Here you have a strait walk extending itself along the banks of the lake; there, a spacious terrace that falls by a gentle descent towards it. The former does not feel the force of the waves; the latter breaks them; from that you see the fishing-vessels; from this you may fish yourself, and throw your line out of your room, and almost from your bed, as from off a boat. It is the beauties therefore these agreeable villas possess that tempt me to add to them those which are wanting.—But I need not assign a reason to you; who, undoubtedly, will think it a sufficient one that I follow your example. Farewell.

TO GEMINUS

YOUR LETTER WAS PARTICULARLY acceptable to me, as it mentioned your desire that I would send you something of mine, addressed to you, to insert in your works. I shall find a more appropriate occasion of complying with your request than that which you propose, the subject you point out to me being attended with some objections; and when you reconsider it, you will think so.—As I did not imagine there were any booksellers at

---

135 Now called Castello di Baia, in Terra di Lavoro. It was the place the Romans chose for their winter retreat; and which they frequented upon account of its warm baths. Some few ruins of the beautiful villas that once covered this delightful coast still remain; and nothing can give one a higher idea of the prodigious expense and magnificence of the Romans in their private buildings than the manner in which some of these were situated. It appears from this letter, as well as from several other passages in the classic writers, that they actually projected into the sea, being erected upon vast piles, sunk for that purpose.

136 The buskin was a kind of high shoe worn upon the stage by the actors of tragedy, in order to give them a more heroical elevation of stature; as the sock was something between a shoe and stocking, it was appropriated to the comic players. M.

Lugdunum,[137] I am so much the more pleased to learn that my works are sold there. I rejoice to find they maintain the character abroad which they raised at home, and I begin to flatter myself they have some merit, since persons of such distant countries are agreed in their opinion with regard to them. Farewell.

TO JUNIOR

A CERTAIN FRIEND OF mine lately chastised his son, in my presence, for being somewhat too expensive in the matter of dogs and horses. "And pray," I asked him, when the youth had left us, "did you never commit a fault yourself which deserved your father's correction? Did you never? I repeat. Nay, are you not sometimes even now guilty of errors which your son, were he in your place, might with equal gravity reprove? Are not all mankind subject to indiscretions? And have we not each of us our particular follies in which we fondly indulge ourselves?"[138]

The great affection I have for you induced me to set this instance of unreasonable severity before you—a caution not to treat your son with too much harshness and severity. Consider, he is but a boy, and that there was a time when you were so too. In exerting, therefore, the authority of a father, remember always that you are a man, and the parent of a man. Farewell.

---

137   Lyons.
138   He was accused of treason, under pretence that in a dramatic piece which he composed he had, in the characters of Paris and Oenone, reflected upon Domitian for divorcing his wife Domitia. Suet, in Vit. Domit. C. 10. M.

TO QUADRATUS

THE PLEASURE AND ATTENTION with which you read the vindication
I published of Helvidius,[139] has greatly raised your curiosity, it seems,
to be informed of those particulars relating to that affair, which are
not mentioned in the defence; as you were too young to be present
yourself at that transaction. When Domitian was assassinated, a glorious opportunity, I thought, offered itself to me of pursuing the guilty,
vindicating the injured, and advancing my own reputation. But amidst
an infinite variety of the blackest crimes, none appeared to me more
atrocious than that a senator, of praetorian dignity, and invested with
the sacred character of a judge, should, even in the very senate itself,
lay violent hands upon a member[140] of that body, one of consular rank,
and who then stood arraigned before him. Besides this general consideration, I also happened to be on terms of particular intimacy with
Helvidius, as far as this was possible with one who, through fear of the
times, endeavoured to veil the lustre of his fame, and his virtues, in
obscurity and retirement. Arria likewise, and her daughter Fannia, who
was mother-in-law to Helvidius, were in the number of my friends.
But it was not so much private attachments as the honour of the public, a just indignation at the action, and the danger of the example if
it should pass unpunished, that animated me upon the occasion. At
the first restoration of liberty every man singled out his own particular
enemy (though it must be confessed, those only of a lower rank), and,
in the midst of much clamour and confusion, no sooner brought the
charge than procured the condemnation. But for myself, I thought it
would be more reasonable and more effectual, not to take advantage of
the general resentment of the public, but to crush this criminal with the
single weight of his own enormous guilt. When therefore the first heat
of public indignation began to cool, and declining passion gave way to
justice, though I was at that time under great affliction for the loss of
my wife,[141] I sent to Anteia, the widow of Helvidius, and desired her
to come to me, as my late misfortune prevented me from appearing in
public. When she arrived, I said to her, "I am resolved not to suffer the

139   Helvidius.
140   Upon the accession of Nerva to the empire, after the death of
Domitian. M.
141   Our authors first wife; of whom we have no particular account. After
her death, he married his favourite Calpurnia. M.

injuries your husband has received, to pass unrevenged; let Arria and Fannia" (who were just returned from exile) "know this; and consider together whether you would care to join with me in the prosecution. Not that I want an associate, but I am not so jealous of my own glory as to refuse to share it with you in this affair." She accordingly carried this message; and they all agreed to the proposal without the least hesitation. It happened very opportunely that the senate was to meet within three days. It was a general rule with me to consult, in all my affairs, with Corellius, a person of the greatest far-sightedness and wisdom this age has produced. However, in the present case, I relied entirely upon my own discretion, being apprehensive he would not approve of my design, as he was very cautious and deliberate. But though I did not previously take counsel with him (experience having taught me, never to do so with a person concerning a question we have already determined, where he has a right to expect that one shall be decided by his judgment), yet I could not forbear acquainting him with my resolution at the time I intended to carry it into execution. The senate being assembled, I came into the house, and begged I might have leave to make a motion; which I did in few words, and with general assent. When I began to touch upon the charge, and point out the person I intended to accuse (though as yet without mentioning him by name), I was attacked on all sides. "Let us know," exclaims one, "who is the subject of this informal motion?" "Who is it," (asked another) "that is thus accused, without acquainting the house with his name, and his crime?" "Surely," (added a third) "we who have survived the late dangerous times may expect now, at least, to remain in security." I heard all this with perfect calmness, and without being in the least alarmed. Such is the effect of conscious integrity; and so much difference is there with respect to inspiring confidence or fear, whether the world had only rather one should forbear a certain act, or absolutely condemn it. It would be too tedious to relate all that was advanced, by different parties, upon this occasion. At length the consul said, "You will be at liberty, Secundus, to propose what you think proper when your turn comes to give your opinion upon the order of the day."[142] I replied, "You must allow me a liberty which you never yet refused to any;" and so sat down: when immediately the house went upon another business. In the meanwhile, one of my consular friends took me aside, and, with great earnestness

142   It is very remarkable that, when any senator was asked his opinion in the house, he had the privilege of speaking as long as he pleased upon any other affair before he came to the point in question. Aul. Gell. IV. C. 10. M.

telling me he thought I had carried on this affair with more boldness than prudence, used every method of reproof and persuasion to prevail with me to desist; adding at the same time that I should certainly, if I persevered, render myself obnoxious to some future prince. "Be it so," I returned, "should he prove a bad one." Scarcely had he left me when a second came up: "Whatever," said he, "are you attempting? Why ever will you ruin yourself? Do you consider the risks you expose yourself to? Why will you presume too much on the present situation of public affairs, when it is so uncertain what turn they may hereafter take? You are attacking a man who is actually at the head of the treasury, and will shortly be consul. Besides, recollect what credit he has, and with what powerful friendships he is supported?" Upon which he named a certain person, who (not without several strong and suspicious rumours) was then at the head of a powerful army in the east. I replied,

"'All I've foreseen, and oft in thought revolv'd;[143] and am willing, if fate shall so decree, to suffer in an honest cause, provided I can draw vengeance down upon a most infamous one." The time for the members to give their opinions was now arrived. Domitius Apollinaris, the consul elect, spoke first; after him Fabricius Vejento, then Fabius Maximinus, Vettius Proculus next (who married my wife's mother, and who was the colleague of Publicius Certus, the person on whom the debate turned), and last of all Ammius Flaccus. They all defended Certus, as if I had named him (though I had not yet so much as once mentioned him), and entered upon his justification as if I had exhibited a specific charge. It is not necessary to repeat in this place what they respectively said, having given it all at length in their words in the speech above-mentioned. Avidius Quietus and Cornutus Tertullus answered them. The former observed, "that it was extremely unjust not to hear the complaints of those who thought themselves injured, and therefore that Arria and Fannia ought not to be denied the privilege of laying their grievances before the house; and that the point for the consideration of the senate was not the rank of the person, but the merit of the cause."

Then Cornutus rose up and acquainted the house, "that, as he was appointed guardian to the daughter of Helvidius by the consuls, upon the petition of her mother and her father-in-law, he felt himself compelled to fulfil the duty of his trust. In the execution of which, however, he would endeavour to set some bounds to his indignation by following that great example of moderation which those excellent

---

143   Aeneid, LIB. VI. V. 105.

women[144] had set, who contented themselves with barely informing the senate of the cruelties which Certus committed in order to carry on his infamous adulation; and therefore," he said, "he would move only that, if a punishment due to a crime so notoriously known should be remitted, Certus might at least be branded with some mark of the displeasure of that august assembly." Satrius Rufus spoke next, and, meaning to steer a middle course, expressed himself with considerable ambiguity. "I am of opinion," said he, "that great injustice will be done to Certus if he is not acquitted (for I do not scruple to mention his name, since the friends of Arria and Fannia, as well as his own, have done so too), nor indeed have we any occasion for anxiety upon this account. We who think well of the man shall judge him with the same impartiality as the rest; but if he is innocent, as I hope he is, and shall be glad to find, I think this house may very justly deny the present motion till some charge has been proved against him." Thus, according to the respective order in which they were called upon, they delivered their several opinions. When it came to my turn, I rose up, and, using the same introduction to my speech as I have published in the defence, I replied to them severally. It is surprising with what attention, what clamorous applause I was heard, even by those who just before were loudest against me: such a wonderful change was wrought either by the importance of the affair, the successful progress of the speech, or the resolution of the advocate. After I had finished, Vejento attempted to reply; but the general clamour raised against him not permitting him to go on, "I entreat you, conscript fathers,"[145] said he, "not to oblige me to implore the assistance of the tribunes."[146] Immediately the tribune Murena cried out, "You have my permission, most illustrious Vejento, to go on." But still the clamour was renewed. In the interval, the consul ordered the house to divide, and having counted the voices, dismissed the senate, leaving Vejento in the midst, still attempting to speak. He made great complaints of this affront (as he called it), applying the following lines of Homer to himself:

"Great perils, father, wait the unequal fight;

---

144   Arria and Fannia.
145   The appellation by which the senate was addressed. M.
146   The tribunes were magistrates chosen at first out of the body of the commons, for the defence of their liberties, and to interpose in all grievances offered by their superiors. Their authority extended even to the deliberations of the senate. M.

Those younger champions will thy strength o'ercome."[147]

There was hardly a man in the senate that did not embrace and kiss me, and all strove who should applaud me most, for having, at the cost of private enmities, revived a custom so long disused, of freely consulting the senate upon affairs that concern the honour of the public; in a word, for having wiped off that reproach which was thrown upon it by other orders in the state, "that the senators mutually favoured the members of their own body, while they were very severe in animadverting upon the rest of their fellow-citizens." All this was transacted in the absence of Certus; who kept out of the way either because he suspected something of this nature was intended to be moved, or (as was alleged in his excuse) that he was really unwell. Cæsar, however, did not refer the examination of this matter to the senate. But I succeeded, nevertheless, in my aim, another person being appointed to succeed Certus in the consulship, while the election of his colleague to that office was confirmed. And thus, the wish with which I concluded my speech, was actually accomplished: "May he be obliged," said I, "to renounce, under a virtuous prince,[148] that reward he received from an infamous one!"[149] Some time after I recollected, as well as I could, the speech I had made upon this occasion; to which I made several additions. It happened (though indeed it had the appearance of being something more than casual) that a few days after I had published this piece, Certus was taken ill and died. I was told that his imagination was continually haunted with this affair, and kept picturing me ever before his eyes, as a man pursuing him with a drawn sword. Whether there was any truth in this rumour, I will not venture to assert; but, for the sake of example, however, I could wish it might gain credit. And now I have sent you a letter which (considering it is a letter) is as long as the defence you say you have read: but you must thank yourself for not being content with such information as that piece could afford you. Farewell.

---

147   Diomed's speech to Nestor, advising him to retire from the field of battle. Iliad, VIII. 302. Pope. M.

148   Nerva.

149   Domitian; by whom he had been appointed consul elect, though he had not yet entered upon that office. M.

TO GENITOR

I HAVE RECEIVED YOUR letter, in which you complain of having been highly disgusted lately at a very splendid entertainment, by a set of buffoons, mummers, and wanton prostitutes, who were dancing about round the tables.[150] But let me advise you to smooth your knitted brow somewhat. I confess, indeed, I admit nothing of this kind at my own house; however, I bear with it in others. "And why, then," you will be ready to ask, "not have them yourself?"

The truth is, because the gestures of the wanton, the pleasantries of the buffoon, or the extravagancies of the mummer, give me no pleasure, as they give me no surprise. It is my particular taste, you see, not my judgment, that I plead against them. And indeed, what numbers are there who think the entertainments with which you and I are most delighted no better than impertinent follies! How many are there who, as soon as a reader, a lyrist, or a comedian is introduced, either take their leave of the company or, if they remain, show as much dislike to this sort of thing as

---

150   These persons were introduced at most of the tables of the great, for the purposes of mirth and gaiety, and constituted an essential part in all polite entertainments among the Romans. It is surprising how soon this great people fell off from their original severity of manners, and were tainted with the stale refinements of foreign luxury. Livy dates the rise of this and other unmanly delicacies from the conquest of Scipio Asiaticus over Antiochus; that is when the Roman name had scarce subsisted above a hundred and threescore years. "Luxuriae peregrinae origio," says he, "exercitu Asiatico in urbem invecta est." This triumphant army caught, it seems, the contagious softness of the people it subdued; and, on its return to Rome, spread an infection among their countrymen, which worked by slow degrees, till it effected their total destruction. Thus did Eastern luxury revenge itself on Roman arms. It may be wondered that Pliny should keep his own temper, and check the indignation of his friends at a scene which was fit only for the dissolute revels of the infamous Trimalchio. But it will not, perhaps, be doing justice to our author to take an estimate of his real sentiments upon this point from the letter before us. Genitor, it seems, was a man of strict, but rather of too austere morals for the free turn of the age: "emendatus et gravis: paulo etiam horridior et durior ut in hac licentia teniporuni" (Ep. III. 1. 3). But as there is a certain seasonable accommodation to the manners of the times, not only extremely Consistent with, but highly conducive to, the interests of virtue, Pliny, probably, may affect a greater latitude than he in general approved, in order to draw off his friend from that stiffness and unyielding disposition which might prejudice those of a gayer turn against him, and consequently lessen the beneficial influence of his virtues upon the world. M.

you did to those monsters, as you call them! Let us bear therefore, my friend, with others in their amusements, that they, in return, may show indulgence to ours. Farewell.

TO SABINIANUS

YOUR FREEDMAN, whom you lately mentioned to me with displeasure, has been with me, and threw himself at my feet with as much submission as he could have fallen at yours. He earnestly requested me with many tears, and even with all the eloquence of silent sorrow, to intercede for him; in short, he convinced me by his whole behaviour that he sincerely repents of his fault. I am persuaded he is thoroughly reformed, because he seems deeply sensible of his guilt. I know you are angry with him, and I know, too, it is not without reason; but clemency can never exert itself more laudably than when there is the most cause for resentment. You once had an affection for this man, and, I hope, will have again; meanwhile, let me only prevail with you to pardon him. If he should incur your displeasure hereafter, you will have so much the stronger plea in excuse for your anger as you show yourself more merciful to him now. Concede something to his youth, to his tears, and to your own natural mildness of temper: do not make him uneasy any longer, and I will add too, do not make yourself so; for a man of your kindness of heart cannot be angry without feeling great uneasiness. I am afraid, were I to join my entreaties with his, I should seem rather to compel than request you to forgive him. Yet I will not scruple even to write mine with his; and in so much the stronger terms as I have very sharply and severely reproved him, positively threatening never to interpose again in his behalf. But though it was proper to say this to him, in order to make him more fearful of offending, I do not say so to you. I may perhaps, again have occasion to entreat you upon this account, and again obtain your forgiveness; supposing, I mean, his fault should be such as may become me to intercede for, and you to pardon. Farewell.

TO MAXIMUS

IT HAS FREQUENTLY HAPPENED, as I have been pleading before the Court of the Hundred, that these venerable judges, after having preserved for a long period the gravity and solemnity suitable to their character, have suddenly, as though urged by irresistible impulse, risen up to a man and applauded me. I have often likewise gained as much glory in the senate as my utmost wishes could desire: but I never felt a more sensible pleasure than by an account which I lately received from Cornelius Tacitus. He informed me that, at the last Circensian games, he sat next to a Roman knight, who, after conversation had passed between them upon various points of learning, asked him, "Are you an Italian, or a provincial?" Tacitus replied, "Your acquaintance with literature must surely have informed you who I am." "Pray, then, is it Tacitus or Pliny I am talking with?" I cannot express how highly I am pleased to find that our names are not so much the proper appellatives of men as a kind of distinction for learning herself; and that eloquence renders us known to those who would otherwise be ignorant of us. An accident of the same kind happened to me a few days ago. Fabius Rufinus, a person of distinguished merit, was placed next to me at table; and below him a countryman of his, who had just then come to Rome for the first time. Rufinus, calling his friend's attention to me, said to him, "You see this man?" and entered into a conversation upon the subject of my pursuits: to whom the other immediately replied, "This must undoubtedly be Pliny." To confess the truth, I look upon these instances as a very considerable recompense of my labours. If Demosthenes had reason to be pleased with the old woman of Athens crying out, "This is Demosthenes!" may not I, then, be allowed to congratulate myself upon the celebrity my name has acquired? Yes, my friend, I will rejoice in it, and without scruple admit that I do. As I only mention the judgment of others, not my own, I am not afraid of incurring the censure of vanity; especially from you, who, whilst envying no man's reputation, are particularly zealous for mine. Farewell.

.

TO SABINIANUS

I GREATLY APPROVE OF your having, in compliance with my letter,[151] received again into your favour and family a discarded freedman, who you once admitted into a share of your affection. This will afford you, I doubt not, great satisfaction. It certainly has me, both as a proof that your passion can be controlled, and as an instance of your paying so much regard to me, as either to yield to my authority or to comply with my request. Let me, therefore, at once both praise and thank you. At the same time I must advise you to be disposed for the future to pardon the faults of your people, though there should be none to

---

151   See letter CIII.

intercede in their behalf. Farewell.

TO LUPERCUS

I SAID ONCE (and, I think, not inaptly) of a certain orator of the present age, whose compositions are extremely regular and correct, but deficient in grandeur and embellishment, "His only fault is that he has none." Whereas he, who is possessed of the true spirit of oratory, should be bold and elevated, and sometimes even flame out, be hurried away, and frequently tread upon the brink of a precipice: for danger is generally near whatever is towering and exalted. The plain, it is true, affords a safer, but for that reason a more humble and inglorious, path: they who run are more likely to stumble than they who creep; but the latter gain no honour by not slipping, while the former even fall with glory. It is with eloquence as with some other arts; she is never more pleasing than when she risks most. Have you not observed what acclamations our rope-dancers excite at the instant of imminent danger? Whatever is most entirely unexpected, or as the Greeks more strongly express it, whatever is most perilous, most excites our admiration. The pilot's skill is by no means equally proved in a calm as in a storm: in the former case he tamely enters the port, unnoticed and unapplauded; but when the cordage cracks, the mast bends, and the rudder groans, then it is that he shines out in all his glory, and is hailed as little inferior to a sea-god.

The reason of my making this observation is, because, if I mistake not, you have marked some passages in my writings for being tumid, exuberant, and over-wrought, which, in my estimation, are but adequate to the thought, or boldly sublime. But it is material to consider whether your criticism turns upon such points as are real faults, or only striking and remarkable expressions. Whatever is elevated is sure to be observed; but it requires a very nice judgment to distinguish the bounds between true and false grandeur; between loftiness and exaggeration. To give an instance out of Homer, the author who can, with the greatest propriety, fly from one extreme of style to another.

> *"Heav'n in loud thunder bids the trumpet sound;*
> *And wide beneath them groans the rending ground."*[152]

Again,

---

152   Iliad, XXI. 387. Pope. M.

"Reclin'd on clouds his steed and armour lay."[153]

So in this passage:

"As torrents roll, increas'd by numerous rills,
With rage impetuous down their echoing hills,
Rush to the vales, and pour'd along the plain,
Roar through a thousand channels to the main."

It requires, I say, the nicest balance to poise these metaphors, and determine whether they are incredible and meaningless, or majestic and sublime. Not that I think anything which I have written, or can write, admits of comparison with these. I am not quite so foolish; but what I would be understood to contend for is, that we should give eloquence free rein, and not restrain the force and impetuosity of genius within too narrow a compass. But it will be said, perhaps, that one law applies to orators, another to poets. As if, in truth, Marc Tully were not as bold in his metaphors as any of the poets! But not to mention particular instances from him, in a point where, I imagine, there can be no dispute; does Demosthenes[154] himself, that model and standard of true oratory, does Demosthenes check and repress the fire of his indignation, in that well-known passage which begins thus: "These wicked men, these flatterers, and these destroyers of mankind," &c. And again: "It is neither with stones nor bricks that I have fortified this city," &c. — And afterwards: "I have thrown up these out-works before Attica, and pointed out to you all the resources which human prudence can suggest," &c.— And in another place: "O Athenians, I swear by the immortal gods that he is intoxicated with the grandeur of his own actions," &c.[155] — But what can be more daring and beautiful than that long digression, which begins in this manner: "A terrible disease?" — The following passage

153   Iliad, V. 356, speaking of Mars. M.; Iliad, IV. 452. Pope.
154   The design of Pliny in this letter is to justify the figurative expressions he had employed, probably, in same oration, by instances of the same warmth of colouring from those great masters of eloquence, Demosthenes and his rival Aesehines. But the force of the passages which he produces from those orators must necessarily be greatly weakened to a mere modern reader, some of them being only hinted at, as generally well known; and the metaphors in several of the others have either lost much of their original spirit and boldness, by being introduced and received in Common language, or cannot, perhaps, he preserved in an English translation. M.
155   See 1st Philippic.

likewise, though somewhat shorter, is equally boldly conceived: — "Then it was I rose up in opposition to the daring Pytho, who poured forth a torrent of menaces against you," &c.[156] — The subsequent stricture is of the same stamp: "When a man has strengthened himself, as Philip has, in avarice and wickedness, the first pretence, the first false step, be it ever so inconsiderable, has overthrown and destroyed all," &c.[157] —So in the same style with the foregoing is this: — "Railed off, as it were, from the privileges of society, by the concurrent and just judgments of the three tribunals in the city." — And in the same place: "O Aristogiton! you have betrayed that mercy which used to be shown to offences of this nature, or rather, indeed, you have wholly destroyed it. In vain then would you fly for refuge to a port, which you have shut up, and encompassed with rocks."—He has said before: "I am afraid, therefore, you should appear in the judgment of some, to have erected a public seminary of faction: for there is a weakness in all wickedness which renders it apt to betray itself!" — And a little lower: "I see none of these resources open to him; but all is precipice gulf, and profound abyss."—And again: "Nor do I imagine that our ancestors erected those courts of judicature that men of his character should be planted there, but on the contrary', eradicated, that none may emulate their evil actions."—And afterwards: "If he is then the artificer of every wickedness, if he only makes it his trade and traffic," &c.—And a thousand other passages which I might cite to the same purpose; not to mention those expressions which Aeschines calls not words, but wonders.—You will tell me, perhaps, I have unwarily mentioned Aeschines, since Demosthenes is condemned even by him, for running into these figurative expressions. But observe, I entreat you, how far superior the former orator is to his critic, and superior too in the very passage to which he objects; for in others, the force of his genius, in those above quoted, its loftiness, makes itself manifest. But does Aeschines himself avoid those errors which he reproves in Demosthenes? "The orator," says he, "Athenians, and the law, ought to speak the same language; but when the voice of the law declares one thing, and that of the orator another we should give our vote to the justice of the law, not to the impudence of the orator."[158]—And in another place: "He afterwards manifestly discovered the design he had, of concealing his fraud under cover of the decree, having expressly declared therein that the ambassadors sent

---

156   See Demosthenes' speech in defence of Cteisphon.
157   See end Olynthiac.
158   See Aesehines' speech against Ctesiphon.

to the Oretae gave the five talents, not to you, but to Callias. And that you may be convinced of the truth of what I say (after having stripped the decree of its gallies, its trim, and its arrogant ostentation) the clause itself." — And in another part: "Suffer him not to break cover and escape out of the limits of the question." A metaphor he is so fond of that he repeats it again. "But remaining firm and confident in the assembly, drive him into the merits of the question, and observe well how he doubles."—Is his style more reserved and simple when he says: "But you are ever wounding our ears, and are more concerned in the success of your daily harangues than for the salvation of the city?"—What follows is conceived in a yet higher strain of metaphor: "Will you not expel this man as the common calamity of Greece? Will you not seize and punish this pirate of the state, who sails about in quest of favourable conjunctures," &c.—With many other passages of a similar nature. And now I expect you will make the same attacks upon certain expressions in this letter as you did upon those I have been endeavouring to defend. The rudder that groans, and the pilot compared to a sea-god, will not, I imagine, escape your criticism: for I perceive, while I am suing for indulgence to my former style, I have fallen into the same kind of figurative diction which you condemn. But attack them if you please provided you will immediately appoint a day when we may meet to discuss these matters in person: you will then either teach me to be less daring or I shall teach you to be more bold. Farewell.

TO CANINIUS

I HAVE MET WITH a story, which, although authenticated by undoubted evidence, looks very like fable, and would afford a worthy field for the exercise of so exuberant, lofty, and truly poetical a genius as your own. It was related to me the other day over the dinner table, where the conversation happened to run upon various kinds of marvels. The person who told the story was a man of unsuspected veracity:—but what has a poet to do with truth? However, you might venture to rely upon his testimony, even though you had the character of a faithful historian to support. There is in Africa a town called Hippo, situated not far from the sea-coast: it stands upon a navigable lake, communicating with an estuary in the form of a river, which alternately flows into the lake, or into the ocean, according to the ebb and flow of the tide. People of all ages amuse themselves here with fishing, sailing, or swimming; especially boys, whom love of play brings to the spot. With these it is a fine and manly achievement to be able to swim the farthest; and he that leaves the shore and his companions at the greatest distance gains the victory. It happened, in one of these trials of skill, that a certain boy, bolder than the rest, launched out towards the opposite shore. He was met by a dolphin, who sometimes swam before him, and sometimes behind him, then played round him, and at last took him upon his back, and set him down, and afterwards took him up again; and thus he carried the poor frightened fellow out into the deepest part; when immediately he turns back again to the shore, and lands him among his companions. The fame of this remarkable accident spread through the town, and crowds of people flocked round the boy (whom they viewed as a kind of prodigy) to ask him questions and hear him relate the story. The next day the shore was thronged with spectators, all attentively watching the ocean, and (what indeed is almost itself an ocean) the lake. Meanwhile the boys swam as usual, and among the rest, the boy I am speaking of went into the lake, but with more caution than before. The dolphin appeared again and came to the boy, who, together with his companions, swam away with the utmost precipitation. The dolphin, as though to invite and call them back, leaped and dived up and down, in a series of circular movements. This he practised the next day, the day after, and for several days together, till the people (accustomed from their infancy to the sea) began to be ashamed of their timidity. They ventured, therefore, to advance nearer, playing with him and calling him to them, while he, in return, suffered himself to be touched and stroked. Use rendered them courageous. The boy, in particular, who first made the experiment, swam by the side of him, and, leaping upon his back, was carried backwards and forwards in that manner, and thought the dolphin knew him and was fond of him, while he too had grown fond of the dolphin. There seemed, now, indeed, to be no fear on either side, the confidence of the one and tameness of the other mutually increasing; the rest of the boys, in the meanwhile, surrounding and encouraging their companion. It is very remarkable that this dolphin was followed by a second, which seemed only as a spectator and attendant on the former; for he did not at all submit to the same familiarities as the first, but only escorted him backwards and forwards, as the boys did their comrade. But what is further surprising, and no less true than what I have already related, is that this dolphin, who thus played with the boys and carried them upon his back, would come upon the shore, dry himself in the sand, and, as soon as he grew warm, roll back into the sea. It is a fact that Octavius Avitus, deputy governor of the province, actuated by an absurd piece of superstition, poured some ointment[159] over him as he lay on the shore: the novelty and smell of which made him retire into the ocean, and it was not till several days after that he was seen again, when he appeared dull and languid; however, he recovered his strength and continued his usual playful tricks. All the magistrates round flocked hither to view this sight, whose arrival, and prolonged stay, was an additional expense, which the slender finances of this little community would ill afford; besides, the quiet and retirement of the place was utterly destroyed. It was thought proper, therefore, to remove the occasion of this concourse, by privately killing the poor dolphin. And now, with what a flow of tenderness will you describe this affecting catastrophe![160] and how will your genius adorn and heighten this moving story! Though, indeed, the subject does not require any fictitious embellishments; it will be sufficient to describe the actual facts of the case without suppression or diminution. Farewell.

TO FUSCUS

You want to know how I portion out my day, in my summer villa at Tuscum? I get up just when I please; generally about sunrise, often earlier, but seldom later than this. I keep the shutters closed, as darkness and silence wonderfully promote meditation. Thus free and abstracted from these outward objects which dissipate attention, I am left to my

---

159   It was a religious ceremony practised by the ancients to pour precious ointments upon the statues of their gods: Avitus, it is probable, imagined this dolphin was some sea-divinity, and therefore expressed his veneration of him by the solemnity of a sacred unction. M.

160   The overflowing humanity of Pliny's temper breaks out upon all occasions, but he discovers it in nothing more strongly than by the impression which this little story appears to have made upon him. True benevolence, indeed, extends itself through the whole compass of existence, and sympathises with the distress of every creature of sensation. Little minds may be apt to consider a compassion of this inferior kind as an instance of weakness; but it is undoubtedly the evidence of a noble nature. Homer thought it not unbecoming the character even of a hero to melt into tears at a distress of this sort, and has given us a most amiable and affecting picture of Ulysses weeping over his faithful dog Argus, when he expires at his feet:

"Soft pity touch'd the mighty master's soul;
Adown his cheek the tear unbidden stole,
Stole unperceived; he turn'd his head and dry'd
The drop humane.".
(Odyss. XVII. Pope.) M.]

own thoughts; nor suffer my mind to wander with my eyes, but keep my eyes in subjection to my mind, which, when they are not distracted by a multiplicity of external objects, see nothing but what the imagination represents to them. If I have any work in hand, this is the time I choose for thinking it out, word for word, even to the minutest accuracy of expression. In this way I compose more or less, according as the subject is more or less difficult, and I find myself able to retain it. I then call my secretary, and, opening the shutters, dictate to him what I have put into shape, after which I dismiss him, then call him in again, and again dismiss him. About ten or eleven o'clock (for I do not observe one fixed hour), according to the weather, I either walk upon my terrace or in the covered portico, and there I continue to meditate or dictate what remains upon the subject in which I am engaged. This completed, I get into my chariot, where I employ myself as before, when I was walking, or in my study; and find this change of scene refreshes and keeps up my attention. On my return home, I take a little nap, then a walk, and after that repeat out loud and distinctly some Greek or Latin speech, not so much for the sake of strengthening my voice as my digestion;[161] though indeed the voice at the same time is strengthened by this practice. I then take another walk, am anointed, do my exercises, and go into the bath. At supper, if I have only my wife or a few friends with me, some author is read to us; and after supper we are entertained either with music or an interlude. When that is finished, I take my walk with my family, among whom I am not without some scholars. Thus we pass our evenings in varied conversation; and the day, even when at the longest, steals imperceptibly away. Upon some occasions I change the order in certain of the articles abovementioned. For instance, if I have studied longer or walked more than usual, after my second sleep, and reading a speech or two aloud, instead of using my chariot I get on horseback; by which means I ensure as much exercise and lose less time. The visits of my friends from the neighbouring villages claim some part of the day; and sometimes, by an agreeable interruption, they come in very seasonably to relieve me when I am feeling tired. I now and then amuse myself with hunting, but always take my tablets into the field, that, if I should meet with no game, I may at least bring home something. Part of my time too (though not so much as they desire) is allotted to my tenants; whose rustic complaints,

---

161   By the regimen which Pliny here follows, one would imagine, if he had not told us who were his physicians, that the celebrated Celsus was in the number. That author expressly recommends reading aloud, and afterwards walking, as beneficial in disorders of the stomach: "Si quis stomacho laborat, leqere clare debet; post lectionem ambulare," &c. Celsi Medic. 1. I. C. 8. M.

along with these city occupations, make my literary studies still more delightful to me. Farewell. —

TO PAULINUS

As you are not of a disposition to expect from your friends the ordinary ceremonial observances of society when they cannot observe them without inconvenience to themselves, so I love you too steadfastly to be apprehensive of your taking otherwise than I wish you should my not waiting upon you on the first day of your entrance upon the consular office, especially as I am detained here by the necessity of letting my farms upon long leases. I am obliged to enter upon an entirely new plan with my tenants: for under the former leases, though I made them very considerable abatements, they have run greatly in arrear. For this reason several of them have not only taken no sort of care to lessen a debt which they found themselves incapable of wholly discharging, but have even seized and consumed all the produce of the land, in the belief that it would now be of no advantage to themselves to spare it. I must therefore obviate this increasing evil, and endeavour to find out some remedy against it. The only one I can think of is, not to reserve my rent in money, but in kind, and so place some of my servants to overlook the tillage, and guard the stock; as indeed there is no sort of revenue more agreeable to reason than what arises from the bounty of the soil, the seasons, and the climate. It is true, this method will require great honesty, sharp eyes, and many hands. However, I must risk the experiment, and, as in an inveterate complaint, try every change of remedy. You see, it is not any pleasurable indulgence that prevents my attending you on the first day of your consulship. I shall celebrate it nevertheless, as much as if I were present, and pay my vows for you here, with all the warmest tokens of joy and congratulation. Farewell.

TO FUSCUS

You are much pleased, I find, with the account I gave you in my former letter of how I spend the summer season at Tuscum, and desire to know what alteration I make in my method when I am at Laurentum in the winter. None at all, except abridging myself of my sleep at noon, and borrowing a good piece of the night before daybreak and after sunset for study: and if business is very urgent (which in winter very frequently happens), instead of having interludes or music after supper, I reconsider whatever I have previously dictated, and improve my memory at the same time by this frequent mental revision. Thus I have given you a general sketch of my mode of life in summer and winter; to which you may add the intermediate seasons of spring and autumn, in which, while losing nothing out of the day, I gain but little from the night. Farewell.

Correspondence with the Emperor Trajan

TO THE EMPEROR TRAJAN[1]

THE PIOUS AFFECTION YOU bore, most sacred Emperor, to your august father induced you to wish it might be late ere you succeeded him. But the immortal gods thought proper to hasten the advancement of those virtues to the helm of the commonwealth which had already shared in the steerage.[2] May you then, and the world through your

---

1   The greater part of the following letters were written by Pliny during his administration in the province of Bithynia. They are of a style and character extremely different from those in the preceding collection; whence some critics have injudiciously inferred that they are the production of another hand: not considering that the occasion necessarily required a different manner. In letters of business, as these chiefly are, turn and sentiment would be foreign and impertinent; politeness and elegance of expression being the essentials that constitute perfection in this kind: and in that view, though they may be less entertaining, they have not less merit than the former. But besides their particular excellence as letters, they have a farther recommendation as so many valuable pieces of history, by throwing a strong light upon the character of one of the most amiable and glorious princes in the Roman annals. Trajan appears throughout in the most striking attitude that majesty can be placed in; in the exertion of power to the godlike purposes of justice and benevolence: and what one of the ancient historians has said of him is here clearly verified, that "he rather chose to be loved than flattered by his people." To have been distinguished by the favour and friendship of a monarch of so exalted a character is an honour that reflects the brightest lustre upon our author; as to have been served and celebrated by a courtier of Pliny's genius and virtues is the noblest monunient of glory that could have been raised to Trajan. M.

2   Nerva, who succeeded Domitian, reigned but sixteen months and a few days. Before his death he not only adopted Trajan, and named him for his

means, enjoy every prosperity worthy of your reign: to which let me add my wishes, most excellent Emperor, upon a private as well as public account, that your health and spirits may be preserved firm and unbroken.

TO THE EMPEROR TRAJAN

You HAVE OCCASIONED ME, Sir, an inexpressible pleasure in deeming me worthy of enjoying the privilege which the laws confer on those who have three children. For although it was from an indulgence to the request of the excellent Julius Servianus, your own most devoted servant, that you granted this favour, yet I have the satisfaction to find by the words of your rescript that you complied the more willingly as his application was in my behalf. I cannot but look upon myself as in possession of my utmost wish, after having thus received, at the beginning of your most auspicious reign, so distinguishing a mark of your peculiar favour; at the same time that it considerably heightens my desire of leaving a family behind me. I was not entirely without this desire even in the late most unhappy times: as my two marriages will induce you to believe. But the gods decreed it better, by reserving every valuable privilege to the bounty of your generous dispensations. And indeed the pleasure of being a father will be so much more acceptable to me now, that I can enjoy it in full security and happiness.

TO THE EMPEROR TRAJAN

The EXPERIENCE, most excellent Emperor, I have had of your unbounded generosity to me, in my own person, encourages me to hope I may be yet farther obliged to it, in that of my friends. Voconius Romanus (who was my schoolfellow and companion from our earliest years) claims the first rank in that number; in consequence of which I petitioned your sacred father to promote him to the dignity of the senatorial order. But the completion of my request is reserved to your goodness; for his mother had not then advanced, in the manner the law directs, the liberal gift[3] of four hundred thousand sesterces, which she engaged to give him, in her

---

successor, but actually admitted him into a share of the government; giving him the titles of Cæsar, Germanicus and Imperator. Vid. Plin. Paneg. M.

3    $16,000.

letter to the late emperor, your father. This, however, by my advice she has since done, having made over certain estates to him, as well as completed every other act necessary to make the conveyance valid. The difficulties therefore being removed which deferred the gratification of our wishes, it is with full confidence I venture to assure you of the worth of my friend Romanus, heightened and adorned as it is not only by liberal culture, but by his extraordinary tenderness to his parents as well. It is to that virtue he owes the present liberality of his mother; as well as his immediate succession to his late father's estate, and his adoption by his father-in-law. To these personal qualifications, the wealth and rank of his family give additional lustre; and I persuade myself it will be some further recommendation that I solicit in his behalf. Let me, then, entreat you, Sir, to enable me to congratulate Romanus on so desirable an occasion, and at the same time to indulge an eager and, I hope, laudable ambition, of having it in my power to boast that your favourable regards are extended not only to myself, but also to my friend.

TO THE EMPEROR TRAJAN

WHEN BY YOUR GRACIOUS indulgence, Sir, I was appointed to preside at the treasury of Saturn, I immediately renounced all engagements of the bar (as indeed I never blended business of that kind with the functions of the state), that no avocations might call off my attention from the post to which I was appointed. For this reason, when the province of Africa petitioned the senate that I might undertake their cause against Marius Priscus, I excused myself from that office; and my excuse was allowed. But when afterwards the consul elect proposed that the senate should apply to us again, and endeavour to prevail with us to yield to its inclinations, and suffer our names to be thrown into the urn, I thought it most agreeable to that tranquillity and good order which so happily distinguishes your times not to oppose (especially in so reasonable an instance) the will of that august assembly. And, as I am desirous that all my words and actions may receive the sanction of your exemplary virtue, I hope you approve of my compliance.

TRAJAN TO PLINY

YOU ACTED AS BECAME a good citizen and a worthy senator, by paying obedience to the just requisition of that august assembly: and I have full confidence you will faithfully discharge the business you have undertaken.

TO THE EMPEROR TRAJAN

HAVING BEEN ATTACKED LAST year by a very severe and dangerous illness, I employed a physician, whose care and diligence, Sir, I cannot sufficiently reward, but by your gracious assistance. I entreat you therefore to make him a denizen of Rome; for as he is the freedman of a foreign lady, he is, consequently, himself also a foreigner. His name is Harpocras; his patroness (who has been dead a considerable time) was Thermuthis, the daughter of Theon. I further entreat you to bestow the full privileges of a Roman citizen upon Hedia and Antonia Harmeris, the freedwomen of Antonia Maximilla, a lady of great merit. It is at her desire I make this request.

TO THE EMPEROR TRAJAN

I RETURN YOU THANKS, Sir, for your ready compliance with my desire, in granting the complete privileges of a Roman to the freedwomen of a lady to whom I am allied and also for making Harpocras, my physician, a denizen of Rome. But when, agreeably to your directions, I gave in an account of his age, and estate, I was informed by those who are better skilled in the affairs than I pretend to be that, as he is an Egyptian, I ought first to have obtained for him the freedom of Alexandria before he was made free of Rome. I confess, indeed, as I was ignorant of any difference in this case between those of Egypt and other countries, I contented myself with Only acquainting you that he had been manumitted by a foreign lady long since deceased. However, it is an ignorance I cannot regret, since it affords me an opportunity of receiving from you a double obligation in favour of the same person. That I may legally therefore enjoy the benefit of your goodness, I beg you would be pleased to grant him the freedom of the city of Alexandria, as well as that of Rome. And that your gracious intentions may not meet with any further obstacles, I have taken care, as you directed, to send an account to your freedman of his age and possessions.

TRAJAN TO PLINY

IT IS MY RESOLUTION, in pursuance of the maxim observed by the princes my predecessors, to be extremely cautious in granting the freedom of the city of Alexandria: however, since you have obtained of me the freedom of Rome for your physician Harpocras, I cannot refuse you this other request. You must let me know to what district he belongs, that I may give you a letter to my friend Pompeius Planta, governor of Egypt.

TO THE EMPEROR TRAJAN

I CANNOT EXPRESS, Sir, the pleasure your letter gave me, by which I am informed that you have made my physician Harpocras a denizen of Alexandria; notwithstanding your resolution to follow the maxim of your predecessors in this point, by being extremely cautious in granting that privilege. Agreeably to your directions, I acquaint you that Harpocras belongs to the district of Memphis.[4] I entreat you then, most gracious Emperor, to send me, as you promised, a letter to your friend Pompeius Planta, governor of Egypt. As I purpose (in order to have the earliest enjoyment of your presence, so ardently wished for here) to come to meet you, I beg, Sir, you would permit me to extend my journey as far as possible.

TO THE EMPEROR TRAJAN

I WAS GREATLY OBLIGED, Sir, in my late illness, to Posthumius Marinus, my physician; and I cannot make him a suitable return, but by the assistance of your wonted gracious indulgence. I entreat you then to make Chrysippus Mithridates and his wife Stratonica (who are related to Marinus) denizens of Rome. I entreat likewise the same privilege in favour of Epigonus and Mithridates, the two sons of Chrysippus; but with this restriction' that they may remain under the dominion of their father, and yet reserve their right of patronage over their own freedmen. I further entreat you to grant the full privileges of a Roman to L.

---

4   One of the four governments of Lower Egypt. M.

Satrius Abascantius, P. Caesius Phosphorus, and Pancharia Soteris. This request I make with the consent of their patrons.[5]

TO THE EMPEROR TRAJAN

AFTER YOUR LATE SACRED father, Sir, had, in a noble speech, as well as by his own generous example, exhorted and encouraged the public to acts of munificence, I implored his permission to remove the several statues which I had of the former emperors to my corporation, and at the same time requested permission to add his own to the number. For as I had hitherto let them remain in the respective places in which they stood when they were left to me by several different inheritances, they were dispersed in distant parts of my estate. He was pleased to grant my request, and at the same time to give me a very ample testimony of his approbation. I immediately, therefore, wrote to the decurii, to desire they would allot a piece of ground, upon which I might build a temple at my own expense; and they, as a mark of honour to my design, of-fered me the choice of any site I might think proper. However, my own ill-health in the first place, and later that of your father, together with the duties of that employment which you were both pleased to entrust me, prevented my proceeding with that design. But I have now, I think, a convenient opportunity of making an excursion for the purpose, as my monthly attendances ends on the 1st of September, and there are several festivals in the month following. My first request, then, is that you would permit me to adorn the temple I am going to erect with your statue, and next (in order to the execution of my design with all the expedition possible) that you would indulge me with leave of absence. It would ill become the sincerity I profess, were I to dissemble that

---

5   The extensive power of paternal authority was (as has been observed in the notes above) peculiar to the Romans. But after Chrysippus was made a denizen of Rome, he was not, it would seem, consequentially entitled to that privilege over those children which were born before his denization. On the other hand, if it was expressly granted him, his children could not preserve their right of patronage over their own freedmen, because that right would of course devolve to their father, by means of this acquired dominion over them. The denization therefore of his children is as expressly solicited as his own. But both parties becoming quirites, the children by this creation, and not pleading in right of their father, would be patres fam. To prevent which the clause is added, "ita ut sint in patris potestate:" as there is another to save to them their rights of patronage over their freedmen, though they were reduced in patrmam potestate. M.

your goodness in complying with this desire will at the same time be extremely serviceable to me in my own private affairs. It is absolutely necessary I should not defer any longer the letting of my lands in that province; for, besides that they amount to above four hundred thousand sesterces,[6] the time for dressing the vineyards is approaching, and that business must fall upon my new tenants.[7] The unfruitfulness of the seasons besides, for several years past, obliges me to think of making some abatements in my rents; which I cannot possibly settle unless I am present. I shall be indebted then to your indulgence, Sir, for the expedition of my work of piety, and the settlement of my own private affairs, if you will be pleased to grant me leave of absence[8] for thirty days. I cannot give myself a shorter time, as the town and the estate of which I am speaking lie above a hundred and fifty miles from Rome.

TRAJAN TO PLINY

YOU HAVE GIVEN ME many private reasons, and every public one, why you desire leave of absence; but I need no other than that it is your desire: and I doubt not of your returning as soon as possible to the duty of an office which so much requires your attendance. As I would not seem to check any instance of your affection towards me, I shall not oppose your erecting my statue in the place you desire; though in general I am extremely cautious in giving any encouragement to honours of that kind.

---

6   Pliny enjoyed the office of treasurer in conjunction with Cornutus Tertullus. It was the custom at Rome for those who had colleagues to administer the duties of their posts by monthly turns. Buchner. M.

7   About $16,000; the annual income of Pliny's estate in Tuscany. He mentions another near Comum in Milan, the yearly value of which does not appear. We find him likewise meditating the purchase of an estate, for which he was to give about $117,000 of our money; but whether he ever completed that purchase is uncertain. This, however, we are sure of, that his fortunes were but moderate, considering his high station and necessary expenses: and yet, by the advantage of a judicious economy, we have seen him in the course of these letters, exercising a liberality of which after ages have furnished no parallel. M.

8   The senators were not allowed to go from Rome into the provinces without having first obtained leave of the emperor. Sicily, however, had the privilege to be excepted out of that law; as Gallia Narbonensis afterwards was, by Claudius Cæsar. Tacit. Ann. XII. C. 23. M.

TO THE EMPEROR TRAJAN[9]

As I am sensible, Sir, that the highest applause my actions can receive is to be distinguished by so excellent a prince, I beg you would be graciously pleased to add either the office of augur or septemvir' (both which are now vacant) to the dignity I already enjoy by your indulgence; that I may have the satisfaction of publicly offering up those vows for your prosperity, from the duty of my office, which I daily prefer to the gods in private, from the affection of my heart.

TO THE EMPEROR TRAJAN

Having safely passed the promontory of Malea, I am arrived at Ephesus with all my retinue, notwithstanding I was detained for some time by contrary winds: a piece of information, Sir, in which, I trust, you will feel yourself concerned. I propose pursuing the remainder of my journey to the province[10] partly in light vessels, and partly in post-chaises: for as the excessive heats will prevent my travelling altogether by land, so the Etesian winds,[11] which are now set in, will not permit me to proceed entirely by sea.

TRAJAN TO PLINY

Your information, my dear Pliny, was extremely agreeable to me, as it does concern me to know in what manner you arrive at your province. It is a wise intention of yours to travel either by sea or land, as you shall find most convenient.

---

9   One of the seven priests who presided over the feasts appointed in honour of Jupiter and the other gods, an office, as appears, of high dignity, since Pliny ranks it with the augurship.

10   Bithynia, a province in Anatolia, or Asia Minor, of which Pliny was appointed governor by Trajan, in the sixth year of his reign, A. D. 103, not as an ordinary proconsul, but as that emperor's own lieutenant, with powers extraordinary. (See Dio.) The following letters were written during his administration of that province. M.

11   A north wind in the Grecian seas, which rises yearly some time in July, and continues to the end of August; though others extend it to the middle of September. They blow only in the day-time. Varenius's Geogr. V.I. p. 513. M.

TO THE EMPEROR TRAJAN

As I HAD A very favourable voyage to Ephesus, so in travelling by post-chaise from thence I was extremely troubled by the heats, and also by some slight feverish attacks, which kept me some time at Pergamus. From there, Sir, I got on board a coasting vessel, but, being again detained by contrary winds, did not arrive at Bithynia so soon as I had hoped. However, I have no reason to complain of this delay, since (which indeed was the most auspicious circumstance that could attend me) I reached the province in time to celebrate your birthday. I am at present engaged in examining the finances of the Prusenses,[12] their expenses, revenues, and credits; and the farther I proceed in this work, the more I am convinced of the necessity of my enquiry. Several large sums of money are owing to the city from private persons, which they neglect to pay upon various pretences; as, on the other hand, I find the public funds are, in some instances, very unwarrantably applied. This, Sir, I write to you immediately on my arrival. I entered this province on the 17th of September,[13] and found in it that obedience and loyalty towards yourself which you justly merit from all mankind. You will consider, Sir, whether it would not be proper to send a surveyor here; for I am inclined to think much might be deducted from what is charged by those who have the conduct of the public works if a faithful admeasurement were to be taken: at least I am of that opinion from what I have already seen of the accounts of this city, which I am now going into as fully as is possible.

TRAJAN TO PLINY

I SHOULD HAVE REJOICED to have heard that you arrived at Bithynia without the smallest inconvenience to yourself or any of your retinue, and that your journey from Ephesus had been as easy as your voyage to that place was favourable. For the rest, your letter informs me, my dearest Secundus, on what day you reached Bithynia. The people of that province will be convinced, I persuade myself, that I am attentive to their

12   The inhabitants of Prusa (Brusa), a principal city of Bithynia.
13   In the sixth year of Trajan's reign, A. D. 103, and the 41st of our author's age: he continued in this province about eighteen months. Vid. Mass, in Vit. Phin. 129. M.

interest: as your conduct towards them will make it manifest that I could have chosen no more proper person to supply my place. The examination of the public accounts ought certainly to be your first employment, as they are evidently in great disorder. I have scarcely surveyors sufficient to inspect those works[14] which I am carrying on at Rome, and in the neighbourhood; but persons of integrity and skill in this art may be found, most certainly, in every province, so that they will not fail you if only you will make due enquiry.

TO THE EMPEROR TRAJAN

THOUGH I AM WELL assured, Sir, that you, who never omit any opportunity of exerting your generosity, are not unmindful of the request I lately made to you, yet, as you have often indulged me in this manner, give me leave to remind and earnestly entreat you to bestow the praetorship now vacant upon Attius Sura. Though his ambition is extremely moderate, yet the quality of his birth, the inflexible integrity he has preserved in a very narrow fortune, and, more than all, the felicity of your times, which encourages conscious virtue to claim your favour, induce him to hope he may experience it in the present instance.

TO THE EMPEROR TRAJAN

I CONGRATULATE BOTH YOU and the public, most excellent Emperor, upon the great and glorious victory you have obtained; so agreeable to the heroism of ancient Rome. May the immortal gods grant the same happy success to all your designs, that, under the administration of so many princely virtues, the splendour of the empire may shine out, not only in its former, but with additional lustre.[15]

---

14   Among other noble works which this glorious emperor executed, the forum or square which went by his name seems to have been the most magnificent. It was built with the foreign spoils he had taken in war. The covering of this edifice was all brass, the porticoes exceedingly beautiful and magnificent, with pillars of more than ordinary height and dimensions. In the centre of this forum was erected the famous pillar which has been already described.

15   It is probable the victory here alluded to was that famous one which Trajan gained over the Daciaiss; some account of which has been given in the notes above. It is certain, at least, Pliny lived to see his wish accomplished, this emperor having carried the Roman splendour to its highest pitch, and

TO THE EMPEROR TRAJAN

MY LIEUTENANT, Servilius Pudens, came to Nicomedia,[16] Sir, on the 24th of November, and by his arrival freed me, at length, from the anxiety of a very uneasy expectation.

TO THE EMPEROR TRAJAN

YOUR GENEROSITY TO ME, Sir, was the occasion of uniting me to Rosianus Geminus, by the strongest ties; for he was my quaestor when I was consul. His behaviour to me during the continuance of our offices was highly respectful, and he has treated me ever since with so peculiar a regard that, besides the many obligations I owe him upon a public account, I am indebted to him for the strongest pledges of private friendship. I entreat you, then, to comply with my request for the advancement of one whom (if my recommendation has any weight) you will even distinguish with your particular favour; and whatever trust you shall repose in him, he will endeavour to show himself still deserving of an higher. But I am the more sparing in my praises of him, being persuaded his integrity, his probity, and his vigilance are well known to you, not only from those high posts which he has exercised in Rome within your immediate inspection, but from his behaviour when he served under you in the army. One thing, however, my affection for him inclines me to think, I have not yet sufficiently done; and therefore, Sir, I repeat my entreaties that you will give me the pleasure, as early as possible, of rejoicing in the advancement of my quaestor, or, in other words, of receiving an addition to my own honours, in the person of my friend.

TO THE EMPEROR TRAJAN

IT IS NOT EASY, Sir, to express the joy I received when I heard you had, in compliance with the request of my mother-in-law and myself, granted

---

extended the dominions of the empire farther than any of his predecessors; as after his death it began to decline. M.

16   The capital of Bithynia; its modern name is Izmid.

Coelius Clemens the proconsulship of this province after the expiration of his consular office; as it is from thence I learn the full extent of your goodness towards me, which thus graciously extends itself through my whole family. As I dare not pretend to make an equal return to those obligations I so justly owe you, I can only have recourse to vows, and ardently implore the gods that I may not be found unworthy of those favours which you are repeatedly conferring upon me.

TO THE EMPEROR TRAJAN

I RECEIVED, Sir, a dispatch from your freedman, Lycormas, desiring me, if any embassy from Bosporus[17] should come here on the way to Rome, that I would detain it till his arrival. None has yet arrived, at least in the city[18] where I now am. But a courier passing through this place from the king of Sarmatia,[19] I embrace the opportunity which accidentally offers itself, of sending with him the messenger which Lycormas despatched hither, that you might be informed by both their letters of what, perhaps, it may be expedient you should be acquainted with at one and the same time.

TO THE EMPEROR TRAJAN

I AM INFORMED BY a letter from the king of Sarmatia that there are certain affairs of which you ought to be informed as soon as possible. In order, therefore, to hasten the despatches which his courier was charged with to you, I granted him an order to make use of the public post.[20]

---

17   The town of Panticapoeum, also called Bosporus, standing on the European side of the Cimmerian Bosporus (Straits of Kaffa), in the modern Crimea.
18   Nicea (as appears by the 15th letter of this book), a city in Bithynia, now called Iznik. M.
19   Sarmatia was divided into European, Asiatic, and German Sarmatia. It is not exactly known what bounds the ancients gave to this extensive region; however, in general, it comprehended the northern part of Russia, and the greater part of Poland, &c. M.
20   The first invention of public couriers is ascribed to Cyrus, who, in order to receive the earliest intelligence from the governors of the several provinces, erected post-houses throughout the kingdom of Persia, at equal distances, which supplied men and horses to forward the public despatches. Augustus was the first who introduced this most useful institution among the Romans,

TO THE EMPEROR TRAJAN

THE AMBASSADOR FROM THE king of Sarmatia having remained two days, by his own choice, at Nicea, I did not think it reasonable, Sir, to detain him any longer: because, in the first place, it was still uncertain when your freedman, Lycormas, would arrive, and then again some indispensable affairs require my presence in a different part of the province. Of this I thought it necessary that you should be informed, because I lately acquainted you in a letter that Lycormas had desired, if any embassy should come this way from Bosporus, that I would detain it till his arrival. But I saw no plausible pretext for keeping him back any longer, especially as the despatches from Lycormas, which (as I mentioned before) I was not willing to detain, would probably reach you some days sooner than this ambassador.

TO THE EMPEROR TRAJAN

I RECEIVED A LETTER, Sir, from Apuleius, a military man, belonging to the garrison at Nicomedia, informing me that one Callidromus, being arrested by Maximus and Dionysius (two bakers, to whom he had hired himself), fled for refuge to your statue;[21] that, being brought before a magistrate, he declared he, was formerly slave to Laberius Maximus,

---

by employing post-chaises, disposed at convenient distances, for the purpose of political intelligence. The magistrates of every city were obliged to furnish horses for these messengers, upon producing a diploma, or a kind of warrant, either from the emperor himself or from those who had that authority under him. Sometimes, though upon very extraordinary occasions, persons who travelled upon their private affairs, were allowed the use of these post-chaises. It is surprising they were not sooner used for the purposes of commerce and private communication. Louis XI. first established them in France, in the year 1414; but it was not till later (date uncertain) that the post-office was settled in England by Act of Parliament, M.

21   Particular temples, altars, and statues were allowed among the Romans as places of privilege and sanctuary to slaves, debtors and malefactors. This custom was introduced by Romulus, who borrowed it probably from the Greeks; but during the free state of Rome, few of these asylums were permitted. This custom prevailed most under the emperors, till it grew so scandalous that the Emperor Pius found it necessary to restrain those privileged places by an edict. See Lipsii Excurs. ad Taeiti Ann. III, C. 36, M.

but being taken prisoner by Susagus[22] in Moesia,[23] he was sent as a present from Decebalus to Pacorus, king of Parthia, in whose service he continued several years, from whence he made his escape, and came to Nicomedia. When he was examined before me, he confirmed this account, for which reason I thought it necessary to send[24] him to you. This I should have done sooner, but I delayed his journey in order to make an inquiry concerning a seal ring which he said was taken from him, upon which was engraven the figure of Pacorus in his royal robes; I was desirous (if it could have been found) of transmitting this curiosity to you, with a small gold nugget which he says he brought from out of the Parthian mines. I have affixed my seal to it, the impression of which is a chariot drawn by four horses.

TO THE EMPEROR TRAJAN

YOUR FREEDMAN AND PROCURATOR,[25] Maximus, behaved, Sir, during all the time we were together, with great probity, attention, and diligence; as one strongly attached to your interest, and strictly observant of discipline. This testimony I willingly give him; and I give it with all the fidelity I owe you.

TO THE EMPEROR TRAJAN

AFTER HAVING EXPERIENCED, Sir, in Gabius Bassus, who commands on the Pontic[26] coast, the greatest integrity, honour, and diligence, as well as the most particular respect to myself, I cannot refuse him my best wishes and suffrage; and I give them to him with all that fidelity which is due to you. I have found him abundantly qualified by having served in the army under you; and it is owing to the advantages of your discipline that he has learned to merit your favour. The soldiery and the

---

22   General under Deeebalus, king of the Dacians. M.
23   A province in Daeia, comprehending the southern parts of Servia and part of Bulgaria. M.
24   The second expedition of Trajan against Decebalus was undertaken the same year that Pliny went governor into this province; the reason therefore why Pliny sent this Calhidromus to the emperor seems to be that some use might possibly be made of him in favour of that design, M.
25   Receiver of the finances. M.
26   The coast round the Black Sea.

people here, who have had full experience of his justice and humanity, rival each other in that glorious testimony they give of his conduct, both in public and in private; and I certify this with all the sincerity you have a right to expect from me.

TO THE EMPEROR TRAJAN

NYMPHIDIUS LUPUS,[27] Sir, and myself, served in the army together; he commanded a body of the auxiliary forces at the same time that I was military tribune; and it was from thence my affection for him began. A long acquaintance has since mutually endeared and strengthened our friendship. For this reason I did violence to his repose, and insisted upon his attending me into Bithynia, as my assessor in council. He most readily granted me this proof of his friendship; and without any regard to the plea of age, or the ease of retirement, he shared, and continues to share, with me, the fatigue of public business. I consider his relations, therefore, as my own; in which number Nymphidius Lupus, his son, claims my particular regard. He is a youth of great merit and indefatigable application, and in every respect well worthy of so excellent a father. The early proof he gave of his merit, when he commanded a regiment of foot, shows him to be equal to any honour you may think proper to confer upon him; and it gained him the strongest testimony of approbation from those most illustrious personages, Julius Ferox and Fuscus Salinator. And I will add, Sir, that I shall rejoice in any accession of dignity which he shall receive as an occasion of particular satisfaction to myself.

TO THE EMPEROR TRAJAN

I BEG YOUR DETERMINATION, Sir, on a point I am exceedingly doubtful about: it is whether I should place the public slaves[28] as sentries round the prisons of the several cities in this province (as has been hitherto the practice) or employ a party of soldiers for that purpose? On the one hand, I am afraid the public slaves will not attend this duty with the fidelity they

---

27   The text calls him primipilarem, that is, one who had been Prirnipilus, in officer in the army, whose post was both highly honourable and profitable; among other parts of his office he had the care of the eagle, or chief standard of the legion. M.

28   Slaves who were purchased by the public. M.

ought; and on the other, that it will engage too large a body of the soldiery. In the meanwhile I have joined a few of the latter with the former. I am apprehensive, however, there may be some danger that this method will occasion a general neglect of duty, as it will afford them a mutual opportunity of throwing the blame upon each other.

TRAJAN TO PLINY

THERE IS NO OCCASION, my dearest Secundus, to draw off any soldiers in order to guard the prisons. Let us rather persevere in the ancient customs observed in this province, of employing the public slaves for that purpose; and the fidelity with which they shall execute their duty will depend much upon your care and strict discipline. It is greatly to be feared, as you observe, if the soldiers should be mixed with the public slaves, they will mutually trust to each other, and by that means grow so much the more negligent. But my principal objection is that as few soldiers as possible should be withdrawn from their standard.

TO THE EMPEROR TRAJAN

GABIUS BASSUS, who commands upon the frontiers of Pontica, in a manner suitable to the respect and duty which he owes you, came to me, and has been with me, Sir, for several days. As far as I could observe, he is a person of great merit and worthy of your favour. I acquainted him it was your order that he should retain only ten beneficiary[29] soldiers, two horse-guards, and one centurion out of the troops which you were pleased to assign to my command. He assured me those would not be sufficient, and that he would write to you accordingly; for which reason I thought it proper not immediately to recall his supernumeraries.

---

29   The most probable conjecture (for it is a point of a good deal of obscurity) concerning the beneficiary seems to be that they were a certain number of soldiers exempted from the usual duty of their office, in order to be employed as a sort of body-guards to the general. These were probably foot; as the equites here mentioned were perhaps of the same nature, only that they served on horseback. Equites singulares Cæsaris Augusti, &c., are frequently met with upon ancient inscriptions, and are generally supposed to mean the bodyguards of the emperor. M.

TRAJAN TO PLINY

I HAVE RECEIVED FROM Gabius Bassus the letter you mention, acquainting me that the number of soldiers I had ordered him was not sufficient; and for your information I have directed my answer to be hereunto annexed. It is very material to distinguish between what the exigency of affairs requires and what an ambitious desire of extending power may think necessary. As for ourselves, the public welfare must be our only guide: accordingly it is incumbent upon us to take all possible care that the soldiers shall not be absent from their standard.

TO THE EMPEROR TRAJAN

THE PRUSENSES, Sir, having an ancient bath which lies in a ruinous state, desire your leave to repair it; but, upon examination, I am of opinion it ought to be rebuilt. I think, therefore, you may indulge them in this request, as there will be a sufficient fund for that purpose, partly from those debts which are due from private persons to the public which I am now collecting in; and partly from what they raise among themselves towards furnishing the bath with oil, which they are willing to apply to the carrying on of this building; a work which the dignity of the city and the splendour of your times seem to demand.

TRAJAN TO PLINY

IF THE ERECTING A public bath will not be too great a charge upon the Prusenses, we may comply with their request; provided, however, that no new tax be levied for this purpose, nor any of those taken off which are appropriated to necessary services.

TO THE EMPEROR TRAJAN

I AM ASSURED, Sir, by your freedman and receiver-general Maximus, that it is necessary he should have a party of soldiers assigned to him, over and besides the beneficiarii, which by your orders I allotted to the very worthy Gemellinus. Those therefore which I found in his service, I thought proper he should retain, especially as he was going into Paphlagonia,[30] in order to procure corn. For his better protection likewise, and because it was his request, I added two of the cavalry. But I beg you would inform me, in your next despatches, what method you would have me observe for the future in points of this nature.

TRAJAN TO PLINY

As my freedman Maximus was going upon an extraordinary commission to procure corn, I approve of your having supplied him with a file of soldiers. But when he shall return to the duties of his former post, I think two from you and as many from his coadjutor, my receiver-general Virdius Gemelhinus, will be sufficient.

TO THE EMPEROR TRAJAN

The very excellent young man Sempronius Caelianus, having discovered two slaves[31] among the recruits, has sent them to me. But I deferred passing sentence till I had consulted you, the restorer and upholder of military discipline, concerning the punishment proper to be inflicted upon them. My principal doubt is that, whether, although they have taken the military oath, they are yet entered into any particular legion. I request you therefore, Sir, to inform me what course I should pursue in this affair, especially as it concerns example.

---

30   A province in Asia Minor, bounded by the Black Sea on the north, Bithynia on the west, Pontus on the east, and Phrygia on the south.
31   The Roman policy excluded slaves from entering into military service, and it was death if they did so. However, upon cases of great necessity, this maxim was dispensed with; but then they were first made free before they were received into the army, excepting only (as Servius in his notes upon Virgil) observes after the fatal battle of Cannae; when the public distress was so great that the Romans recruited their army with their slaves, though they had not time to give them their freedom. One reason, perhaps, of this policy might be that they did not think it safe to arm so considerable a body of men, whose numbers, in the times when the Roman luxury was at its highest, we may have some idea of by the instance which Pun the naturalist mentions of Claudius Isodorus, who at the time of his death was possessed of no less than 4,116 slaves, notwithstanding he had lost great numbers in the civil wars. Pun. Hist. Nat. XXXIII. 10. M.

TRAJAN TO PLINY

SEMPRONIUS CAELINUS HAS ACTED agreeably to my orders, in sending such persons to be tried before you as appear to deserve capital
punishment. It is material however, in the case in question, to inquire
whether these slaves in-listed themselves voluntarily, or were chosen
by the officers, or presented as substitutes for others. If they were chosen, the officer is guilty; if they are substitutes, the blame rests with
those who deputed them; but if, conscious of the legal inabilities of
their station, they presented themselves voluntarily, the punishment
must fall upon their own heads. That they are not yet entered into any
legion, makes no great difference in their case; for they ought to have
given a true account of themselves immediately, upon their being approved as fit for the service.

TO THE EMPEROR TRAJAN

As I HAVE YOUR permission, Sir, to address myself to you in all my
doubts, you will not consider it beneath your dignity to descend to
those humbler affairs which concern my administration of this province. I find there are in several cities, particularly those of Nicomedia
and Nicea, certain persons who take upon themselves to act as public
slaves, and receive an annual stipend accordingly; notwithstanding
they have been condemned either to the mines, the public games,[32]
or other punishments of the like nature. Having received information
of this abuse I have been long debating with myself what I ought
to do. On the one hand, to send them back again to their respective
punishments (many of them being now grown old, and behaving,
as I am assured, with sobriety and modesty) would, I thought, be
proceeding against them too severely; on the other, to retain convicted criminals in the public service, seemed not altogether decent.
I considered at the same time to support these people in idleness
would be an useless expense to the public; and to leave them to starve
would be dangerous. I was obliged therefore to suspend the deter-

---

32   A punishment among the Romans, usually inflicted upon slaves, by
which they were to engage with wild beasts, or perform the part of gladiators,
in the public shows. M.

mination of this matter till I could consult with you. You will be desirous, perhaps, to be informed how it happened that these persons escaped the punishments to which they were condemned. This enquiry I have also made, but cannot return you any satisfactory answer. The decrees against them were indeed produced; but no record appears of their having ever been reversed. It was asserted, however, that these people were pardoned upon their petition to the proconsuls, or their lieutenants; which seems likely to be the truth, as it is improbable any person would have dared to set them at liberty without authority.

TRAJAN TO PLINY

YOU WILL REMEMBER YOU were sent into Bithynia for the particular purpose of correcting those many abuses which appeared in need of reform. Now none stands more so than that of criminals who have been sentenced to punishment should not only be set at liberty (as your letter informs me) without authority; but even appointed to employments which ought only to be exercised by persons whose characters are irreproachable. Those therefore among them who have been convicted within these ten years, and whose sentence has not been reversed by proper authority, must be sent back again to their respective punishments: but where more than ten years have elapsed since their conviction, and they are grown old and infirm, let them he disposed of in such employments as are but few degrees removed from the punishments to which they were sentenced; that is, either to attend upon the public baths, cleanse the common sewers, or repair the streets and highways, the usual offices assigned to such persons.

TO THE EMPEROR TRAJAN

WHILE I WAS MAKING a progress in a different part of the province, a most extensive fire broke out at Nicomedia, which not only consumed several private houses, but also two public buildings; the town-house and the temple of Isis, though they stood on contrary sides of the street. The occasion of its spreading thus far was partly owing to the violence of the wind, and partly to the indolence of the people, who, manifestly, stood idle and motionless spectators of this terrible calamity. The truth is the city was not furnished with either engines,[33] buckets, or any single instrument suitable for extinguishing fires; which I have now however given directions to have prepared. You will consider, Sir, whether it may not be advisable to institute a company of fire-men, consisting only of one hundred and fifty members. I will take care none but those of that business shall be admitted into it, and that the privileges granted them shall not be applied to any other purpose. As this corporate body will be restricted to so small a number of members, it will be easy to keep them under proper regulation.

TRAJAN TO PLINY

YOU ARE OF OPINION it would be proper to establish a company of firemen in Nicomedia, agreeably to what has been practised in several other cities. But it is to be remembered that societies of this sort have greatly disturbed the peace of the province in general, and of those cities in particular. Whatever name we give them, and for whatever purposes they may be founded, they will not fail to form themselves into factious assemblies, however short their meetings may be. It will therefore be safer to provide such machines as are of service in extinguishing fires, enjoining the owners of houses to assist in preventing the mischief from spreading, and, if it should be necessary, to call in the aid of the populace.

---

33   It has been generally imagined that the ancients had not the art of raising water by engines; but this passage seems to favour the contrary opinion. The word in the original is sipho, which Hesychius explains (as one of the commentators observes) "instrumentuns ad jaculandas aquas adversas incendia; an instrument to throw up water against fires." But there is a passage in Seneca which seems to put this matter beyond conjecture, though none of the critics upon this place have taken notice of it: "Solemiss," says he, "duabus manibus inter se junctis aguam concipere, et com pressa utrinque palma in modum ciphonis exprimere" (Q. N. 1. II. 16) where we plainly see the use of this sipho was to throw UP water, and consequently the Romans were acquainted with that art. The account which Pliny gives of his fountains at Tuscum is likewise another evident proof. M.

TO THE EMPEROR TRAJAN

WE HAVE ACQUITTED, Sir, and renewed our annual vows[34] for your prosperity, in which that of the empire is essentially involved, imploring the gods to grant us ever thus to pay and thus to repeat them.

TRAJAN TO PLINY

I RECEIVED THE SATISFACTION, my dearest Secundus, of being informed by your letter that you, together with the people under your government, have both discharged and renewed your vows to the immortal gods for my health and happiness.

TO THE EMPEROR TRAJAN

THE CITIZENS OF NICOMEDIA, Sir, have expended three millions three hundred and twenty-nine sesterces[35] in building an aqueduct; but, not being able to finish it, the works are entirely falling to ruin. They made a second attempt in another place, where they laid out two millions.[36] But this likewise is discontinued; so that, after having been at an immense charge to no purpose, they must still be at a further expense, in order to be accommodated with water. I have examined a fine spring from whence the water may be conveyed over arches (as was attempted in their first design) in such a manner that the higher as well as level and low parts of the city may be supplied. There are still remaining a very few of the old arches; and the square stones, however, employed in the former building, may be used in turning the new arches. I am of opinion part should be raised with brick, as that will be the easier and cheaper material. But that this work may not meet with the same ill-success as the former, it will be necessary to send here an architect, or some one skilled in the construction of this kind of waterworks. And I will venture to say, from the beauty and usefulness of the design, it will be an erection well worthy the splendour of your times.

---

34   This was an anniversary custom observed throughout the empire on the 30th of December. M.

35   About $132,000.

36   About $80,000.

TRAJAN TO PLINY

CARE MUST BE TAKEN to supply the city of Nicomedia with water; and that business, I am well persuaded, you will perform with all the diligence you ought. But really it is no less incumbent upon you to examine by whose misconduct it has happened that such large sums have been thrown away upon this, lest they apply the money to private purposes, and the aqueduct in question, like the preceding, should be begun, and afterwards left unfinished. You will let me know the result of your inquiry.

TO THE EMPEROR TRAJAN

THE CITIZENS OF NICEA, Sir; are building a theatre, which, though it is not yet finished, has already exhausted, as I am informed (for I have not examined the account myself), above ten millions of sesterces;[37] and, what is worse, I fear to no purpose. For either from the foundation being laid in soft, marshy ground, or that the stone itself is light and crumbling, the walls are sinking, and cracked from top to bottom. It deserves your consideration, therefore, whether it would be best to carry on this work, or entirely discontinue it, or rather, perhaps, whether it would not be most prudent absolutely to destroy it: for the buttresses and foundations by means of which it is from time to time kept up appear to me more expensive than solid. Several private persons have undertaken to build the compartment of this theatre at their own expense, some engaging to erect the portico, others the galleries over the pit:[38] but this design cannot be executed, as the principal building which ought first to be completed is now at a stand. This city is also

---

37   About $400,000. To those who are not acquainted with the immense riches of the ancients, it may seem incredible that a city, and not the capital one either, of a conquered province should expend so large a sum of money upon only the shell (as it appears to be) of a theatre: but Asia was esteemed the most considerable part of the world for wealth; its fertility and exportations (as Tully observes) exceeding that of all other countries. M.

38   The word carte, in the original, comprehends more than what we call the pit in our theatres, as at means the whole space lit which the spectators sat. These theatres being open at the top, the galleries here mentioned were for the convenience of retiring in bad weather. M.

rebuilding, upon a far more enlarged plan, the gymnasium,[39] which was burnt down before my arrival in the province. They have already been at some (and, I rather fear, a fruitless) expense. The structure is not only irregular and ill-proportioned, but the present architect (who, it must be owned, is a rival to the person who was first employed) asserts that the walls, although twenty-two feet[40] in thickness, are not strong enough to support the superstructure, as the interstices are filled up with quarrystones, and the walls are not overlaid with brickwork. Also the inhabitants of Claudiopolis[41] are sinking (I cannot call it erecting) a large public bath, upon a low spot of ground which lies at the foot of a mountain. The fund appropriated for the carrying on of this work arises from the money which those honorary members you were pleased to add to the senate paid (or, at least, are ready to pay whenever I call upon them) for their admission.[42] As I am afraid, therefore, the public money in the city of Nicea, and (what is infinitely more valuable than any pecuniary consideration) your bounty in that of Nicopolis, should be ill applied, I must desire you to send hither an architect to inspect, not only the theatre, but the bath; in order to consider whether, after all the expense which has already been laid out, it will be better to finish them upon the present plan, or alter the one, and remove the other, in as far as may seem necessary: for otherwise we may perhaps throw away our future cost in endeavoring not to lose what we have already expended.

TRAJAN TO PLINY

You, who are upon the spot, will best be able to consider and determine what is proper to be done concerning the theatre which the inhabitants of Nicea are building; as for myself, it will be sufficient if you let me know your determination. With respect to the particular parts of this theatre which are to be raised at a private charge, you will see those engagements fulfilled when the body of the building to which they are

---

39   A place in which the athletic exercises were performed, and where the philosophers also used to read their lectures. M.
40   The Roman foot consisted of 11.71 inches of our standard, M.
41   A colony in the district of Cataonia, in Cappadocia.
42   The honorary senators, that is, such who were not received into the council of the city by election, but by the appointment of the emperor, paid a certain sum of money upon their admission into the senate. M.

to be annexed shall be finished. — These paltry Greeks[43] are, I know, immoderately fond of gymnastic diversions, and therefore, perhaps, the citizens of Nicea have planned a more magnificent building for this purpose than is necessary; however, they must be content with such as will be sufficient to answer the purpose for which it is intended. I leave it entirely to you to persuade the Claudiopolitani as you shall think proper with regard to their bath, which they have placed, it seems, in a very improper situation. As there is no province that is not furnished with men of skill and ingenuity, you cannot possibly want architects; unless you think it the shortest way to procure them from Rome, when it is generally from Greece that they come to us.

TO THE EMPEROR TRAJAN

WHEN I REFLECT UPON the splendour of your exalted station, and the magnanimity of your spirit, nothing, I am persuaded, can be more suitable to both than to point out to you such works as are worthy of your glorious and immortal name, as being no less useful than magnificent. Bordering upon the territories of the city of Nicomedia is a most extensive lake; over which marbles, fruits, woods, and all kinds of materials, the commodities of the country, are brought over in boats up to the high-road, at little trouble and expense, but from thence are conveyed in carriages to the sea-side, at a much greater charge and with great labour. To remedy this inconvenience, many hands will be in request; but upon such an occasion they cannot be wanting: for the country, and particularly the city, is exceedingly populous; and one may assuredly hope that every person will readily engage in a work which will be of universal benefit. It only remains then to send hither, if you shall think proper, a surveyor or an architect, in order to examine whether the lake lies above the level of the sea; the engineers of this province being of opinion that the former is higher by forty cubits,[44] I find there is in the neighbourhood of this place a large canal, which was cut by a king of this country; but as it is left unfinished, it is uncertain whether it was for the purpose of draining the adjacent fields, or making a communication between the lake and the river. It is equally

43   "Graeculi. Even under the empire, with its relaxed morality and luxurious tone, the Romans continued to apply this contemptuous designation to people to whom they owed what taste for art and culture they possessed." Church and Brodribb.
44   A Roman cubit is equal to a foot 5.406 inches of our measure. Arbuthanot's Tab. M.

doubtful too whether the death of the king, or the despair of being able to accomplish the design, prevented the completion of it. If this was the reason, I am so much the more eager and warmly desirous, for the sake of your illustrious character (and I hope you will pardon me the ambition), that you may have the glory of executing what kings could only attempt.

TRAJAN TO PLINY

THERE IS SOMETHING IN the scheme you propose of opening a communication between the lake and the sea, which may, perhaps, tempt me to consent. But you must first carefully examine the situation of this body of water, what quantity it contains, and from whence it is supplied; lest, by giving it an opening into the sea, it should be totally drained. You may apply to Calpurnius Macer for an engineer, and I will also send you from hence some one skilled in works of this nature.

TO THE EMPEROR TRAJAN

UPON EXAMINING INTO THE public expenses of the city of Byzantium, which, I find, are extremely great, I was informed, Sir, that the appointments of the ambassador whom they send yearly to you with their homage, and the decree which passes in the senate upon that occasion, amount to twelve thousand sesterces.[45] But knowing the generous maxims of your government, I thought proper to send the decree without the ambassador, that, at the same time they discharged their public duty to you, their expense incurred in the manner of paying it might be lightened. This city is likewise taxed with the sum of three thousand sesterces[46] towards defraying the expense of an envoy, whom they annually send to compliment the governor of Moesia: this expense I have also directed to be spared. I beg, Sir, you would deign either to confirm my judgment or correct my error in these points, by acquainting me with your sentiments.

---

45   About $480.
46   About $120.

TRAJAN TO PLINY

I ENTIRELY APPROVE, my dearest Secundus, of your having excused the Byzantines that expense of twelve thousand sesterces in sending an ambassador to me. I shall esteem their duty as sufficiently paid, though I only receive the act of their senate through your hands. The governor of Moesia must likewise excuse them if they compliment him at a less expense.

TO THE EMPEROR TRAJAN

I BEG, SIR, you would settle a doubt I have concerning your diplomas;[47] whether you think proper that those diplomas the dates of which are expired shall continue in force, and for how long? For I am apprehensive I may, through ignorance, either confirm such of these instruments as are illegal or prevent the effect of those which are necessary.

TRAJAN TO PLINY

THE DIPLOMAS WHOSE DATES are expired must by no means be made use of. For which reason it is an inviolable rule with me to send new instruments of this kind into all the provinces before they are immediately wanted.

TO THE EMPEROR TRAJAN

UPON INTIMATING, Sir, my intention to the city of Apamea,[48] of examining into the state of their public dues, their revenue and expenses, they told me they were all extremely willing I should inspect their accounts, but that no proconsul had ever yet looked them over, as they had a privilege (and that of a very ancient date) of administering the affairs of their corporation in the manner they thought proper. I required them to draw

---

47   A diploma is properly a grant of certain privileges either to particular places or persons. It signifies also grants of other kinds; and it sometimes means post-warrants, as, perhaps, it does in this place. M.
48   A city in Bithynia. M.

up a memorial of what they then asserted, which I transmit to you precisely as I received it; though I am sensible it contains several things foreign to the question. I beg you will deign to instruct me as to how I am to act in this affair, for I should be extremely sorry either to exceed or fall short of the duties of my commission.

TRAJAN TO PLINY

THE MEMORIAL OF THE Apanieans annexed to your letter has saved me the necessity of considering the reasons they suggest why the former proconsuls forbore to inspect their accounts, since they are willing to submit them to your examination. Their honest compliance deserves to be rewarded; and they may be assured the enquiry you are to make in pursuance of my orders shall be with a full reserve to their privileges.

TO THE EMPEROR TRAJAN

THE NICOMEDIANS, Sir, before my arrival in this province, had begun to build a new forum adjoining their former, in a corner of which stands an ancient temple dedicated to the mother of the gods.[49] This fabric must either be repaired or removed, and for this reason chiefly, because it is a much lower building than that very lofty one which is now in process of erection. Upon enquiry whether this temple had been consecrated, I was informed that their ceremonies of dedication differ from ours. You will be pleased therefore, Sir, to consider whether a temple which has not been consecrated according to our rites may be removed,[50] consistently with the reverence due to religion: for, if there should be no objection from that quarter, the removal in every other respect would be extremely convenient.

TRAJAN TO PLINY

YOU MAY WITHOUT SCRUPLE, my dearest Secundus, if the situation requires it, remove the temple of the mother of the gods, from the place

---

49   Cybele, Rhea, or Ops, as she is otherwise called; from whom, according to the pagan creed, the rest of the gods are supposed to have descended. M.
50   Whatever was legally consecrated was ever afterwards unapplicable to profane uses. M.

where it now stands, to any other spot more convenient. You need be under no difficulty with respect to the act of dedication; for the ground of a foreign city[51] is not capable of receiving that kind of consecration which is sanctified by our laws.

TO THE EMPEROR TRAJAN

WE HAVE CELEBRATED, Sir (with those sentiments of joy your virtues so justly merit), the day of your accession to the empire, which was also its preservation, imploring the gods to preserve you in health and prosperity; for upon your welfare the security and repose of the world depends. I renewed at the same time the oath of allegiance at the head of the army, which repeated it after me in the usual form, the people of the province zealously concurring in the same oath.

TRAJAN TO PLINY

YOUR LETTER, my dearest Secundus, was extremely acceptable, as it informed me of the zeal and affection with which you, together with the army and the provincials, solemnised the day of my accession to the empire.

TO THE EMPEROR TRAJAN

THE DEBTS WHICH WE are owing to the public are, by the prudence, Sir, of your counsels, and the care of my administration, either actually paid in or now being collected: but I am afraid the money must lie unemployed. For as on one side there are few or no opportunities of purchasing land, so, on the other, one cannot meet with any person who is willing to borrow of the public[52] (especially at 12 per cent, interest) when they can raise money upon the same terms from private sources. You will consider then,

---

51   That is, a city not admitted to enjoy the laws and privileges of Rome. M.

52   The reason why they did not choose to borrow of the public at the same rate of interest which they paid to private persons was (as one of the Commentators observes) because in the former instance they were obliged to give security, whereas in the latter they could raise money upon their personal credit. M.

Sir, whether it may not be advisable, in order to invite responsible persons to take this money, to lower the interest; or if that scheme should not succeed, to place it in the hands of the decurii, upon their giving sufficient security to the public. And though they should not be willing to receive it, yet as the rate of interest will be diminished, the hardship will be so much the less.

TRAJAN TO PLINY

I AGREE WITH YOU, my dear Pliny, that there seems to be no other method of facilitating the placing out of the public money than by lowering the interest; the measure of which you will determine according to the number of the borrowers. But to compel persons to receive it who are not disposed to do so, when possibly they themselves may have no opportunity of employing it, is by no means consistent with the justice of my government.

TO THE EMPEROR TRAJAN

I RETURN YOU MY warmest acknowledgments, Sir, that, among the many important occupations in which you are engaged you have condescended to be my guide on those points on which I have consulted you: a favour which I must now again beseech you to grant me. A certain person presented himself with a complaint that his adversaries, who had been banished for three years by the illustrious Servilius Calvus, still remained in the province: they, on the contrary, affirmed that Calvus had revoked their sentence, and produced his edict to that effect. I thought it necessary therefore to refer the whole affair to you. For as I have your express orders not to restore any person who has been sentenced to banishment either by myself or others so I have no directions with respect to those who, having been banished by some of my predecessors in this government, have by them also been restored. It is necessary for me, therefore, to beg you would inform me, Sir, how I am to act with regard to the above- mentioned persons, as well as others, who, after having been condemned to perpetual banishment, have been found in the province without permission to return; for cases of that nature have likewise fallen under my cognisance. A person was brought before me who had been sentenced to perpetual exile by the proconsul Julius

Bassus, but knowing that the acts of Bassus, during his administration, had been rescinded, and that the senate had granted leave to all those who had fallen under his condemnation of appealing from his decision at any time within the space of two years, I enquired of this man whether he had, accordingly, stated his case to the proconsul. He replied he had not. I beg then you would inform me whether you would have him sent back into exile or whether you think some more severe and what kind of punishment should be inflicted upon him, and such others who may hereafter be found under the same circumstances. I have annexed to my letter the decree of Calvus, and the edict by which the persons above-mentioned were restored, as also the decree of Bassus.

TRAJAN TO PLINY

I WILL LET YOU know my determination concerning those exiles which were banished for three years by the proconsul P. Servilius Calvus, and soon afterwards restored to the province by his edict, when I shall have informed myself from him of the reasons of this proceeding. With respect to that person who was sentenced to perpetual banishment by Julius Bassus, yet continued to remain in the province, without making his appeal if he thought himself aggrieved (though he had two years given him for that purpose), I would have sent in chains to my praetorian prefects:[53] for, only to remand him back to a punishment which he has contumaciously eluded will by no means be a sufficient punishment.

TO THE EMPEROR TRAJAN

WHEN I CITED THE judges, Sir, to attend me at a sessions[54] which I was going to hold, Flavius Archippus claimed the privilege of being

---

53   These, in the original institution as settled by Augustus, were only commanders of his body-guards; but in the later times of the Roman empire they were next in authority under the emperor, to whom they seem to have acted as a sort of prime ministers. M.

54   The provinces were divided into, a kind of circuits called conventus, whither the proconsuls used to go in order to administer justice. The judges here mentioned must not be understood to mean the same sort of judicial officers as with us: they rather answered to our juries. M.

excused as exercising the profession of a philosopher.[55] It was alleged by some who were present that he ought not only to be excused from that office, but even struck out of the rolls of judges, and remanded back to the punishment from which he had escaped, by breaking his chains. At the same time a sentence of the proconsul Velius Paullus was read, by which it appeared that Archippus had been condemned to the mines for forgery. He had nothing to produce in proof of this sentence having ever been reversed. He alleged, however, in favour of his restitution, a petition which he presented to Domitian, together with a letter from that prince, and a decree of the Prusensians in his honour. To these he subjoined a letter which he had received from you; as also an edict and a letter of your august father confirming the grants which had been made to him by Domitian. For these reasons, notwithstandng crimes of so atrocious a nature were laid to his charge, I did not think proper to determine anything concerning him, without first consulting with you, as it is an affair which seems to merit your particular decision. I have transmitted to you, with this letter, the several allegations on both sides.

DOMITIAN'S LETTER TO TERENTIUS MAXIMUS

"FLAVIUS ARCHIPPUS THE philosopher has prevailed with me to give an order that six hundred thousand sesterces[56] be laid out in the purchase of an estate for the support of him and his family, in the neighbourhood of Prusias,[57] his native country. Let this be accordingly done; and place that sum to the account of my benefactions."

FROM THE SAME TO L. APPIUS MAXIMUS

"I RECOMMEND, my dear Maximus, to your protection that worthy philosopher Archippus; a person whose moral conduct is agreeable to the principles of the philosophy he professes; and I would have you pay entire regard to whatever he shall reasonably request."

---

55   By the imperial constitutions the philosophers were exempted from all public functions. Catariscus. M.

56   About $24,000.

57   Geographers are not agreed where to place this city; Cellarius conjectures it may possibly be the same with Prusa ad Olympum, Prusa at the foot of Mount Olympus in Mysia.

THE EDICT OF THE EMPEROR NERVA

"There are some points no doubt, Quirites, concerning which the happy tenour of my government is a sufficient indication of my sentiments; and a good prince need not give an express declaration in matters wherein his intention cannot but be clearly understood. Every citizen in the empire will bear me witness that I gave up my private repose to the security of the public, and in order that I might have the pleasure of dispensing new bounties of my own, as also of confirming those which had been granted by predecessors. But lest the memory of him[58] who conferred these grants, or the diffidence of those who received them, should occasion any interruption to the public joy, I thought it as necessary as it is agreeable to me to obviate these suspicions by assuring them of my indulgence. I do not wish any man who has obtained a private or a public privilege from one of the former emperors to imagine he is to be deprived of such a privilege, merely that he may owe the restoration of it to me; nor need any who have received the gratifications of imperial favour petition me to have them confirmed. Rather let them leave me at leisure for conferring new grants, under the assurance that I am only to be solicited for those bounties which have not already been obtained, and which the happier fortune of the empire has put it in my power to bestow."

FROM THE SAME TO TULLIUS JUSTUS

"Since I have publicly decreed that all acts begun and accomplished in former reigns should be confirmed, the letters of Domitian must remain valid."

TO THE EMPEROR TRAJAN

Flavius Archippus has conjured me, by all my vows for your prosperity, and by your immortal glory, that I would transmit to you the memorial which he presented to me. I could not refuse a request couched in such terms; however, I acquainted the prosecutrix with this my in-

---

58   Domitian.

tention, from whom I have also received a memorial on her part. I have annexed them both to this letter; that by hearing, as it were, each party, you may the better be enabled to decide.

TRAJAN TO PLINY

IT IS POSSIBLE THAT Domitian might have been ignorant of the circumstances in which Archippus was when he wrote the letter so much to that philosopher's credit. However, it is more agreeable to my disposition to suppose that prince designed he should be restored to his former situation; especially since he so often had the honour of a statue decreed to him by those who could not be ignorant of the sentence pronounced against him by the proconsul Paullus. But I do not mean to intimate, my dear Pliny, that if any new charge should be brought against him, you should be the less disposed to hear his accusers. I have examined the memorial of his prosecutrix, Furia Prima, as well as that of Archippus himself, which you sent with your last letter.

TO THE EMPEROR TRAJAN

THE APPREHENSIONS YOU EXPRESS, Sir, that the lake will be in danger of being entirely drained if a communication should be opened between that and the sea, by means of the river, are agreeable to that prudence and forethought you so eminently possess; but I think I have found a method to obviate that inconvenience. A channel may be cut from the lake up to the river so as not quite to join them, leaving just a narrow strip of land between, preserving the lake; by this means it will not only be kept quite separate from the river, but all the same purposes will be answered as if they were united: for it will be extremely easy to convey over that little intervening ridge whatever goods shall be brought down by the canal. This is a scheme which may be pursued, if it should be found necessary; but I hope there will be no occasion to have recourse to it. For, in the first place, the lake itself is pretty deep; and in the next, by damming up the river which runs from it on the opposite side and turning its course as we shall find expedient, the same quantity of water may be retained. Besides, there are several brooks near the place where it is proposed the channel shall be cut which, if skilfully collected, will supply the lake with water in proportion to what it shall discharge. But if you should rather approve of the channel's being extended farther and cut narrower, and so conveyed directly into the sea, without running into the river, the reflux of the tide will return whatever it receives from the lake. After all, if the nature of the place should not admit of any of these schemes, the course of the water may be checked by sluices. These, however, and many other particulars, will be more skilfully examined into by the engineer, whom, indeed, Sir, you ought to send, according to your promise, for it is an enterprise well worthy of your attention and magnificence. In the meanwhile, I have written to the illustrious Calpurnius Macer, in pursuance of your orders, to send me the most skilful engineer to be had.

TRAJAN TO PLINY

IT IS EVIDENT, my dearest Secundus, that neither your prudence nor your care has been wanting in this affair of the lake, since, in order to render it of more general benefit, you have provided so many expedients against the danger of its being drained. I leave it to your own choice to pursue whichever of the schemes shall be thought most proper. Calpurnius Macer will furnish you, no doubt, with an engineer, as artificers of that kind are not wanting in his province.

TO THE EMPEROR TRAJAN

A VERY CONSIDERABLE QUESTION, Sir, in which the whole province is interested, has been lately started, concerning the state[59] and maintenance of deserted children.[60] I have examined the constitutions of former princes upon this head, but not finding anything in them relating, either in general or particular, to the Bithynians, I thought it necessary to apply to you for your directions: for in a point which seems to require the special interposition of your authority, I could not content myself with following precedents. An edict of the emperor Augustus (as pretended) was read to me, concerning one Annia; as also a letter from

---

59 That is, whether they should be considered in a state of freedom or slavery. M.

60 "Parents throughout the entire ancient world had the right to expose their children and leave them to their fate. Hence would sometimes arise the question whether such a child, if found and brought up by another, was entitled to his freedom, whether also the person thus adopting him must grant him his freedom without repayment for the cost of maintenance." Church and Brodribb.

Vespasian to the Lacedaemonians, and another from Titus to the same, with one likewise from him to the Achaeans, also some letters from Domitian, directed to the proconsuls Avidius Nigrinus and Armenius Brocchus, together with one from that prince to the Lacedaemonians: but I have not transmitted them to you, as they were not correct (and some of them too of doubtful authenticity), and also because I imagine the true copies are preserved in your archives.

TRAJAN TO PLINY

THE QUESTION CONCERNING CHILDREN who were exposed by their parents, and afterwards preserved by others, and educated in a state of servitude, though born free, has been frequently discussed; but I do not find in the constitutions of the princes my predecessors any general regulation upon this head, extending to all the provinces. There are, indeed, some rescripts of Domitian to Avidius Nigrinus and Armenhis Brocchus, which ought to be observed; but Bithynia is not comprehended in the provinces therein mentioned. I am of opinion therefore that the claims of those who assert their right of freedom upon this footing should be allowed; without obliging them to purchase their liberty by repaying the money advanced for their maintenance.[61]

TO THE EMPEROR TRAJAN

HAVING BEEN PETITIONED BY some persons to grant them the liberty (agreeably to the practice of former proconsuls) of removing the relics of their deceased relations, upon the suggestion that either their monuments were decayed by age or ruined by the inundations of the river, or for other reasons of the same kind, I thought proper, Sir, knowing that in cases of this nature it is usual at Rome to apply to the college of priests, to consult you, who are the sovereign of that sacred order, as to how you would have me act in this case.

---

61   "This decision of Trajan, the effect of which would be that persons would be slow to adopt an abandoned child which, when brought up, its natural parents could claim back without any compensation for its nurture, seems harsh, and we find that it was disregarded by the later emperors in their legal decisions on the subject." Church and Brodribb.

TRAJAN TO PLINY

IT WILL BE A HARDSHIP upon the provincials to oblige them to address themselves to the college of priests whenever they may have just reasons for removing the ashes of their ancestors. In this case, therefore, it will be better you should follow the example of the governors your predecessors, and grant or deny them this liberty as you shall see reasonable.

TO THE EMPEROR TRAJAN

I HAVE ENQUIRED, Sir, at Prusa, for a proper place on which to erect the bath you were pleased to allow that city to build, and I have found one to my satisfaction. It is upon the site where formerly, I am told, stood a very beautiful mansion, but which is now entirely fallen into ruins. By fixing upon that spot, we shall gain the advantage of ornamenting the city in a part which at present is exceedingly deformed, and enlarging it at the same time without removing any of the buildings; only restoring one which is fallen to decay. There are some circumstances attending this structure of which it is proper I should inform you. Claudius Polyaenus bequeathed it to the emperor Claudius Cæsar, with directions that a temple should be erected to that prince in a colonnade-court, and that the remainder of the house should be let in apartments. The city received the rents for a considerable time; but partly by its having been plundered, and partly by its being neglected, the whole house, colonnade-court, and all, is entirely gone to ruin, and there is now scarcely anything remaining of it but the ground upon which it stood. If you shall think proper, Sir, either to give or sell this spot of ground to the city, as it lies so conveniently for their purpose, they will receive it as a most particular favour. I intend, with your permission, to place the bath in the vacant area, and to extend a range of porticoes with seats in that part where the former edifice stood. This new erection I purpose dedicating to you, by whose bounty it will rise with all the elegance and magnificence worthy of your glorious name. I have sent you a copy of the will, by which, though it is inaccurate, you will see that Polyaenus left several articles of ornament for the embellishment of this house; but these also are lost with all the rest: I will, however, make the strictest enquiry after them that I am able.

TRAJAN TO PLINY

I HAVE NO OBJECTION to the Prusenses making use of the ruined court and house, which you say are untenanted, for the erection of their bath. But it is not sufficiently clear by your letter whether the temple in the centre of the colonnade-court was actually dedicated to Claudius or not; for if it were, it is still consecrated ground.[62]

TO THE EMPEROR TRAJAN

I HAVE BEEN PRESSED by some persons to take upon myself the enquiry of causes relating to claims of freedom by birth-right, agreeably to a rescript of Domitian's to Minucius Rufus, and the practice of former proconsuls. But upon casting my eye on the decree of the senate concerning cases of this nature, I find it only mentions the proconsular provinces.[63] I have therefore, Sir, deferred interfering in this affair, till I shall receive your instructions as to how you would have me proceed.

TRAJAN TO PLINY

IF YOU WILL SEND me the decree of the senate, which occasioned your doubt, I shall be able to judge whether it is proper you should take upon yourself the enquiry of causes relating to claims of freedom by birth-right.

---

62   And consequently by the Roman laws unapplicable to any other purpose. M.
63   The Roman provinces in the times of the emperors were of two sorts: those which were distinguished by the name of the provinciae Cæsaris and the provinciae senatus. The provinciae Cæsaris, or imperial provinces, were such as the emperor, for reasons of policy, reserved to his own immediate administration, or of those whom he thought proper to appoint: the provinciae senatus, or proconsular provinces, were such as he left to the government of proconsuls or praetors, chosen in the ordinary method of election. (Vid. Suet. in Aug. V. 47.) Of the former kind was Bithynis, at the time when our author presided there. (Vid. Masson. Vit. Plin. p. 133.) M.

TO THE EMPEROR TRAJAN

JULIUS LARGUS, of Ponus[64] (a person whom I never saw nor indeed ever heard his name till lately), in confidence, Sir, of your distinguishing judgment in my favour, has entrusted me with the execution of the last instance of his loyalty towards you. He has left me, by his will, his estate upon trust, in the first place to receive out of it fifty thousand sesterces[65] for my own use, and to apply the remainder for the benefit of the cities of Heraclea and Tios,[66] either by erecting some public edifice dedicated to your honour or instituting athletic games, according as I shall judge proper. These games are to be celebrated every five years, and to be called Trajan's games. My principal reason for acquainting you with this bequest is that I may receive your directions which of the respective alternatives to choose.

TRAJAN TO PLINY

BY THE PRUDENT CHOICE Julius Largus has made of a trustee, one would imagine he had known you perfectly well. You will consider then what will most tend to perpetuate his memory, under the circumstances of the respective cities, and make your option accordingly.

TO THE EMPEROR TRAJAN

YOU ACTED AGREEABLY, Sir, to your usual prudence and foresight in ordering the illustrious Calpurnius Macer to send a legionary centurion to Byzantium: you will consider whether the city of Juliopolis' does not deserve the same regard, which, though it is extremely small, sustains very great burthens, and is so much the more exposed to injuries as it is less capable of resisting them. Whatever benefits you shall confer upon that city will in effect be advantageous to the whole country; for it is situated at the entrance of Bithynia, and is the town through which all who travel into this province generally pass.

---

64   A province in Asia, bordering upon the Black Sea, and by some ancient geographers considered as one province with Bithynia. M.
65   About $2,000. M.
66   Cities of Pontus near the Euxine or Black Sea. M.

TRAJAN TO PLINY

THE CIRCUMSTANCES OF THE city of Byzantium are such, by the great confluence of strangers to it, that I held it incumbent upon me, and consistent with the customs of former reigns, to send thither a legionary centurion's guard to preserve the privileges of that state. But if we should distinguish the city of Juliopolis[67] in the same way, it will be introducing a precedent for many others, whose claim to that favour will rise in proportion to their want of strength. I have so much confidence, however, in your administration as to believe you will omit no method of protecting them from injuries. If any persons shall act contrary to the discipline I have enjoined, let them be instantly corrected; or if they happen to be soldiers, and their crimes should be too enormous for immediate chastisement, I would have them sent to their officers, with an account of the particular misdemeanour you shall find they have been guilty of; but if the delinquents should be on their way to Rome, inform me by letter.

TO THE EMPEROR TRAJAN

BY A LAW OF Pompey's[68] concerning the Bithynians, it is enacted, Sir, that no person shall be a magistrate, or be chosen into the senate, under the age of thirty. By the same law it is declared that those who have exercised the office of magistrate are qualified to be members of the senate. Subsequent to this law, the emperor Augustus published an edict, by which it was ordained that persons of the age of twenty-two should be capable of being magistrates. The question therefore is whether those who have exercised the functions of a magistrate before the age of thirty may be legally chosen into the senate by the censors?[69] And if so, whether, by the same kind

---

67   Gordium, the old capital of Phrygia. It afterwards, in the reign of the Emperor Augustus, received the name of Juliopolis. (See Smith's Classical Diet.)

68   Pompey the Great having subdued Mithridates, and by that means enlarged the Roman empire, passed several laws relating to the newly conquered provinces, and, among others, that which is here mentioned. M.

69   The right of electing Senators did not originally belong to the censors, who were only, as Cicero somewhere calls them, guardians of the discipline and manners of the city; but in process of time they engrossed the whole privilege of conferring that honour. M.

of construction, they may be elected senators, at the age which entitles them to be magistrates, though they should not actually have borne any office? A custom which, it seems, has hitherto been observed, and is said to be expedient, as it is rather better that persons of noble birth should be admitted into the senate than those of plebeian rank. The censors elect having desired my sentiments upon this point, I was of opinion that both by the law of Pompey and the edict of Augustus those who had exercised the magistracy before the age of thirty might be chosen into the senate; and for this reason, because the edict allows the office of magistrate to be undertaken before thirty; and the law declares that whoever has been a magistrate should be eligible for the senate. But with respect to those who never discharged any office in the state, though they were of the age required for that purpose, I had some doubt: and therefore, Sir, I apply to you for your directions. I have subjoined to this letter the heads of the law, together with the edict of Augustus.

TRAJAN TO PLINY

I AGREE WITH YOU, my dearest Secundus, in your construction, and am of opinion that the law of Pompey is so far repealed by the edict of the emperor Augustus that those persons who are not less than twenty-two years of age may execute the office of magistrates, and, when they have, may be received into the senate of their respective cities. But I think that they who are under thirty years of age, and have not discharged the function of a magistrate, cannot, upon pretence that in point of years they were competent to the office, legally be elected into the senate of their several communities.

TO THE EMPEROR TRAJAN

WHILST I WAS DESPATCHING some public affairs, Sir, at my apartments in Prusa, at the foot of Olympus, with the intention of leaving that city the same day, the magistrate Asclepiades informed me that Eumolpus had appealed to me from a motion which Cocceianus Dion made in their senate. Dion, it seems, having been appointed supervisor of a public building, desired that it might be assigned[70] to the city in form. Eumolpus, who was

---

70   This, probably, was some act whereby the city was to ratify and confirm the proceedings of Dion under the commission assigned to him.

counsel for Flavius Archippus, insisted that Dion should first be required to deliver in his accounts relating to this work, before it was assigned to the corporation; suggesting that he had not acted in the manner he ought. He added, at the same time, that in this building, in which your statue is erected, the bodies of Dion's wife and son are entombed,[71] and urged me to hear this cause in the public court of judicature. Upon my at once assenting to his request, and deferring my journey for that purpose, he desired a longer day in order to prepare matters for hearing, and that I would try this cause in some other city. I appointed the city of Nicea; where, when I had taken my seat, the same Eumolpus, pretending not to be yet sufficiently instructed, moved that the trial might be again put off: Dion, on the contrary, insisted it should be heard. They debated this point very fully on both sides, and entered a little into the merits of the cause; when being of opinion that it was reasonable it should be adjourned, and thinking it proper to consult with you in an affair which was of consequence in point of precedent, I directed them to exhibit the articles of their respective allegations in writing; for I was desirous you should judge from their own representations of the state of the question between them. Dion promised to comply with this direction and Eumolpus also assured me he would draw up a memorial of what he had to allege on the part of the community. But he added that, being only concerned as advocate on behalf of Archippus, whose instructions he had laid before me, he had no charge to bring with respect to the sepulchres. Archippus, however, for whom Eulnolpus was counsel here, as at Prusa, assured me he would himself present a charge in form upon this head. But neither Eumolpus nor Archippus (though I have waited several days for that purpose) have yet performed their engagement: Dion indeed has; and I have annexed his memorial to this letter. I have inspected the buildings in question, where I find your statue is placed in a library, and as to the edifice in which the bodies of Dion's wife and son are said to be deposited, it stands in the middle of a court, which is enclosed with a colonnade. Deign, therefore, I entreat you, Sir, to direct my judgment in the determination of this cause above all others as it is a point to which the public is greatly attentive, and necessarily so, since the fact is not only acknowledged, but countenanced

---

71   It was a notion which generally prevailed with the ancients, in the Jewish as well as heathen world, that there was a pollution in the contact of dead bodies, and this they extended to the very house in which the corpse lay, and even to the uncovered vessels that stood in the same room. (Vid. Pot. Antiq. V. II. 181.) From some such opinion as this it is probable that the circumstance, here mentioned, of placing Trajan's statue where these bodies were deposited, was esteemed as a mark of disrespect to his person.

by many precedents.

TRAJAN TO PLINY

You well know, my dearest Secundus, that it is my standing maxim not to create an awe of my person by severe and rigorous measures, and by construing every slight offence into an act of treason; you had no reason, therefore, to hesitate a moment upon the point concerning which you thought proper to consult me. Without entering therefore into the merits of that question (to which I would by no means give any attention, though there were ever so many instances of the same kind), I recommend to your care the examination of Dion's accounts relating to the public works which he has finished; as it is a case in which the interest of the city is concerned, and as Dion neither ought nor, it seems, does refuse to submit to the examination.

TO THE EMPEROR TRAJAN

The Niceans having, in the name of their community, conjured me, Sir, by all my hopes and wishes for your prosperity and immortal glory (an adjuration which is and ought to be most sacred to me), to present to you their petition, I did not think myself at liberty to refuse them: I have therefore annexed it to this letter.

TRAJAN TO PLINY

The Niceans I find, claim a right, by an edict of Augustus, to the estate of every citizen who dies intestate. You will therefore summon the several parties interested in this question, and, examining these pretensions, with the assistance of the procurators Virdius Gemellinus, and Epimachus, my freedman (having duly weighed every argument that shall be alleged against the claim), determine as shall appear most equitable.

TO THE EMPEROR TRAJAN

May this and many succeeding birthdays be attended, Sir, with the highest felicity to you; and may you, in the midst of an uninterrupted course of health and prosperity, be still adding to the increase of that immortal glory which your virtues justly merit!

TRAJAN TO PLINY

YOUR WISHES, MY DEAREST Secundus, for my enjoyment of many happy birthdays amidst the glory and prosperity of the republic were extremely agreeable to me.

TO THE EMPEROR TRAJAN

THE INHABITANTS OF SINOPE[72] are ill supplied, Sir, with water, which however may be brought thither from about sixteen miles' distance in great plenty and perfection. The ground, indeed, near the source of this spring is, for rather over a mile, of a very suspicious and marshy nature; but I have directed an examination to be made (which will be effected at a small expense) whether it is sufficiently firm to support any superstructure. I have taken care to provide a sufficient fund for this purpose, if you should approve, Sir, of a work so conducive to the health and enjoyment of this colony, greatly distressed by a scarcity of water.

TRAJAN TO PLINY

I WOULD HAVE YOU proceed, my dearest Secundus, in carefully examining whether the ground you suspect is firm enough to support an aqueduct. For I have no manner of doubt that the Sinopian colony ought to be supplied with water; provided their finances will bear the expense of a work so conducive to their health and pleasure.

TO THE EMPEROR TRAJAN

THE FREE AND CONFEDERATE city of the Amiseni[73] enjoys, by your in-

---

72   A thriving Greek colony in the territory of Sinopis, on the Euxine.
73   A colony of Athenians in the province of Pontus. Their town, Amisus, on the coast, was one of the residences of Mithridates.

dulgence, the privilege of its own laws. A memorial being presented to me there, concerning a charitable institution,[74] I have subjoined it to this letter, that you may consider, Sir, whether, and how far, this society ought to be licensed or prohibited.

TRAJAN TO PLINY

IF THE PETITION OF the Amiseni which you have transmitted to me, concerning the establishment of a charitable society, be agreeable to their own laws, which by the articles of alliance it is stipulated they shall enjoy, I shall not oppose it; especially if these contributions are employed, not for the purpose of riot and faction, but for the support of the indigent. In other cities, however, which are subject to our laws, I would have all assemblies of this nature prohibited.

TO THE EMPEROR TRAJAN

SUETONIUS TRANQUILLUS, Sir, is a most excellent, honour-able, and learned man. I was so much pleased with his tastes and disposition that I have long since invited him into my family, as my constant guest and domestic friend; and my affection for him increased the more I knew of him. Two reasons concur to render the privileges which the law grants to those who have three children particularly neces-sary to him; I mean the bounty of his friends, and the ill-success of his marriage. Those advantages, therefore, which nature has denied to him, he hopes to obtain from your goodness, by my intercession. I am thoroughly sensible, Sir, of the value of the privilege I am asking; but I know, too, I am asking it from one whose gracious compliance with all my desires I have amply experienced. How passionately I wish to do so in the present instance, you will judge by my thus requesting it in my absence; which I would not, had it not been a favour which I am more than ordinarily anxious to obtain.[75]

---

74   Casaubon, in his observations upon Theophrastus (as cited by one of the commentators) informs us that there were at Athens and other cities of Greece Certain fraternities which paid into a common chest a monthly contribution towards the support of such of their members who had fallen into misfortunes; upon condition that, if ever they arrived to more prosperous circumstances, they should repay into the general fund the money so advanced. M.

75   By the law for encouragement of matrimony (some account of which

TRAJAN TO PLINY

YOU CANNOT BUT BE sensible, my dearest Secundus, how reserved I am in granting favours of the kind you desire; having frequently declared in the senate that I had not exceeded the number of which I assured that illustrious order I would be contented with. I have yielded, however, to your request, and have directed an article to be inserted in my register, that I have conferred upon Tranquillus, on my usual conditions, the privilege which the law grants to these who have three children.

TO THE EMPEROR TRAJAN[76]

IT IS MY INVARIABLE rule, Sir, to refer to you in all matters where I feel doubtful; for who is more capable of removing my scruples, or informing my ignorance? Having never been present at any trials concerning those who profess Christianity, I am unacquainted not only with the nature of their crimes, or the measure of their punishment, but how far it is proper to enter into an examination concerning them. Whether, therefore, any difference is usually made with respect to ages, or no distinction is to be observed between the young and the adult; whether repentance entitles them to a pardon; or if a man has been once a Christian, it avails nothing to desist from his error; whether the very profession of Christianity, unattended with any criminal act, or only the crimes themselves inherent in the profession are punishable; on all these points I am in great doubt. In the meanwhile, the method I have observed towards those who have been brought before me as Christians is this: I asked them whether they were Christians; if they admitted it, I repeated the question twice, and threatened them with punishment; if they persisted, I ordered them to

---

has already been given in the notes above), as a penalty upon those who lived bachelors, they were declared incapable of inheriting any legacy by will; so likewise, if being married, they had no children, they could not claim the full advantage of benefactions of that kind.

76   This letter is esteemed as almost the only genuine monument of ecclesiastical antiquity relating to the times immediately succeeding the Apostles, it being written at most not above forty years after the death of St. Paul. It was preserved by the Christians themselves as a clear and unsuspicious evidence of the purity of their doctrines, and is frequently appealed to by the early writers of the Church against the calumnies of their adversaries. M.

be at once punished: for I was persuaded, whatever the nature of their opinions might be, a contumacious and inflexible obstinacy certainly deserved correction. There were others also brought before me possessed with the same infatuation, but being Roman citizens,[77] I directed them to be sent to Rome. But this crime spreading (as is usually the case) while it was actually under prosecution, several instances of the same nature occurred. An anonymous information was laid before me containing a charge against several persons, who upon examination denied they were Christians, or had ever been so. They repeated after me an invocation to the gods, and offered religious rites with wine and incense before your statue (which for that purpose I had ordered to be brought, together with those of the gods), and even reviled the name of Christ: whereas there is no forcing, it is said, those who are really Christians into any of these compliances: I thought it proper, therefore, to discharge them. Some among those who were accused by a witness in person at first confessed themselves Christians, but immediately after denied it; the rest owned indeed that they had been of that number formerly, but had now (some above three, others more, and a few above twenty years ago) renounced that error. They all worshipped your statue and the images of the gods, uttering imprecations at the same time against the name of Christ. They affirmed the whole of their guilt, or their error, was, that they met on a stated day before it was light, and addressed a form of prayer to Christ, as to a divinity, binding themselves by a solemn oath, not for the purposes of any wicked design, but never to commit any fraud, theft, or adultery, never to falsify their word, nor deny a trust when they should be called upon to deliver it up; after which it was their custom to separate, and then reassemble, to eat in common a harmless meal. From this custom, however, they desisted after the publication of my edict, by which, according to your commands, I forbade the meeting of any assemblies. After receiving this account, I judged it so much the more necessary to endeavor to extort the real truth, by putting two female slaves to the torture, who were said to officiate' in their religious rites: but all I could discover was evidence of an absurd and extravagant superstition. I deemed it expedient, therefore, to adjourn all further proceedings, in order to consult you. For it appears to be a matter highly deserving your consideration, more especially as great numbers must be involved in the danger of these prosecutions, which have already extended, and are still

---

77   It was one of the privileges of a Roman citizen, secured by the Semprorian law, that he could not be capitally convicted but by the suffrage of the people; which seems to have been still so far in force as to make it necessary to send the persons here mentioned to Rome. M.

likely to extend, to persons of all ranks and ages, and even of both sexes. In fact, this contagious superstition is not confined to the cities only, but has spread its infection among the neighbouring villages and country. Nevertheless, it still seems possible to restrain its progress. The temples, at least, which were once almost deserted, begin now to be frequented; and the sacred rites, after a long intermission, are again revived; while there is a general demand for the victims, which till lately found very few purchasers. From all this it is easy to conjecture what numbers might be reclaimed if a general pardon were granted to those who shall repent of their error.[78]

TRAJAN TO PLINY

YOU HAVE ADOPTED THE right course, my dearest Secundtis, in investigating the charges against the Christians who were brought before you. It is not possible to lay down any general rule for all such cases. Do not go out of your way to look for them. If indeed they should be brought before you, and the crime is proved, they must be punished;[79] with the restriction, however, that where the party denies he is a Christian, and shall make it evident that he is not, by invoking our gods, let him (notwithstanding any former suspicion) be pardoned upon his repentance. Anonymous informations ought not to be received in any sort of prosecution. It is introducing a very dangerous precedent, and is quite foreign to the spirit of our age.

---

78   These women, it is supposed, exercised the same office as Phoebe mentioned by St. Paul, whom he styles deaconess of the church of Cenchrea. Their business was to tend the poor and sick, and other charitable offices; as also to assist at the ceremony of female baptism, for the more decent performance of that rite: as Vossius observes upon this passage. M.
79   If we impartially examine this prosecution of the Christians, we shall find it to have been grounded on the ancient constitution of the state, and not to have proceeded from a cruel or arbitrary temper in Trajan. The Roman legislature appears to have been early jealous of any innovation in point of public worship; and we find the magistrates, during the old republic frequently interposing in cases of that nature. Valerius Maximus has collected some instances to that purpose (L. I. C. 3), and Livy mentions it as an established principle of the earlier ages of the commonwealth, to guard against the introduction of foreign ceremonies of religion. It was an old and fixed maxim likewise of the Roman government not to suffer any unlicensed assemblies of the people. From hence it seems evident that the Christians had rendered themselves obnoxious not so much to Trajan as to the ancient and settled laws of the state, by introducing a foreign worship, and assembling themselves without authority. M.

TO THE EMPEROR TRAJAN

THE ELEGANT AND BEAUTIFUL city of Amastris,[80] Sir, has, among other principal constructions, a very fine street and of considerable length, on one entire side of which runs what is called indeed a river, but in fact is no other than a vile common sewer, extremely offensive to the eye, and at the same time very pestilential on account of its noxious smell. It will be advantageous, therefore, in point of health, as well as decency, to have it covered; which shall be done with your permission: as I will take care, on my part, that money be not wanting for executing so noble and necessary a work.

TRAJAN TO PLINY

IT IS HIGHLY REASONABLE, my dearest Secundus, if the water which runs through the city of Amastris is prejudicial, while uncovered, to the health of the inhabitants, that it should be covered up. I am well assured you will, with your usual application, take care that the money necessary for this work shall not be wanting.

TO THE EMPEROR TRAJAN

WE HAVE CELEBRATED, Sir, with great joy and festivity, those votive soleninities which were publicly proclaimed as formerly, and renewed them the present year, accompanied by the soldiers and provincials, who zealously joined with us in imploring the gods that they would be graciously pleased to preserve you and the republic in that state of prosperity which your many and great virtues, particularly your piety and reverence towards them, so justly merit.

TRAJAN TO PLINY

IT WAS AGREEABLE TO me to learn by your letter that the army and the provincials seconded you, with the most joyful unanimity, in those vows

---

80   On the coast of Paphlagonia.

which you paid and renewed to the immortal gods for my preservation and prosperity.

TO THE EMPEROR TRAJAN

WE HAVE CELEBRATED, with all the warmth of that pious zeal we justly ought, the day on which, by a most happy succession, the protection of mankind was committed over into your hands; recommending to the gods, from whom you received the empire, the object of your public vows and congratulations.

TRAJAN TO PLINY

I WAS EXTREMELY WELL pleased to be informed by your letter that you had, at the head of the soldiers and the provincials, solemnised my accession to the empire with all due joy and zeal.

TO THE EMPEROR TRAJAN

VALERIUS PAULINUS, Sir, having bequeathed to me the right of patronage[81] over all his freedmen, except one, I intreat you to grant the freedom of Rome to three of them. To desire you to extend this favour to all of them would, I fear, be too unreasonable a trespass upon your indulgence; which, in proportion as I have amply experienced, I ought to be so much the more cautious in troubling. The persons for whom I make this request are C. Valerius Astraeus, C. Valerius Dionysius, and C. Valerius Aper.

TRAJAN TO PLINY

YOU ACT MOST GENEROUSLY in so early soliciting in favour of those

---

81   By the Papian law, which passed in the consulship of M. Papius Mutilus and Q. Poppeas Secundus, u. c. 761, if a freedman died worth a hundred thousand sesterces (or about $4,000 of our money), leaving only one child, his patron (that is, the master from whom he received his liberty) was entitled to half his estate; if he left two children, to one-third; but if more than two, then the patron was absolutely excluded. This was afterwards altered by Justinian, Inst. 1. III. tit. 8. M.

whom Valerius Paulinus has confided to your trust. I have accordingly granted the freedom of the city to such of his freedmen for whom you requested it, and have directed the patent to be registered: I am ready to confer the same on the rest, whenever you shall desire me.

TO THE EMPEROR TRAJAN

P. ATTIUS AQUILA, a centurion of the sixth equestrian cohort, request-ed me, Sir, to transmit his petition to you, in favour of his daughter. I thought it would be unkind to refuse him this service, knowing, as I do, with what patience and kindness you attend to the petitions of the soldiers.

TRAJAN TO PLINY

I HAVE READ THE petition of P. Attius Aquila, centurion of the sixth equestrian cohort, which you sent to me; and in compliance with his request, I have conferred upon his daughter the freedom of the city of Rome. I send you at the same time the patent, which you will deliver to him.

TO THE EMPEROR TRAJAN

I REQUEST, SIR, your directions with respect to the recovering those debts which are due to the cities of Bithynia and Pontus, either for rent, or goods sold, or upon any other consideration. I find they have a privilege conceded to them by several proconsuls, of being preferred to other credi-tors; and this custom has prevailed as if it had been established by law. Your prudence, I imagine, will think it necessary to enact some settled rule, by which their rights may always be secured. For the edicts of others, how wisely however founded, are but feeble and temporary ordinances, unless confirmed and sanctioned by your authority.

TRAJAN TO PLINY

THE RIGHT WHICH THE cities either of Pontus or Bithynia claim relating to the recovery of debts of whatever kind, due to their several communities, must be determined agreeably to their respective laws. Where any of these communities enjoy the privilege of being preferred to other creditors, it must be maintained; but, where no such privilege prevails, it is not just I should establish one, in prejudice of private property.

TO THE EMPEROR TRAJAN

THE SOLICITOR TO THE treasury of the city of Amisis instituted a claim, Sir, before me against Julius Piso of about forty thousand denarii,[82] presented to him by the public above twenty years ago, with the consent of the general council and assembly of the city: and he founded his demand upon certain of your edicts, by which donations of this kind are prohibited. Piso, on the other hand, asserted that he had conferred large sums of money upon the community, and, indeed, had thereby expended almost the whole of his estate. He insisted upon the length of time which had intervened since this donation, and hoped that he should not be compelled, to the ruin of the remainder of his fortunes, to refund a present which had been granted him long since, in return for many good offices he had done the city. For this reason, Sir, I thought it necessary to suspend giving any judgment in this cause till I shall receive your directions.

TRAJAN TO PLINY

THOUGH BY MY EDICTS I have ordained that no largesses shall be given out of the public money, yet, that numberless private persons may not be disturbed in the secure possession of their fortunes, those donations which have been made long since ought not to be called in question or revoked. We will not therefore enquire into anything that has been transacted in this affair so long ago as twenty years; for I would be no less attentive to secure the repose of every private man than to preserve the treasure of every public community.

TO THE EMPEROR TRAJAN

THE POMPEIAN LAW, Sir, which is observed in Pontus and Bithynia, does not direct that any money for their admission shall be paid in by those who

---

82   About $7,000.

are elected into the senate by the censors. It has, however, been usual for
such members as have been admitted into those assemblies, in pursuance
of the privilege which you were pleased to grant to some particular cities,
of receiving above their legal number, to pay one[83] or two thousand denarii[84] on their election. Subsequent to this, the proconsul Anicius Maximus
ordained (though indeed his edict related to some few cities only) that
those who were elected by the censors should also pay into the treasury a
certain sum, which varied in different places. It remains, therefore, for your
consideration whether it would not be proper to settle a certain sum for
each member who is elected into the councils to pay upon his entrance;
for it well becomes you, whose every word and action deserves to be im-
mortalized, to establish laws that shall endure for ever.

TRAJAN TO PLINY

I CAN GIVE NO general directions applicable to all the cities of Bithynia,
in relation to those who are elected members of their respective councils, whether they shall pay an honorary fee upon their admittance or
not. I think that the safest method which can be pursued is to follow
the particular laws of each city; and I also think that the censors ought
to make the sum less for those who are chosen into the senate contrary
to their inclinations than for the rest.

TO THE EMPEROR TRAJAN

THE POMPEIAN LAW, Sir, allows the Bithynians to give the freedom of
their respective cities to any person they think proper, provided he is not
a foreigner, but native of some of the cities of this province. The same
law specifies the particular causes for which the censors may expel any
member of the senate, but makes no mention of foreigners. Certain of the
censors therefore have desired my opinion whether they ought to expel a
member if he should happen to be a foreigner. But I thought it necessary
to receive your instructions in this case; not only because the law, though
it forbids foreigners to be admitted citizens, does not direct that a senator shall be expelled for the same reason, but because I am informed that
in every city in the province a great number of the senators are foreign-

---

83   About $175
84   About $350.

ers. If, therefore, this clause of the law, which seems to be antiquated by a long custom to the contrary, should be enforced, many cities, as well as private persons, must be injured by it. I have annexed the heads of this law to my letter.

TRAJAN TO PLINY

You MIGHT WELL BE doubtful, my dearest Secundus, what reply to give to the censors, who consulted you concerning their right to elect into the senate foreign citizens, though of the same province. The authority of the law on one side, and long custom prevailing against it on the other, might justly occasion you to hesitate, The proper mean to observe in this case will be to make no change in what is past, but to allow those senators who are already elected, though contrary to law, to keep their seats, to whatever city they may belong; in all future elections, however, to pursue the directions of the Pompeian law: for to give it a retrospective operation would necessarily introduce great confusion.

TO THE EMPEROR TRAJAN

It IS CUSTOMARY HERE upon any person taking the manly robe, solemnising his marriage, entering upon the office of a magistrate, or dedicating any public work, to invite the whole senate, together with a considerable part of the commonalty, and distribute to each of the company one or two denarii.[85] I request you to inform me whether you think proper this ceremony should be observed, or how far you approve of it. For myself, though I am of opinion that upon some occasions, especially those of public festivals, this kind of invitation may be permitted, yet, when carried so far as to draw together a thousand persons, and sometimes more, it seems to be going beyond a reasonable number, and has somewhat the appearance of ambitious largesses.

TRAJAN TO PLINY

---

85   The denarius=7 cents. The sum total, then, distributed among one thousand persons at the rate of, say, two denara a piece would amount to about $350.

YOU VERY JUSTLY APPREHENDED that those public invitations which extend to an immoderate number of people, and where the dole is distributed, not singly to a few acquaintances, but, as it were, to whole collective bodies, may be turned to the factious purposes of ambition. But I appointed you to your present government, fully relying upon your prudence, and in the persuasion that you would take proper measures for regulating the manners and settling the peace of the province.

TO THE EMPEROR TRAJAN

THE ATHLETIC VICTORS, Sir, in the Iselastic[86] games, conceive that the stipend you have established for the conquerors becomes due from the day they are crowned: for it is not at all material, they say, what time they were triumphantly conducted into their country, but when they merited that honour. On the contrary, when I consider the meaning of the term Iselastic, I am strongly inclined to think that it is intended the stipend should commence from the time of their public entry. They likewise petition to be allowed the treat you give at those combats which you have converted into Iselastic, though they were conquerors before the appointment of that institution: for it is but reasonable, they assert, that they should receive the reward in this instance, as they are deprived of it at those games which have been divested of the honour of being Iselastic, since their victory. But I am very doubtful, whether a retrospect should be admitted in the case in question, and a reward given, to which the claimants had no right at the time they obtained the victory. I beg, therefore, you would be pleased to direct my judgment in these points, by explaining the intention of your own benefactions.

TRAJAN TO PLINY

THE STIPEND APPOINTED FOR the conqueror in the Iselastic games ought not, I think, to commence till he makes his triumphant entry

---

86   These games are called Iselastic from the Greek word invehor, because the victors, drawn by white horses, and wearing crowns on their heads, were conducted with great pomp into their respective cities, which they entered through a breach in the walls made for that purpose; intimating, as Plutarch observes, that a City which produced such able and victorious citizens, had little occasion for the defence of walls (Catanaeus). They received also annually a certain honourable stipend from the public. M.

into his city. Nor are the prizes, at those combats which I thought proper to make Iselastic, to be extended backwards to those who were victors before that alteration took place. With regard to the plea which these athletic combatants urge, that they ought to receive the Iselastic prize at those combats which have been made Iselastic subsequent to their conquests, as they are denied it in the same case where the games have ceased to be so, it proves nothing in their favour; for notwithstanding any new arrangements which has been made relating to these games, they are not called upon to return the recompense which they received prior to such alteration.

TO THE EMPEROR TRAJAN

I have hitherto never, Sir, granted an order for post-chaises to any person, or upon any occasion, but in affairs that relate to your administration. I find myself, however, at present under a sort of necessity of breaking through this fixed rule. My wife having received an account of her grandfather's death, and being desirous to wait upon her aunt with all possible expedition, I thought it would be unkind to deny her the use of this privilege; as the grace of so tender an office consists in the early discharge of it, and as I well knew a journey which was founded in filial piety could not fail of your approbation. I should think myself highly ungrateful therefore, were I not to acknowledge that, among other great obligations which I owe to your indulgence, I have this in particular, that, in confidence of your favour, I have ventured to do, without consulting you, what would have been too late had I waited for your consent.

TRAJAN TO PLINY

You did me justice, my dearest Secundus, in confiding in my affection towards you. Without doubt, if you had waited for my consent to forward your wife in her journey by means of those warrants which I have entrusted to your care, the use of them would not have answered your purpose; since it was proper this visit to her aunt should have the additional recommendation of being paid with all possible expedition.

Index

REVIVE *classics*

"There is no friend as loyal as a book." Ernest Hemingway

REVIVE *classics*

"A room without books is like a body without a soul." Cicero

⬡ REVIVE *classics*

"If a book is well written, I always find it too short." Jane Austen

The Hound of the Baskervilles BY ARTHUR CONAN DOYLE
The House of Mirth BY EDITH WHARTON
The House of the Seven Gables BY NATHANIEL HAWTHORNE
The Hunchback of Notre-Dame BY VICTOR HUGO
The Idiot BY FYODOR DOSTOEVSKY
The Iliad BY HOMER
The Imitation of Christ BY THOMAS À KEMPIS
The Importance of Being Earnest BY OSCAR WILDE
The Innocents Abroad BY MARK TWAIN
The Interesting Narrative of the Life of Olaudah Equiano BY O. EQUIANO
The Island of Doctor Moreau BY H. G. WELLS
The Jungle BY UPTON SINCLAIR
The Jungle Book BY RUDYARD KIPLING
The Kama Sutra BY VĀTSYĀYANA
The King in Yellow BY ROBERT W. CHAMBERS
The Kybalion BY THREE INITIATES
The Lady of the Camellias BY ALEXANDRE DUMAS
The Lais of Marie de France BY MARIE DE FRANCE
The Last Man BY MARY SHELLEY
The Last of the Mohicans BY JAMES FENIMORE COOPER
The Law and the Lady BY WILKIE COLLINS
The Legend of Sleepy Hollow BY WASHINGTON IRVING
The Letters of Abelard and Heloise BY H. D'ARGENTEUIL & P. ABELARD
The Letters of Pliny the Younger BY PLINY THE YOUNGER
The Life and Opinions of Tristram Shandy BY LAURENCE STERNE
The Light Princess BY GEORGE MACDONALD
The Longest Journey BY E. M. FORSTER
The Lost World BY ARTHUR CONAN DOYLE
The Mabinogion BY ANONYMOUS
The Man in the Brown Suit BY AGATHA CHRISTIE
The Man in the Iron Mask BY ALEXANDRE DUMAS
The Man Who Was Thursday BY GILBERT K. CHESTERTON
The Mayor of Casterbridge BY THOMAS HARDY
The Memoirs of Sherlock Holmes BY ARTHUR CONAN DOYLE
The Merry Adventures of Robin Hood BY HOWARD PYLE
The Metamorphosis BY FRANZ KAFKA
The Mill on the Floss BY GEORGE ELIOT
The Monk: A Romance BY MATTHEW LEWIS
The Moonstone BY WILKIE COLLINS
The Murder of Roger Ackroyd BY AGATHA CHRISTIE
The Murder on the Links BY AGATHA CHRISTIE
The Mysterious Affair at Styles BY AGATHA CHRISTIE
The Mysterious Island BY JULES VERNE
The Mystery of the Blue Train BY AGATHA CHRISTIE
The Nature of Things BY TITUS LUCRETIUS CARUS
The Odyssey BY HOMER
The Old Curiosity Shop BY CHARLES DICKENS
The Origin of Species BY CHARLES DARWIN
The Painted Veil BY W. SOMERSET MAUGHAM
The Phantom of the Opera BY GASTON LEROUX
The Pickwick Papers BY CHARLES DICKENS
The Picture of Dorian Gray BY OSCAR WILDE
The Portrait of a Lady BY HENRY JAMES
The Prince BY NICCOLÒ MACHIAVELLI
The Prince and the Pauper BY MARK TWAIN
The Princess and the Goblin BY GEORGE MACDONALD
The Problems of Philosophy BY BERTRAND RUSSELL
The Prophet BY KAHLIL GIBRAN

The Pursuit of God BY A. W. TOZER
The Railway Children BY E. NESBIT
The Red Badge of Courage BY STEPHEN CRANE
The Republic BY PLATO
The Return of the Native BY THOMAS HARDY
The Richest Man In Babylon BY GEORGE S CLASON
The Rough Riders BY THEODORE ROOSEVELT
The Rule of Saint Benedict BY SAINT BENEDICT
The Scarlet Letter BY NATHANIEL HAWTHORNE
The Scarlet Pimpernel BY BARONESS ORCZY
The Science of Getting Rich BY WALLACE D. WATTLES
The Sea-Wolf BY JACK LONDON
The Secret Adversary BY AGATHA CHRISTIE
The Secret Garden BY FRANCES HODGSON BURNETT
The Secret of Chimneys BY AGATHA CHRISTIE
The Sign of the Four BY ARTHUR CONAN DOYLE
The Social Contract BY JEAN-JACQUES ROUSSEAU
The Song of the Lark BY WILLA CATHER
The Souls of Black Folk BY W. E. B. DU BOIS
The Strange Case of Dr. Jekyll & Mr. Hyde BY ROBERT LOUIS STEVENSON
The Story of a Soul: The Autobiography of SAINT THÉRÈSE OF LISIEUX
The Sun Also Rises BY ERNEST HEMINGWAY
The Swiss Family Robinson BY JOHANN DAVID WYSS
The Tenant of Wildfell Hall BY ANNE BRONTË
The Theory of Moral Sentiments BY ADAM SMITH
The Three Musketeers BY ALEXANDRE DUMAS
The Time Machine BY H. G. WELLS
The Turn of the Screw BY HENRY JAMES
The Twelve Caesars BY SUETONIUS
The Upanishads BY ANONYMOUS
The War of the Worlds BY H. G. WELLS
The Wealth of Nations BY ADAM SMITH
The Wind in the Willows BY KENNETH GRAHAME
The Woman in White BY WILKIE COLLINS
The Yoga Sutras OF PATANJALI
Theodore Roosevelt: An Autobiography BY THEODORE ROOSEVELT
Theogony and Works and Days BY HESIOD
Thérèse Raquin BY ÉMILE ZOLA
This Side of Paradise BY F. SCOTT FITZGERALD
Through the Looking-Glass BY LEWIS CARROLL
Timaeus and Critias BY PLATO
To the Lighthouse BY VIRGINIA WOOLF
Tom Jones BY HENRY FIELDING
Treasure Island BY ROBERT LOUIS STEVENSON
Twelve Years a Slave BY SOLOMON NORTHUP
Ulysses BY JAMES JOYCE
Uncle Tom's Cabin BY HARRIET BEECHER STOWE
Up From Slavery BY BOOKER T. WASHINGTON
Utilitarianism BY JOHN STUART MILL
Utopia BY SIR THOMAS MORE
Vanity Fair BY WILLIAM MAKEPEACE THACKERAY
Villette BY CHARLOTTE BRONTË
Walden BY HENRY DAVID THOREAU
War and Peace BY LEO TOLSTOY
We BY YEVGENY ZAMYATIN
White Fang BY JACK LONDON
Women in Love BY D. H. LAWRENCE
Wuthering Heights BY EMILY BRONTË

www.ingramcontent.com/pod-product-compliance
Lightning Source LLC
Chambersburg PA
CBHW020443100426
42812CB00036B/3429/J